CONSTRAINTS ON THE WAGING OF WAR

This fully revised fourth edition of *Constraints on the Waging of War* considers the development of the principal rules of international humanitarian law from their origins to the present day. Of particular focus are the rules governing weapons and the legal instruments through which respect for the law can be enforced. Combining theory and actual practice, this book appeals to specialists as well as to students turning to the subject for the first time.

FRITS KALSHOVEN is Professor Emeritus of Public International Law and of International Humanitarian Law at the University of Leiden. In 2003, he was awarded the Henry Dunant Medal of the International Red Cross and Red Crescent Movement for his continued effort to improve the knowledge of and respect for the law of war.

LIESBETH ZEGVELD is a partner at Böhler Advocaten, Amsterdam, where she specialises in legal remedies for war victims. Since September 2006 she has also been Professor of International Humanitarian Law at Leiden University, focusing in particular on the rights of women and children during armed conflict.

I must retrace my steps, and must deprive those who wage war of nearly all the privileges which I seemed to grant, yet did not grant to them. For when I first set out to explain this part of the law of nations I bore witness that many things are said to be 'lawful' or 'permissible' for the reason that they are done with impunity, in part also because coactive tribunals lend to them their authority; things which nevertheless, either deviate from the rule of right (whether this has any basis in law strictly so called, or in the admonitions of other virtues), or at any rate may be omitted on higher grounds and with greater praise among good men.

Grotius: *De jure belli ac pacis*
Book III, Chapter X, Section 1.1.

(English translation: Francis G. Kelsey, Oxford, 1925).

CONSTRAINTS ON THE WAGING OF WAR

An Introduction to International
Humanitarian Law

4TH EDITION

FRITS KALSHOVEN
LIESBETH ZEGVELD

CAMBRIDGE
UNIVERSITY PRESS

CAMBRIDGE UNIVERSITY PRESS
Cambridge, New York, Melbourne, Madrid, Cape Town,
Singapore, São Paulo, Delhi, Tokyo, Mexico City

Cambridge University Press
The Edinburgh Building, Cambridge CB2 8RU, UK

Published in the United States of America by Cambridge University Press, New York

www.cambridge.org
Information on this title: www.cambridge.org/9781107011663

First published 2011

Printed in the United Kingdom at the University Press, Cambridge

A catalogue record for this publication is available from the British Library

Library of Congress Cataloguing in Publication data
Kalshoven, F. (Frits)
Constraints on the waging of war : an introduction to international humanitarian law /
Frits Kalshoven, Liesbeth Zegveld. – 4th ed.
p.   cm.
Includes bibliographical references and index.
ISBN 978-1-107-01166-3 (hardback) – ISBN 978-1-107-60032-4 (paperback)
1. War victims–Legal status, laws, etc.   2. War (International law)
I. Zegveld, Liesbeth.   II. Title.
KZ6475.K35 2011
341.6′7–dc22
2011011808

ISBN 978-1-107-01166-3 Hardback
ISBN 978-1-107-60032-4 Paperback

CONTENTS

v

FOREWORD

Ten years have past since the last edition of Professors Frits Kalshoven and Liesbeth Zegveld's *Constraints on the Waging of War* was published by the International Committee of the Red Cross (ICRC). This time has only reaffirmed the need for such an introductory textbook, which follows the growth of international humanitarian law from its inception to its most recent developments.

Professors Kalshoven and Zegveld – whose expertise in humanitarian law is universally recognized – succeed in bringing together, in a book of limited length, the principal rules of humanitarian law. They do so in an accurate and thorough style, which will undoubtedly appeal to specialists, but also with a clarity that will make the book accessible to students turning to the subject for the first time. The blend of theory and practice renders this book not only extremely useful, but also most interesting to read.

In this new edition, the authors bring *Constraints on the Waging of War* up to date with the challenges of contemporary armed conflict and developments in international humanitarian law. Apart from updated jurisprudence, this edition includes discussion on new treaties – such as the Third Additional Protocol to the Geneva Conventions and the Convention on Cluster Munitions, as well as an analysis of other new doctrinal instruments such as the ICRC's study on Direct Participation in Hostilities.

It is a great pleasure for the ICRC to publish this fourth edition of *Constraints on the Waging of War*, which will do much to promote knowledge of the rules of international humanitarian law on which so many lives depend.

Jakob Kellenberger
President
International Committee of the Red Cross

Introduction

1.1 War and law

Events such as the armed conflicts in the former Yugoslavia; between Iraq and Iran or Ethiopia and Eritrea; in Afghanistan, Iraq, Sudan, Rwanda, the Congo, Somalia, Sri Lanka and Colombia, remind us day after day of the cruelty of war and the suffering, death and destruction it entails. They also raise an obvious question: is the behaviour of the parties to such armed conflicts subject to any restrictions? The answer is that such restrictions do exist, even though they may not always be crystal clear or completely unequivocal. Confining ourselves to the realm of law (rather than that of morality alone) they are found in such diverse branches as the law of the United Nations Charter, human rights law, environmental law, the law of neutrality and, last but not least, the 'law of war' or *jus in bello*: a body of law specifically designed to 'constrain the waging of war'.

The law of war is often referred to as 'international humanitarian law applicable in armed conflict' or, shorter, 'law of armed conflict' or 'humanitarian law'. While the inclusion of 'humanitarian' accentuates the element of protection of victims and its omission that of warfare, the various phrases all refer to the same body of law. We shall be using the terms interchangeably, as we do with 'war' and 'armed conflict'. The book aims to provide information about the origin, character, content and current problems of the law of war. In the process, we shall come across the other aforementioned relevant bodies of law as well, but our main focus is on the law of war in its proper sense.

In the perspective of the law of armed conflict, wars happen: in the past, usually between states; today, more often involving non-state organised armed groups. The legal assessment of recourse to war is a matter for *jus ad bellum*, with the law of the UN Charter as its present centrepiece. For *jus in bello*, i.e. the law relating to the actual waging of war, the occurrence of armed conflict is a matter of fact, and the same goes for the loss of human life and damage to other values it necessarily entails. It should be understood that, rather than granting states or individuals a right to take human lives or bring about such other damage, the *jus in bello* sets limits to acts of war and thereby provides the yardstick by which to measure the justifiability of those acts.

It should also be understood that the limits set by *jus in bello* do not purport to turn armed conflict into a socially acceptable activity like the medieval jousting tournament: their aim goes no further than to prevent wanton cruelty and ruthlessness and to provide essential protection to those most directly affected by the conflict.

The 'limits' of the law of war may be distinguished into principles and rules. Overriding principles are military necessity and humanity. The first principle tells us that for an act of war to be at all justifiable requires that it is militarily necessary: a practical consideration; and the other, that the act cannot be justified if it goes beyond what can be tolerated from a humanitarian point of view: a moral component. Obviously, these are extremely broad principles: over time, they have been elaborated into ever more detailed principles and rules.

One other fundamental principle of the law of war we highlight at the outset is the 'equality' of the belligerent parties. They may be blatantly unequal in many respects, as with last century's wars of national liberation (with a state fighting against a 'people'), today's internal armed conflicts (such as the long-lasting war in Colombia), or the invasion in 2003 of Iraq by the United States of America and its partners: no matter the inequalities, the parties are equally subject to the principles and rules of the law of war.

The principles and rules of the law of war are referred to in the title of this book, with a term borrowed from Grotius' famous treatise *De iure belli ac pacis*, as 'constraints on the waging of war'. Writing at the time of the Thirty Years War (1618–48) Grotius compared the practice of conducting virtually unrestricted war – all the barbaric things belligerents could do, as he said, with impunity as far as the positive law of his time was concerned – with another, more commendable mode of waging war, respecting the "rule of right" and refraining from certain modes of acting "on higher grounds and with greater praise among good men". The *temperamenta belli*, or 'moderations of war', which he then expounded as requirements of a higher, moral order correspond in many respects with the rules of the law of armed conflict as we know it today.

Without such legal restraints, war may all too easily degenerate into utter barbarism. The result need not only be that the impact of the 'scourge of war' referred to with such evident horror in the Charter of the United

Nations becomes immeasurably more devastating and the loss of human dignity for those actively engaged in hostilities commensurately greater; another likely effect is that after the war, the restoration of peace between parties that have fought each other with such utter ruthlessness will be that much more difficult – to the point where it may become virtually impossible.

1.2 Sources of the law of armed conflict

The law of armed conflict has a long history behind it. Even in a distant past, military leaders have been known to order their troops to spare the lives of captured enemies and treat them well, or to spare the enemy civilian population; and upon the termination of hostilities, belligerent parties might agree to exchange the prisoners in their hands. In the course of time, such practices could develop into generally preferred behaviour, whether on the basis of recognised principle or in the shape of customary rules of war: legal norms, that is, which parties to an armed conflict ought to respect even in the absence of a binding unilateral declaration or agreement to that effect.

The scope and content of these non-written rules of war long remained elusive and uncertain. The most effective way for states to remove such uncertainty is by treaty-making, that is, by negotiating agreed versions of the rules and embodying these in internationally accepted, binding instruments. These are generally called treaties; some bear other names, such as convention, declaration or protocol. While treaties can be concluded between two states (bilateral treaties), we are concerned here with treaties concluded between a number of states (multilateral treaties).

Multilateral treaty-making became an important instrument for the regulation of international relations in the nineteenth century. With the number of states much smaller than it is today, and without a United Nations or anything comparable to it, this was done in ad hoc international conferences, whether or not specially convened for that purpose. Two such meetings were convened in the 1860s to deal with a single aspect of the law of war: one, in 1864 in Geneva, on the fate of wounded soldiers on the battlefield; the other, in 1868 in St Petersburg, on the use of explosive rifle bullets. These modest beginnings are at the root of two distinct, though never entirely separate, currents in this body of law, each characterised by its own particular perspective. One, usually (and for reasons to be explained below) known as the law of The Hague, concerns the conduct of war and permissible means and methods of war; the other, styled the law of Geneva, is more particularly concerned with the condition of war victims in enemy hands (such as prisoners of war, or interned civilians).

In the course of time, the treaty law of armed conflict has come to cover ever more ground and gone into ever greater detail (often in reaction to experiences of previous wars). Four major conventions concluded at Geneva in 1949 have now been acceded to by all existing states plus the Vatican. As a consequence, sight might be lost of the fact that a good part of their content rests on generally recognised principles and, on the basis of established practice, may belong to customary law as well. With other treaties in this field having fewer (sometimes far fewer) parties, it is well to remember that treaties bind only the states parties. At the same time, rules in these treaties that already belonged to customary law or that have developed into rules of customary law after the conclusion and entry into force of the treaty, or that reflect generally recognised principles of law, bind non-party states as well.

For long years, treaty-making in the sphere of the law of armed conflict was confined to 'war' in the sense of armed conflicts between states (beginning with the Geneva Conventions of 1949 usually referred to as 'international armed conflicts'). From that date, treaty law also came to include rules applicable in armed conflicts waged within the territory of a state between its armed forces and one or more organised armed groups, or between such groups – or "armed conflicts not of an international character occurring in the territory of one of the High Contracting Parties", as they are styled in common Article 3, the single article of the Conventions that is so applicable. (These conflicts are often referred to as 'non-international armed conflicts'; we prefer the shorter phrase 'internal armed conflicts'.) In later years, in reaction to the ever higher incidence of such conflicts, more and more rules of existing treaty law were made applicable to these conflicts as well. Then again, recent events have given rise to the question of what rules of armed conflict, if any, govern the case of states locked in combat with non-state armed groups that are not, or not exclusively, located in their own territory, so that the conflict is neither 'international' nor 'internal' in the proper sense.

Shortly after the Second World War, the International Military Tribunals of Nuremberg and Tokyo held that the rules on warfare laid down in a treaty concluded in 1899 and revised in 1907, the Hague Convention with annexed Regulations on Land Warfare, had before that war already acquired the status of customary law. More recently, judicial bodies such as the International Court of Justice and the Yugoslavia and

Rwanda Tribunals have in turn found that given rules of recent treaty law possessed the character of customary law as well. In particular, this more recent extension of the scope of the customary law of armed conflict appears to rest on the assumption that for this type of armed conflict, general opinion about preferred behaviour outweighs the requirement of demonstrable practice seen as law. To the extent that this 'general opinion of preferred behaviour' reflects accepted principle, we would prefer to call it that.

In 2005, the International Committee of the Red Cross (or ICRC) published a comprehensive study on 'Customary International Humanitarian Law': a task it had been invited to undertake in 1995 by the 26th International Conference of the Red Cross and Red Crescent. The study, the result of a vast effort, lists a large number of rules the ICRC had identified as belonging to present-day customary law. It may be commented again that in particular with respect to internal armed conflict not all of these rules may rest on the type of actual field practice traditionally required of rules of customary law. Yet they may well reflect existing principles and thus deserve to be promoted under that heading.

1.3   Implementation and enforcement

It is one thing for the representatives of states to negotiate rules of international humanitarian law, and even to be convinced that in doing so they – often, the military officers on the list of states' delegations – have taken realities into account to such a degree that there will be no basis for invoking 'military necessity' in justification of a deviation from the rules. It is another thing to ensure that the rules are applied in practice.

A number of factors may exert a negative influence on the implementation of the rules. Starting at the top: it may be decided at the highest level of authority that certain rules will be disregarded. Examples include the decisions, taken on both sides in the Second World War, to make the enemy civilian population a target of air bombardment, and the decision taken towards the end of that war by President Truman of the United States to use the atomic bomb against Japanese cities. Another important negative factor arises when situations occur that are more than normally conducive to unlawful modes of combat. The phenomenon of 'asymmetrical warfare' might be an example. Other examples include: heavy emphasis on the alleged ideological or religious character of the war; depicting the adversary as barbarian; hostilities carried out as a technical operation at long distance (the bomber operating at high altitudes, the long-range missile) or involving, in a guerrilla-type war, tactics that expose the civilian population to enhanced risk.

For another thing, it would be a sheer miracle if all members of the armed forces were angels, or even simply law-abiding men and women – and even more so if they remained so through every phase of the war. Factors such as insufficient or wrongly oriented training programmes or lack of discipline may play a role in this respect. Yet another factor at the root of many violations of humanitarian law – and which operates at all levels, from the highest political and military leaders to the common soldier – is sheer ignorance of the rules.

In the face of so many adverse factors, what can be done to improve the record of respect for the humanitarian law of armed conflict? A first point to note is that this is first and foremost the responsibility of the states concerned, and, in an internal armed conflict, of the non-state armed groups as well. It has long been realised, however, that this is not enough and outside help is necessary. Reference has already repeatedly been made to the ICRC, the Geneva-based, Swiss organisation, which is active worldwide and which from its inception in 1863 has been the main promoter and guardian, initially, of the law of Geneva in the narrow sense but in more recent times of all humanitarian law. Other instruments and methods have developed, both inter-state and in the context of international organisations, which contribute to the promotion and, if necessary, enforcement of international humanitarian law. We shall come across these various devices and means as they become relevant in the subsequent chapters.

1.4   Structure of this book

It remains to explain the structure of this book. As in the previous editions, the material is divided into historical periods, for two reasons. One is that the body of humanitarian law as we know it today has developed first and foremost as treaty law. Since a treaty applies between the parties to it and is not necessarily set aside by a later treaty on the same subject, the situation may arise where some states are party to the new treaty (for instance, the Protocol of 1977 that deals extensively with combatant behaviour and the protection of civilians) whereas other states are party only to older ones. Therefore, to be useful to all readers, the subject matter of this book is presented in chronological order. Even so we occasionally include a reference to subsequent developments that are more fully dealt with further on in their relevant historical framework.

The chronological approach serves another purpose as well: it enables today's commentators, including the media, to discover what law was applicable to events they are reviewing. This may help prevent the sometimes too easy comment that lays events of the past against the yardstick of today. To give just one example: the treatment of populations under German occupation in the Second World War was governed by the relevant rules of the Hague Regulations of 1899/1907, complemented by such rules of customary law as might have developed since but prior to the war; not, therefore, by the rules of occupation law laid down in the Fourth Geneva Convention of 1949 'Relative to the Protection of Civilian Persons in Time of War', which is subsequent to the war and in effect was drafted to take into account the experiences gained in that unhappy period.

With these considerations in mind, the division of the subject matter across the chapters is as follows: Chapter 2 provides a broad sketch of trends in the historical development of the humanitarian law of war. Chapter 3 deals at greater length with the law as it stood prior to 1977 (the year two protocols additional to the Geneva Conventions of 1949 were adopted). Chapter 4 describes the legal situation as it arises from these protocols. Chapter 5 sets forth the many developments that have occurred since. In conclusion, Chapter 6 briefly summarises some basic features of this body of law.

The main currents: The Hague, Geneva, New York

The present chapter starts out with the birth, in the 1860s, of two 'branches' of the law of armed conflict: the law of The Hague (Section 2.1) and the law of Geneva (Section 2.2).

Just about a century after those early beginnings, in the 1960s and 1970s, the United Nations began to take an active interest in the promotion and development of the law of armed conflict, under the heading 'human rights in armed conflict'. Apart from enabling the General Assembly to incorporate the subject under a previously existing agenda item, this marked the increasingly important relationship between the law of armed conflict and human rights law. This 'current of New York' is the subject of Section 2.3.

Section 2.4 explains how the three 'currents' of The Hague, Geneva and New York, without losing their identities, progressively converged into a single movement and later on, in the 1990s, developed close links with the field of international criminal law as well.

2.1 The Hague

The development of the branch of the law of armed conflict usually referred to as the 'law of The Hague' did not begin in The Hague at all but, rather, at two locations far from that city: Washington and St Petersburg.

Washington was the place where in 1863, in the course of the American Civil War (1861–5), the President of the United States of America (the Northern side in the war) promulgated a famous order entitled 'Instructions for the Government of Armies of the United States in the Field'. The text had been prepared by Francis Lieber, an international lawyer of German origin who had emigrated to America. The Instructions (or Lieber Code, as they are often called) provided detailed rules on the entire range of land warfare, from the conduct of war proper and the treatment of the civilian population to the treatment of specific categories of persons such as prisoners of war, the wounded, *franc-tireurs* and so forth.

Although technically an internal document destined for use by one party in an ongoing civil war, the Lieber Code came to serve as a model and a source of inspiration for the efforts, undertaken later in the nineteenth century at the international level, to arrive at a generally acceptable codification of the laws and customs of war. It thus has exerted great influence on these subsequent developments.

St Petersburg was where, in 1868, another remarkable document saw the light: the Declaration Renouncing the Use, in Time of War, of Explosive Projectiles Under 400 Grammes Weight. In more than one respect, it was the antipode of the Lieber Code. While the Code was a piece of domestic legislation covering an extremely broad range of issues, the Declaration was an international treaty yet bearing on one single, highly specific aspect of the conduct of war. The question at issue was the employment of certain recently developed light explosive or inflammable projectiles. The explosive rifle projectile in particular had already proved its effects on enemy materiel. When used against human beings, it was no more effective than an ordinary rifle bullet: it could put just one adversary out of combat, but owing to its design, it was apt to cause particularly serious wounds to the victim.

The International Military Commission that, on the invitation of the Russian Government, met in St Petersburg in 1868 "to examine the expediency of forbidding the use of certain projectiles in time of war between civilised nations", did not take long to conclude that the new projectiles must be banned from use. Starting from the proposition that "the progress of civilisation should have the effect of alleviating as much as possible the calamities of war", the Commission alleged that "the only legitimate object which states should endeavour to accomplish during war is to weaken the military forces of the enemy". For this purpose it would be "sufficient to disable the greatest possible number of men", and "this object would be exceeded by the employment of arms which uselessly aggravate the sufferings of disabled men, or render their death inevitable". The employment of such weapons "would, therefore, be contrary to the laws of humanity".

Since in the eyes of the Commission the projectiles at issue met these criteria of uselessly aggravating sufferings or rendering death inevitable, its next step was to fix "the technical limits at which the necessities of war ought to yield to the requirements of humanity". This it did with ostensibly mathematical precision: 400 grammes was to be the critical weight. The choice for 400 grammes was random: rifle bullets weighed far less, and the artillery shells of the time were considerably heavier. Yet, the relevant point was the establishment of a fixed dividing line somewhere between these two. Although explosive artillery shells were apt to inflict equally grave wounds, to the point of "rendering the death of disabled men inevitable", they could disable more than one man at a stroke and therefore were not in the same class as rifle bullets. Apart from that, artillery shells were designed to be used against entirely different, 'hard' targets in the first place and therefore had to remain outside the scope of the prohibition: in their case, the balance between military utility and the requirements of humanity worked out differently.

A last point addressed in the Declaration of St Petersburg concerns the question of future developments in weaponry. Here again the text is worthy of note: "The Contracting or Acceding Parties reserve to themselves to come hereafter to an understanding whenever a precise proposition shall be drawn up in view of future improvements which science may effect in the armament of troops, in order to maintain the principles which they have established, and to conciliate the necessities of war with the laws of humanity."

2.1.1   The Hague Peace Conferences

With this we finally arrive at The Hague, where in 1899, once again on the initiative of the Russian Government (though this time on the invitation of the Dutch Government), delegates of twenty-nine states met to discuss matters of peace and war. The stated main purpose of the First Hague Peace Conference was to create conditions precluding further wars. The hope was to bring this about by introducing compulsory inter-state arbitration, coupled with the convening at regular intervals of international conferences to discuss any problems that might arise in connection with the maintenance of peace. The Conference failed to achieve this goal: while it was generally agreed that international arbitration was an excellent means for settling inter-state disputes, a significant number of states were not prepared to waive the right to decide in future, with respect to each dispute as it presented itself and in the light of all prevailing circumstances, whether or not to submit it to arbitration.

While the maintenance of peace might have been its main goal, the initiators of the Conference realistically did not exclude the possibility of future armed conflicts. With a view to that possibility, the Conference discussed a number of proposals relating to the conduct of war.

One proposal was for a codification of the 'laws and customs of war on land'. The proposal was largely based on a text drafted by an earlier international conference, held in Brussels in 1874. This 'Declaration of Brussels of 1874', which had never entered into force, had in turn been strongly influenced by the Lieber Code. Inspired by these earlier examples as, indeed, by the spirit of the Declaration of St Petersburg of 1868, the Conference of 1899 adopted the 'Convention with Respect to the Laws and Customs of War on Land' with annexed Regulations. The Regulations on Land Warfare provide rules concerning all aspects of land warfare on which the contracting states had been able to agree, such as: the types of armed forces that were recognised as 'belligerents'; the treatment of prisoners of war; restrictions on the adoption of means and methods of waging war, including some basic though fragmentary rules on the protection of civilian populations – notably a prohibition to bombard undefended towns – and cultural objects; restrictions on the behaviour of an occupying power. (The Regulations do not include provisions on the treatment of the sick and wounded, as that matter was already the subject of the Geneva Convention of 1864.)

One vexed and ultimately unresolved question before the Conference concerned the position of groups of resistance fighters in occupied territory who take up arms against the occupant: was the occupying power obliged to recognise these groups as belligerents, or could it summarily execute captured resistance fighters as *franc-tireurs*? On this question, the small powers opposed the big ones. The former, realising that their territories would be the probable theatre of military occupation, strongly advocated a right of resistance of the occupied population. As against this, the major powers held that although inhabitants of occupied territory engaging in armed resistance might be heroes in the eyes of their own people, they could not be recognised as legitimate combatants and therefore would always act at their peril.

With the question thus unresolved, a significant spin-off of the debate was the inclusion, in the preamble of the Convention, of a rightly famous paragraph which, as a tribute to the Russian delegate who proposed it, has become known as the Martens clause. Recognising that it had not been possible to resolve all problems, the contracting parties stated that it was not their intention "that unforeseen cases should, in the absence of a written undertaking, be left to the arbitrary judgment of military commanders": on the contrary, in such unforeseen cases both civilians and combatants would "remain under the protection and the rule of the principles of the laws of nations, as they result from the usages established among civilised peoples, from the laws of humanity, and the dictates of the public conscience". This phrase, although formulated especially with

a view to disposing of the thorny problem of armed resistance in occupied territory, has acquired a significance far exceeding that particular
problem. It implies no more or less than that, no matter what states may
fail to agree upon, the conduct of war will always be governed by existing
principles of international law.

While the reference in the Martens clause to the "laws of humanity"
already points to the Declaration of St Petersburg as a source of inspiration, the preamble of the Convention of 1899 refers even more directly
to that document when it states that the wording of the Regulations "has
been inspired by the desire to diminish the evils of war, as far as military
requirements permit". The principle expressed in this paragraph – and
found once again in the Regulations, in the form of a general prohibition
on the use of weapons that cause unnecessary suffering – reflects the principle at the root of the work of the International Military Commission
of 1868: namely, that military necessity must be balanced against the
requirements of humanity.

Continuing the work begun in 1868 in a practical manner as well, the
First Hague Peace Conference adopted a Declaration (IV, 3) prohibiting the use of yet another recently developed type of rifle ammunition,
called dum-dum bullets after the British Indian arsenal Dum-Dum, near
Calcutta, where they had first been developed. These bullets, stated to
"expand or flatten easily in the human body", were apt to cause wounds
as horrible as those of the light explosive or inflammable projectiles prohibited in 1868. The new prohibition was one clear application of the idea,
expressed by the delegates at St Petersburg, that new weapon developments needed to be evaluated "in order to maintain the principles which
they have established, and to conciliate the necessities of war with the
laws of humanity".

Another Hague Declaration worth mentioning (IV, 1) prohibited for
a period of five years "the launching of projectiles and explosives from
balloons, or by other new methods of a similar nature" – a supplement to
the prohibition in the Regulations of bombardment of undefended towns,
and a first premonition of the possible impact of the air arm on the conduct of war.

In 1907, the Second Hague Peace Conference convened according to
plan. The main goal, ensuring international peace, once again remained
beyond reach. Indeed, any existing illusions in this respect were rudely
shattered with the outbreak, in 1914, of the First World War, an event
that also effectively prevented the convening of the planned Third Peace
Conference.

The activities of the Second Peace Conference with respect to the law of land warfare were confined to a minor revision of the Convention and Regulations of 1899. One important item concerned the bombardment of undefended towns. Besides artillery shelling, bombardment from the air was looming ever more clearly as another possibility. Although the existing technique still was limited to bombs thrown from balloons, the mere contemplation of further possibilities was sufficient ground to add the words "by whatever means" to the existing prohibition on bombardment of undefended towns. The Declaration on balloons was renewed as well (XIV), this time "for a period extending to the close of the Third Peace Conference" – a conference that was never held. For the rest, the treatment of what later came to be called 'battlefield law' remained as fragmentary as it had been in 1899.

On the other hand, the Conference dealt extensively with naval warfare. One important result was the Convention (IX) Concerning Bombardment by Naval Forces in Time of War. Its opening article repeats the prohibition to bombard undefended towns, and Article 2 goes on to provide a definition of specific objects (such as naval establishments, or works that could be utilised for the needs of the hostile fleet) which, although situated within such undefended towns, would nonetheless be military objectives and therefore subject to bombardment. This reminds us that at the time, naval guns could perform a task air forces would take over later: the bombardment of military objectives located far from the battlefield. The rule in Article 2 foreshadows those later developments. Unfortunately, Article 3 of the Convention also permitted the bombardment of entire undefended towns, on the mere ground that the local authorities "decline[d] to comply with requisitions for provisions or supplies necessary for the immediate use of the naval force before the place in question": decidedly a rather less felicitous provision in modern eyes.

Always in the sphere of naval warfare, the Conference adopted a Convention (VIII) that placed certain restrictions on the use of automatic submarine contact mines and torpedoes, and several other conventions on (neutral and enemy) commercial shipping interests. Prominent among these was Convention XII on the creation of an International Prize Court. However, states did not agree on the substantive rules the Court should apply with respect to matters such as blockade, contraband, visit and search, and destruction of merchant vessels – an area of disagreement that remained untouched in 1907. A Naval Conference held in London in 1909 did find agreed solutions for these questions, but the resultant Declaration Concerning the Law of Naval War failed to be ratified, and so did the Convention on the International Prize Court. In consequence, the Court was never established, leaving matters of prize law to domestic jurisdictions.

2.1.2   The League of Nations period

The League of Nations, established after the First World War, never paid much attention to the development of the law of armed conflict. After all, the organisation was supposed to maintain peace, and "war would no longer occur", at least in Europe: under the guidance of the League, the world would disarm and the arms trade be brought under control. A conference convened to that end in Geneva in 1925 actually adopted a treaty on supervision of the international arms trade. The treaty failed to be ratified, however, and never entered into force.

The Conference of 1925 had more success with what actually was a by-product of its proceedings: the Protocol for the Prohibition of the Use in War of Asphyxiating, Poisonous or Other Gases, and of Bacteriological Methods of Warfare. The Hague Regulations of 1899 had already codified the ancient prohibition on the use of 'poison or poisoned weapons'; but the use in the First World War of various chemical agents, such as chlorine, phosgene and mustard gas, had demonstrated the inadequacy of this prohibition. As noted in the preamble of the Protocol of 1925, public opinion had sharply condemned this use of chemical means of warfare, and the participants at the Conference of 1925 did not hesitate to ban it once and for all. The prohibition on the use of 'bacteriological means of warfare' was added with foresight: at the time, such means of warfare were no more than a theoretical possibility.

Also worthy of note under the heading 'law of The Hague' is a set of rules of air warfare drafted in 1923 by a commission of jurists set up by virtue of a resolution adopted by the Washington Conference of 1922 on the Limitation of Armaments, and composed of lawyers from the United States, Great Britain, France, Italy, Japan and the Netherlands. Taking into account the experiences of the First World War, the Hague Rules of Aerial Warfare (so called after the venue of the Commission's meetings) inter alia set stringent limits to air bombardment. Although influential, the Rules remained a non-binding instrument. Even so, in September 1938, in reaction to bombardments from the air on localities in Spain and elsewhere, the League Assembly adopted an (equally non-binding) resolution stating the illegality of intentional bombing of the civilian population and formulating ground rules for air attacks on military objectives.

The League of Nations period also saw repeated attempts at curbing the use of submarines against merchant shipping, in view of the great risks these operations posed to "the lives of neutrals and noncombatants at sea in time of war". The quoted words are from the abortive treaty relating to the Use of Submarines and Noxious Gases in Warfare, concluded in 1922 in Washington but which failed to enter into force. In a next attempt, Article 22 of the 1930 Treaty of London for the Limitation and Reduction of Naval Armaments laid down "as established rules of international law" that "[i]n their action with regard to merchant ships, submarines must conform to the rules of international law to which surface vessels are subject" and, except in case of a persistent refusal to stop or active resistance, "may not sink or render incapable of navigation a merchant vessel without having first placed passengers, crew and ship's papers in a place of safety". These 'rules', reaffirmed in the 1936 *Procès-Verbal* of London, although widely accepted, have never proved very effective.

All these efforts in the League period are evidence of a growing concern about developments in the war-making capabilities of states, developments that exposed civilians on land as at sea to ever greater risks from the conduct of hostilities. The ultimate, desperate effort to stem these developments, the League Disarmament Conference of 1932–4, foundered miserably in the political storm gathering over Europe that, when it finally broke in 1939, destroyed many more things, including the League of Nations itself.

2.1.3   *The Post-Second World War period*

The horrors of the Second World War inspired a stream of important developments, both of general international law and in the law of armed conflict. Of outstanding importance and to be mentioned before all others was the adoption, in 1945, of the Charter of the United Nations, establishing the United Nations as successor to the League of Nations.

Another major feat was the creation and work of the International Military Tribunals in Nuremberg and Tokyo for the prosecution of the major war criminals of the Axis countries (already referred to briefly in Section 1.2), highlighting the notion of individual responsibility for war crimes. (See also Section 2.3.1.)

High on the agenda of the United Nations from the first days of its existence, was the 'atomic bomb'. The very first resolution ever adopted by the UN General Assembly, Resolution 1 (I) of 24 January 1946, provided for the establishment of an Atomic Energy Commission, with as one of its tasks the formulation of proposals for the elimination of nuclear weapons from national armaments.

Apart from these and other aspects of contemporary warfare, which because of their wider implications will be discussed hereafter in Sections 2.3 and 2.4, the position of the United Nations initially remained the same as that of the League of Nations: focus on the maintenance of peace, little interest for the development of the law of armed conflict in general, and even less for the 'law of The Hague' in particular.

One notable exception to this lack of interest concerns the protection of cultural property in the event of armed conflict. This was the theme of an intergovernmental conference that met in 1954 at The Hague under the auspices of UNESCO (the United Nations Educational, Scientific and Cultural Organization). The conference adopted the Hague Convention for the Protection of Cultural Property in the Event of Armed Conflict, with annexed Regulations, as well as a protocol specifically dealing with the export of cultural property from occupied territory. Compared with the scant provisions on this subject in the Regulations on Land Warfare, these instruments signified an important step forward in the protection of cultural property in time of war.

2.2   Geneva

Around the middle of the nineteenth century the condition of wounded soldiers on the battlefield left nearly everything to be desired. Care for the wounded was primitive and insufficient in all respects: there was a dearth of medical and auxiliary personnel; surgery and other treatment usually had to be carried out in very primitive conditions; insight into the need for sterile wound treatment was lacking; antibiotics and blood plasma did not exist; and so on. Nor was this all: perhaps worst was that the Napoleonic wars of the early nineteenth century had brought an end to the previous practice of sparing the enemy's field hospitals and leaving both the medical personnel and the wounded untouched. Instead, field hospitals were shelled, and doctors and stretcher bearers on the battlefield subjected to fire; and whoever fell into enemy hands, whether wounded or not and regardless of whether they belonged to the fighting forces or to the medical or auxiliary personnel, was taken prisoner. The net result was that often, upon the approach of enemy forces, or even on the rumour of their approach, doctors and nurses in the field hospitals fled with the primitive ambulances at their disposal, taking with them as many wounded as they could and leaving the others unattended.

Neither could aid for the wounded always be expected from the inhabitants of nearby localities: one never knew which way the fortunes of battle would go, and anyone who tended a wounded soldier of one party ran the risk of being regarded as an active supporter of that party by the other side.

The disastrous consequences of this accumulation of adverse factors were widely known. Yet it took the initiative of a businessman from Geneva, J. Henry Dunant, for the world to take effective steps about it. In 1859, in the aftermath of the Battle of Solferino in northern Italy, Dunant found himself, more or less by accident, amidst the thousands of French and Austrian wounded who had been brought to the nearby village of Castiglione. For days, he and a few other volunteers did what they could to treat the wounded and alleviate the sufferings of the dying.

Then, deeply affected by the misery he had witnessed, he retired for a while from active life and recorded his experiences in a book to which he gave the title *Un souvenir de Solferino* (A Memory of Solferino). Published in 1862, the book created an immediate stir throughout Europe, especially in elite circles where the realisation was sharp that the existing situation could no longer be left unchanged. In effect, Dunant had specified in his book two steps he regarded as indispensable: the establishment, in each country, of a national private aid organisation to assist military medical services in a task they were insufficiently equipped to perform; and the adoption of a treaty that would facilitate the work of these organisations and guarantee a better treatment of the wounded.

The realisation of both ideas took surprisingly little time. As early as 1863 a few citizens from Geneva, with Henry Dunant among them, established the International Committee for Aid to the Wounded, with the self-appointed task of promoting the twin aims of the creation of national aid societies and the adoption of a treaty facilitating their work. The Committee, which initially had also been known as the Committee of Five or Geneva Committee, was soon renamed International Committee of the Red Cross.

Also in 1863, the first national society was established in Württemberg; Oldenburg, Belgium and Prussia followed in 1864, and the Netherlands in 1866. These early national societies were succeeded in the course of time by similar societies in nearly every country, under the name of Red Cross or Red Crescent Society. (On the present state of what has grown into the International Red Cross and Red Crescent Movement, see Section 5.3.9a.)

The desired treaty was hardly longer in coming. A group of enthusiastic propagandists seized every opportunity to spread the idea that such a treaty was urgently needed. As a result of their efforts, and on the invitation of the Swiss Government, a diplomatic conference convened in 1864 in Geneva that, on 22 August of that year, adopted the 'Convention for the Amelioration of the Condition of the Wounded in Armies in the Field'.

The most important features of the Convention (a mere ten articles long!) may be summarised as follows: in war on land, ambulances and military hospitals would be "recognised as neutral, and as such, protected and respected by the belligerents as long as they accommodate wounded and sick"; hospital and ambulance personnel, far from being taken prisoner or made the target of fire, would have "the benefit of the same neutrality when on duty, and while there remain any wounded to be brought in or assisted"; "wounded and sick combatants, to whatever nation they may belong, shall be collected and cared for"; and, last but not least, "hospitals, ambulances and evacuation parties" would be distinguished by a uniform flag bearing "a red cross on a white ground".

This first, modest beginning would be followed by a long list of further steps developing the 'law of Geneva' and either expanding the categories of protected persons or improving the rules in the light of acquired experience. In 1899, a treaty was concluded that rendered the principles of the treaty of 1864 applicable to the wounded, sick and shipwrecked at sea. 1906 saw a first revision of the treaty of 1864, and in 1907 the treaty of 1899 was adjusted to the revision of 1906.

In 1929, on the initiative of the ICRC and once again by invitation of the Swiss Government, a diplomatic conference convened in Geneva. It adopted, first, a much improved treaty on the treatment of the wounded and sick on land, taking into account the experiences of the First World War. Second, it negotiated a separate convention on the treatment of prisoners of war.

The latter treaty significantly expanded the categories of persons protected under the law of Geneva. As mentioned earlier, rules relating to the status of prisoners of war did already exist: having initially developed as rules of customary law, they had been incorporated in 1899 in the Hague Regulations on Land Warfare. Yet, the First World War, with its long duration and large numbers of prisoners of war on both sides, had brought to light the need for more detailed regulation of their protection. The Convention of 1929 achieved this goal. Important improvements included: far greater clarity and completeness of the rules and principles on capture and captivity; the introduction of a categorical ban on reprisals against prisoners of war; and acceptance of the principle that application of the agreed rules would be open to international scrutiny.

The tragic events, successively, of the Spanish Civil War and the Second World War provided the incentive for yet another major revision and further development of the law of Geneva. A diplomatic conference convened in 1949 in Geneva, once again at the instigation of the ICRC and by invitation of the Swiss Government. The three Geneva Conventions in force (one of 1907 and two of 1929) were substituted by new ones, improving many existing rules and filling lacunae practice had brought to light. To give just one example: the often ruthless treatment, in the course of the Second World War, of armed resistance fighters in countries under German occupation led to the express recognition that members of organised resistance movements that fulfil a number of (stringent) conditions would qualify as prisoners of war.

Then, the law of Geneva was enriched with an entirely novel convention on the protection of civilian persons in time of war. It protects two categories of civilians in particular: enemy civilians in the territory of a belligerent party and the inhabitants of occupied territory; categories of civilians, that is, who as a consequence of the armed conflict find themselves in the power of the enemy. With this latest addition the law of Geneva had come to comprise four conventions, dealing with the wounded and sick on land (I); the wounded, sick and shipwrecked at sea (II); prisoners of war (III); and protected civilians (IV).

The Diplomatic Conference of 1949 added two further innovations of crucial importance. One, mentioned briefly in the foregoing, concerns the scope of application of the Conventions. The earlier Geneva Conventions, like the Hague Conventions on land warfare and similar instruments, had been drafted for application in wars between states. The Spanish Civil War had demonstrated the difficulty, and the need, to make the parties to such internal armed conflicts respect basic principles of humanitarian law. In the light of this experience, the Conference introduced into all four Conventions of 1949, common Article 3 "applicable in the case of armed conflict not of an international character occurring in the territory of one of the High Contracting Parties". The Article lays down a list of fundamental rules each party to the conflict is "bound to apply, as a minimum" in the event of such a conflict. Its adoption represented a tremendous step forward in that it demonstrated the possibility of agreeing on rules of international law expressly addressing situations of internal armed conflict. Another intriguing aspect of common Article 3 is the evident influence on its provisions of nascent notions of human rights.

The other major innovation was the introduction, again into all four Conventions, of provisions requiring contracting states to take the necessary penal, disciplinary and organisational measures to deal with grave breaches and other serious violations of the Conventions.

In the course of the years, the four Conventions of Geneva of 1949 in their turn began to show shortcomings, for instance, with respect to the treatment of captured guerrilla fighters in so-called wars of national liberation. Endeavours to cope with these problems coincided with developments in other areas of the law of armed conflict and will therefore be dealt with in Section 2.4.

2.3   New York

As mentioned above, the United Nations in its early years displayed very little interest in the development of the law of armed conflict. In 1949, the International Law Commission, as the organ especially charged with the codification and progressive development of international law, gave expression to this negative attitude when it decided not to place the law of armed conflict on its agenda, on the argument that any attention devoted to that branch of law might be considered as betraying a lack of confidence in the capacity of the United Nations to maintain international peace and security.

Even so, two specific subjects attracted attention in this period: the prosecution of war criminals and the problems posed by the atomic bomb, as the most recent and particularly horrifying addition to arsenals.

2.3.1   The Nuremberg Principles

The issue of individual responsibility for war crimes had been the focus of attention ever since 1943, when the Allied powers, in the course of the war, had made it known that the major war criminals of the Axis powers would be made to answer for their evil deeds. As mentioned above, two tribunals were set up shortly after the war for the prosecution and punishment of these criminals: one, in 1945, for the major war criminals of the European Axis (usually referred to, after its venue, as the Nuremberg Tribunal); the other, in 1946 and with its seat in Tokyo, to try the major Japanese war criminals.

The basis for the prosecution of the war criminals of the European Axis was the Charter establishing the Nuremberg Tribunal, annexed to the London Agreement of August 1945. The Charter defined three categories of crimes falling within the jurisdiction of the Tribunal and for which there would be individual responsibility: crimes against the peace (or aggression), war crimes and crimes against humanity.]It also defined applicable principles of individual criminal liability; notably, the official position of defendants would "not be considered as freeing them from responsibility or mitigating punishment", and a superior order would not free a defendant from responsibility but might be "considered in mitigation of punishment if the Tribunal determines that justice so requires".

In 1946, the UN General Assembly in Resolution 95 (I) reaffirmed these principles, as reformulated by the Tribunal (and therefore usually referred to as the 'Nuremberg Principles'), as generally valid principles of international law. Believing moreover that the time had come to set about drafting a code of international criminal law, the General Assembly in the same resolution directed the International Law Commission to prepare a Draft Code of Offences Against the Peace and Security of Mankind. (As set forth in Section 2.4, it would take until the 1990s to resolve the problems attending these efforts.)

2.3.2 The UN General Assembly and the 'atomic bomb'

As mentioned above, the 'atomic bomb' was the other subject of urgent concern on the early agenda of the UN General Assembly, and it had charged the Atomic Energy Commission with formulating proposals to eliminate nuclear weapons from national arsenals (see Section 2.1.3). In the years that followed, the disarmament aspect apparent in these terms of reference (as opposed to the issue of actual use of the weapons) largely dominated the debate, both in the Commission and in the General Assembly.

By way of exception to this trend the General Assembly on 24 November 1961 adopted Resolution 1635 (XVI), which focused on the use of nuclear weapons, declaring that such use would be unlawful. Considerably reducing the effect of this firm opening statement, part two of the Resolution requested the Secretary-General "to consult the Governments of Member States to ascertain their views on the possibility of convening a special conference for signing a convention on the prohibition of the use of nuclear and thermo-nuclear weapons for war purposes", and to report on the results at its next session. (Needless to say, the consultations remained without result.) The impact of the Resolution was undermined even further by the fact that a significant number of states, including the United States, the United Kingdom and France – all three nuclear powers – voted against or abstained; the vote was fifty-five in favour, twenty against and twenty-six abstentions. Yet, despite these shortcomings, the Resolution gave expression to a majority opinion in the General Assembly.

2.3.3   *The UN General Assembly and 'human rights in armed conflicts'*

1968, baptised the 'Human Rights Year', marked the beginning of a broader and more active interest of the United Nations in the law of armed conflict. The International Conference on Human Rights, which met under UN auspices from 22 April to 15 May in Teheran, adopted towards the end of its sessions, and without much debate, Resolution XXIII on 'human rights in armed conflicts'. The Resolution requested the General Assembly to invite the Secretary-General to study steps "to secure the better application of existing humanitarian international conventions and rules in all armed conflicts".

The Teheran Resolution also requested an enquiry into the "need for additional humanitarian international conventions or for possible revision of existing Conventions to ensure the better protection of civilians, prisoners of war and combatants in all armed conflicts and the prohibition and limitation of the use of certain methods and means of warfare".

The General Assembly on 19 December 1968 passed Resolution 2444 (XXIII), which invited the Secretary-General, in consultation with the ICRC, to undertake the studies requested in the Teheran Resolution. The General Assembly Resolution was entitled 'Respect for Human Rights in Armed Conflicts', and many of the UN activities relating to the law of armed conflict have since been placed under that banner. As noted before, with this title the UN not only indicated the historical origin of its active interest in the law of armed conflict, but provided a justification for its radical change of course: under the Charter, the promotion and protection of human rights are among its main functions.

The activities of the United Nations with respect to the development of the law of armed conflict undertaken since the adoption of Resolution 2444 fall into two separate categories. On the one hand, the Secretary-General in a series of annual reports provided a broad overview of the law of armed conflict (in UN terms, of human rights applicable in armed conflicts), making many interesting suggestions for the development of this body of law. These reports were usually followed by General Assembly resolutions expressing general support for the work in progress. On the other hand, the General Assembly and its various commissions repeatedly engaged in debates and adopted resolutions, focusing on a few narrowly defined specific questions, notably, the protection of women and children, the position of journalists and the condition of liberation fighters in wars of national liberation.

2.3.4 The UN General Assembly and wars of national liberation

So-called wars of national liberation were of particular concern to the General Assembly, and understandably so since they concerned two issues that through the years deeply stirred the organisation. One was the situation in the Middle East (with the various groups constituting the Palestine Liberation Organization acting as liberation fighters); and the other, the decolonisation process with its long drawn-out conflicts in Asia and Africa.

In respect of this process of decolonisation the General Assembly took sides with ever greater insistence. Time and again, its resolutions, and those of other main UN organs as well, underscored the right of self-determination of the peoples involved, and appealed to the authorities in power no longer to oppose its realisation. With the increasing violence accompanying the liberation of the territories under colonial domination, the resolutions declared ever more unambiguously that the use of force in these 'wars of national liberation' was justified, and they appealed to other countries to lend aid and support to the liberation fighters. The resolutions also – and this brings us back to our subject – repeatedly stated that the wars of national liberation were international armed conflicts, and they insisted that captured liberation fighters be regarded as prisoners of war and treated as such. In this manner in particular, the UN had a stimulating effect on the negotiations that meanwhile, under the guidance of the ICRC, had commenced in Geneva, with respect to the position of guerrilla fighters, among other things.

2.3.5 The UN General Assembly and conventional weapons

Another series of resolutions adopted by the General Assembly in the 1970s had a bearing on the question of possible prohibitions or restrictions on the use of specified 'conventional weapons'. The term refers to weapons other than those belonging to the class of so-called weapons of mass destruction – that is to say, nuclear, chemical and bacteriological (NBC) weapons. While, as we shall see, the real debate on this subject too was taking place in a different forum, the resolutions of the General Assembly were important in that they kept the subject in the public eye.

In sum, the activities of the United Nations relating to the reaffirmation and development of the law of war in the 1970s have been significant in three respects. First and foremost, they contributed to cutting through the taboo on the subject. Second, they highlighted the idea of protection of the fundamental rights of human beings even in times of armed conflict. And third, they made a valuable contribution to the debate on a number of specific questions, notably that of the position of guerrilla fighters in wars of national liberation.

2.4   Confluence: 1977 and beyond

The International Committee of the Red Cross, although originally concerned in particular with the 'law of Geneva' in a strict sense, had already in the 1950s embarked on a road that took it on to the domain referred to as the 'law of The Hague': in 1955 and once again in 1956 it published a set of draft rules for the area where this body of law was most blatantly inadequate, namely, the protection of an unoccupied civilian population against the effects of military operations. These proposals, published at the height of the Cold War, had garnered insufficient positive response: at the time, few important governments were prepared to engage in a discussion as delicate as the detailed regulation and limitation of aerial bombardment. The generally negative reactions were enhanced by the fact that the draft rules contained an only thinly veiled condemnation of nuclear weapons.

A decade later, the ICRC took a new initiative along an entirely different line: no detailed proposals this time about precise rules, but a statement of some fundamental principles of the law of war, the validity of which no one would dare to deny. This approach was successful: the 20th International Conference of the Red Cross, held in Vienna in 1965, adopted Resolution XXVIII that "solemnly declares that all Governments and other authorities responsible for action in armed conflicts should conform at least to the following principles":

(a) that the right of the parties to a conflict to adopt means of injuring the enemy is not unlimited;
(b) that it is prohibited to launch attacks against the civilian populations as such;
(c) that distinction must be made at all times between persons taking part in the hostilities and members of the civilian population to the effect that the latter be spared as much as possible;

(d) that the general principles of the law of war apply to nuclear and similar weapons.

The adoption of this Resolution, precisely in the year the United States began its bombardments of North Vietnam, marked an important breakthrough. Governmental delegations of states party to the Geneva Conventions participate with full voting rights in the International Conferences of the Red Cross and Red Crescent – as the conferences have been styled since 1995; and the fact that the Vienna Conference adopted the Resolution was a clear sign that besides Red Cross and Red Crescent circles, governments as well were prepared to take up the matter of the 'reaffirmation and development' of the law of armed conflict.

This readiness was even more evident with the adoption in December 1968 of UNGA Resolution 2444 (XXIII). This not only requested the UN Secretary-General to carry out his studies "in consultation with the International Committee of the Red Cross": it also repeated and reaffirmed the principles for the protection of civilian populations set forth in the Vienna Resolution – except for the fourth and last principle, considered redundant in view of the earlier statement in GA Resolution 1653 (XVI) that the use of nuclear weapons was unlawful. With the adoption of Resolution 2444, the General Assembly had once and for all rejected the idea of war waged against a population in its entirety, in an attempt thus to force the adverse party to surrender. It may be noted in passing that the principles set forth in Resolution 2444 have since been widely recognised as belonging to the realm of customary law.

Resolution 2444 marked the beginning of an accelerated movement that brought the three currents of The Hague, Geneva and New York together into one main stream. With governments and the United Nations participating and the ICRC very much in a leading role, the debate concerned the rules of combat in the sense of Hague law as much as those on the protection of the victims of war in the sense of Geneva law and, indeed, the notion of international protection of human rights in armed conflicts, thus demonstrating the growing interaction between these parts of international law.

This accelerated development eventually culminated in the Diplomatic Conference on the Reaffirmation and Development of International Humanitarian Law Applicable in Armed Conflicts – known by its French acronym, CDDH – which convened in 1974 in Geneva at the invitation of the Swiss Government. In four yearly sessions (1974–7) and on the basis of draft texts submitted by the ICRC, the CDDH drew up the text of two treaties styled Protocols Additional to the Conventions of Geneva of 1949. Protocol I governs the protection of victims of international armed conflicts, and Protocol II, the protection of victims of internal armed conflicts; both contain a mixture of Hague and Geneva law with important human rights elements. The CDDH adopted the Protocols on 8 June 1977. Signed on 12 December 1977 at Bern by numerous states, they have been ratified since by a vast majority of the states. The Protocols entered into force on 7 December 1978, six months after two instruments of ratification had been deposited, with the Swiss Government acting as depositary.

The Protocols of 1977 are silent on the subject mentioned at the end of Section 2.3, of possible prohibitions or restrictions on the use of conventional weapons such as napalm, landmines and booby traps. At the time of the CDDH, the debate on this subject – which again belongs as much to Hague as to Geneva law, with strong human rights overtones – began to assume the character of negotiations; but these could not be brought to a conclusion together with the negotiations on the Protocols. The subject was next taken up by a UN Conference convened for that purpose. After two sessions held in 1979 and 1980, the Conference on 10 October 1980 adopted the Convention on Prohibitions or Restrictions on the Use of Certain Conventional Weapons Which May be Deemed to be Excessively Injurious or to Have Indiscriminate Effects, with three annexed Protocols: on 'non-detectable fragments', 'mines, booby traps and other devices', and 'incendiary weapons'. The Convention with annexed Protocols entered into force on 2 December 1983.

A fourth Protocol was attached to the Convention in 1995, on 'blinding laser weapons', and in 2003 a fifth, on 'explosive remnants of war'. In 1996, the Mines Protocol was thoroughly amended, and in 2001, Article 1 of the Convention, which limited its scope to international armed conflicts, was amended to encompass all armed conflicts.

In a parallel development, two related conventions were adopted in this period: one, in 1997, completely prohibiting the possession and use of anti-personnel mines (the Ottawa Convention, in force since March 1999); and the other, in 2008, equally completely banning the possession and use of cluster munitions (in force since 1 August 2010). See further Section 5.1.2.

The adoption and entry into force of the Additional Protocols of 1977 has inspired several other developments that need to be briefly mentioned here. One concerns the protection of cultural property. The Hague Convention of 1954 and its related instruments, mentioned at the end of Section 2.1, had proved inadequate to achieve its purpose, and this necessitated thorough amendment. Solutions introduced in the 1977 Protocols for the protection of civilians enabled the finding of comparable solutions for problems inherent in the protection of cultural property in times of armed conflict. The combined efforts of UNESCO and a number of actively interested governments resulted in the adoption, on 26 March 1999, of the Second Hague Protocol for the Protection of Cultural Property in the Event of Armed Conflict (in force since 9 March 2004). Between the states parties it largely sets aside the systems of protection of cultural property established under the 1954 Convention. See further Section 5.2.3.

The law of warfare at sea too, had long remained immune to development, except for the Geneva part of the law, crowned in 1949 with the adoption of the Second Convention. In effect, after the abortive attempts of 1907 and 1909 to create an International Prize Court, and the almost equally unsuccessful attempts in the 1930s to curb the dangers submarine warfare posed to merchant shipping, no international conference has been convened to this day to draft rules, say, for the "protection of civilians and civilian objects against the effects of hostilities" at sea. In this predicament, an international group of lawyers and naval officers working under the aegis of the San Remo International Institute of Humanitarian Law and in close cooperation with the ICRC, in 1994 produced a Manual on International Law Applicable to Armed Conflicts at Sea. Although not itself a lawmaking instrument, the Manual provides an authoritative overview of the law of naval warfare. See further Section 5.2.1.

In a similar development, a group of international and military lawyers and air force officers meeting under the aegis of the Harvard Program on Humanitarian Policy and Conflict Research (HPCR) in 2009 produced a Manual on International Law Applicable to Air and Missile Warfare. The last text especially written for air warfare had been the 1923 Draft Rules of Aerial Warfare mentioned in Section 2.1; and although a number of the rules in Protocol I of 1977 and other instruments (such as the Convention on the Protection of Cultural Property in the Event of Armed Conflict) apply to these areas of warfare as well, a document applying the rules to the peculiarities of air and missile warfare could be helpful. Like the San Remo Manual, the HPCR Manual does not purport to create law: it rather aims to provide a detailed exposé of the existing law governing air and missile operations, concerning matters such as the precautions required of a belligerent party attacking from the sky and the precautions expected of the attacked party, the protection of civilian, medical and neutral aircraft, and no-fly zones in belligerent airspace. See further Section 5.2.2.

A last area of 'confluence' of Hague, Geneva and New York law may be seen in the recent developments regarding the prosecution and punishment of war crimes. Mention was made in the foregoing of two events that occurred in the aftermath of the Second World War: the introduction into the 1949 Geneva Conventions of provisions on grave breaches and other violations, and the establishment of the Nuremberg and Tokyo Tribunals. The 'grave breach' provisions in the 1949 Conventions single out specific serious violations contracting states are obliged to prosecute. A similar provision was subsequently included in Protocol I of 1977. The provisions contemplate only violations committed in international conflicts, and neither the Conventions nor the Protocol make provision for an international criminal procedure.

While these instruments leave the prosecution and trial of war criminals to national courts, the opposite was the case with the establishment of the International Military Tribunals in Nuremberg and Tokyo for the prosecution and punishment of the major war criminals of the Axis powers. Subsequent attempts to build on these experiences long continued to be frustrated by political factors, and the work on the topic in the International Law Commission (or ILC, a subsidiary organ of the UN General Assembly) remained completely stalled until the Security Council in the last decade of the twentieth century established two ad hoc International Criminal Tribunals: one, in 1993, for the prosecution of persons responsible for serious violations of international humanitarian law committed since 1991 in the territory of the former Yugoslavia; and the other, in 1994, for the prosecution of persons responsible for genocide and other grave violations committed in that year in the territory of Rwanda, or of Rwandan citizens responsible for such violations elsewhere.

The establishment of these two ad hoc tribunals gave new impetus to the work of the ILC. This resulted in the adoption, by a United Nations Diplomatic Conference in 1998, of the Statute of the International Criminal Court (ICC). This Statute, often referred to as the Rome Statute after the venue of the Conference, applies to crimes committed in both international and non-international armed conflicts, and the Court's jurisdiction encompasses breaches of Hague, Geneva and New York law, thus rendering the distinction between these three fields ever more blurred.

The ICC has its seat at The Hague. Its Statute entered into force in 2002, and a first team of judges, the prosecutor and the registrar took office in 2003. By 2005, with three states and the Security Council having referred cases to the ICC, it has entered into its judicial phase.

Apart from setting up two ad hoc tribunals, the Security Council in the first decade of the twenty-first century has been actively promoting international humanitarian law in other ways as well, in particular with regard to the protection of civilian populations. One specific mode was its involvement in the creation of hybrid jurisdictions, to cope with gross violations of humanitarian law in specified areas (Cambodia, Sierra Leone, East Timor, Kosovo).

By way of conclusion, the reader is reminded once again that except for the Geneva Conventions of 1949, the treaties, conventions and protocols mentioned in the foregoing apply as treaty law only to the states parties. At the same time, rules in these instruments may reflect established principles or customary law as well, and thus be binding in principle on all parties.

3

The law before the Protocols of 1977

This chapter provides an overview of the law of armed conflict as it emerged from the developments described in the previous chapter, up to the Diplomatic Conference of 1974–7. Two topics of general importance are dealt with first: the scope of application of the treaties adopted in this period (Section 3.1), and their relation to military necessity (Section 3.2). These are followed by the main substantive aspects of the law of The Hague and of Geneva, in that order (Sections 3.3 and 3.4). The chapter concludes with a discussion of implementation and sanctions in the event of non-implementation (Section 3.5).

3.1 Scope of application

The law of armed conflict is applicable in the event of war. Thus, Article 2 of the Hague Convention in its 1899 version provides that the annexed Regulations are "binding on the Contracting Powers, in case of war between two or more of them". The article adds that the Regulations "shall cease to be binding from the time when, in a war between Contracting Powers, a non-Contracting Power joins one of the belligerents"; this so-called *si omnes* clause has long lost its relevance: the Nuremberg and Tokyo Tribunals found that the contents of the Convention and Regulations even before the Second World War had become binding on all states as customary law.

The wording of Article 2 makes it clear that the contracting parties of those days were thinking of inter-state war. This is not to say that they would have regarded the rules they were establishing or recognising as unsuitable to be applied in a situation such as the American Civil War. Rather, the idea that treaty rules could be laid down for such an internal situation simply had not yet entered their minds.

Matters were different at the Diplomatic Conference of 1949: the suggestion of making the Geneva Conventions applicable in their entirety to situations of internal armed conflict was expressly raised – and equally expressly rejected. States were not prepared to accept that the detailed and complicated provisions of the Conventions would bind them as treaty law in such internal situations as well. Instead, and as mentioned in Section 2.2, common Article 3 came to lay down a set of minimum rules specifically applicable "in the case of armed conflict not of an international character occurring in the territory of one of the High Contracting Parties". (Article 3 is discussed further in Section 3.4.7.)

The Geneva Conventions of 1949, and subsequent treaties on the law of armed conflict as well, differ from the older treaties also in that they no longer simply refer to 'war'. Common Article 2 of the 1949 Conventions provides that they apply "to all cases of declared war or of any other armed conflict which may arise between two or more of the High Contracting Parties, even if the state of war is not recognised by one of them". While states in the past could argue that a situation not expressly recognised as 'war' did not constitute a war in the legal sense, the authors of the new formula hoped that by adding the objectively ascertainable situation of 'armed conflict' they had done away once and for all with the possibility for states to hide behind a narrow construction of the single word 'war'.

Subsequent events showed that the new formula was not watertight. When in the early 1950s a conflict between the Netherlands and Indonesia about (then) Dutch New Guinea – now a part of Indonesia named Papua – reached its peak and a considerable number of Indonesian armed infiltrators were falling into Dutch hands, the Netherlands denied the applicability of the Prisoners of War Convention of 1949 on the argument that neither party regarded the situation as an armed conflict. The drafters of the 1954 Hague Convention on the Protection of Cultural Property removed this excuse by adding two words at the end of the above phrase: "even if the state of war is not recognised by one *or more* of them" (Art. 18).

The fact remains that even with the objective formula accepted in 1949, the qualification of a situation as an armed conflict in practice remains dependent on the parties' perceived interests in applying their treaty obligations. Apart from that, the formula marks a significant improvement over the previous situation in that it provides third parties – such as states not involved in the conflict, the ICRC or the Security Council – with a tool for exerting pressure on parties that fail to apply the treaties. In effect, in the conflict between the Netherlands and Indonesia, it was the insistence of the ICRC that ultimately resulted in the Dutch authorities changing their position and applying the Prisoners of War Convention to the captured infiltrators.

While the above concerns the application of the law by the parties actually at war, a different matter altogether is the issue of application later on in an international or domestic judicial setting. In such a situation, it is for the forum to determine whether it considers the conflict to be, or to have been, an international or non-international armed conflict in the sense of the relevant rules of treaty or customary law.

Always under the heading of 'scope of application', reference must be made to an issue that arose in the post-Second World War period in connection with UN peacekeeping or peace-enforcing activities. The United Nations cannot become party to the Geneva Conventions, since these are drafted in the traditional manner as inter-state treaties without making provision for accession by non-state entities. The ICRC nonetheless has incessantly urged the UN to find ways formally to subscribe to the Conventions, an urging the UN has equally consistently opposed, accepting only that its forces would be instructed to comply with the 'principles and spirit' of the law. For the rest, it would be for each state contributing forces to a UN operation to ensure compliance by its forces with the rules of humanitarian law in force for that state. As we shall see, the situation changed when in 1999 the Secretary-General issued an instruction that at least partially satisfies the need of greater clarity concerning the specific rules the UN is willing to impose on its forces (see further Section 5.3.1b).

3.2   The law and military necessity

The thesis is sometimes heard that the rules of the law of war have to give in to overriding military necessity. This is incorrect. The preamble to the Hague Convention on Land Warfare of 1899, as reiterated and reaffirmed in 1907, already emphasises that the wording of the Regulations "has been inspired by the desire to diminish the evils of war, *as far as military requirements permit*". The italicised words imply that in drafting the rules as they did, the authors have taken the element of military necessity fully into account. In consequence, a given rule can only be set aside on grounds of military necessity when its text expressly so permits. To give just one example of such an express waiver in the Regulations: Article 23(g) prohibits "To destroy or seize the enemy's property, unless such destruction or seizure be imperatively demanded by the necessities of war".

The language of the Geneva Conventions of 1949 is equally explicit on this point. Common Article 1 obliges states parties "to respect and to ensure respect for the present Convention in all circumstances". The

Conventions likewise provide examples of rules accompanied by a reservation of military necessity. Thus, Article 12 of the First Convention (concerning the wounded and sick of armed forces in the field) provides that a belligerent party "which is compelled to abandon wounded or sick to the enemy shall, *as far as military considerations permit*, leave with them a part of its medical personnel and material to assist in their care". But once again, when no such reservation is specified, the provisions apply without exception.

3.3 The Hague

In this chapter, the traditional, pre-1977 Hague law is discussed under the following headings: qualification as combatant (Section 3.3.1); rules on means and methods of warfare (Sections 3.3.2, 3.3.3); the notion of 'military objective' and, in that connection, the state of affairs with respect to the protection of civilian populations (Section 3.3.4); issues around the notion of the use of nuclear weapons (Section 3.3.5); and protection of cultural property (Section 3.3.6).

3.3.1 *Armed forces, combatants*

It was noted in Section 2.1 that rather than defining individual persons as 'combatants', the Hague Regulations define the categories of armed groups that qualify as 'belligerents' and to whom, as Article 1 specifies, "the laws, rights, and duties of war apply". They are, first, the armed forces of belligerent states (with the exception of non-combatant persons such as military medical and religious personnel). Article 1 next lists 'militia and volunteer corps', provided they fulfil a set of four conditions:

1. to be commanded by a person responsible for his subordinates;
2. to have a fixed distinctive sign recognisable at a distance;
3. to carry arms openly; and
4. to conduct their operations in accordance with the laws and customs of war.

In modern parlance, with its accent on individual participants, the members of these armies, militia and volunteer corps are referred to as combatants. Article 2 adds one further category: "The inhabitants of a territory which has not been occupied, who, on the approach of the enemy, spontaneously take up arms to resist the invading troops without having had time to organise themselves in accordance with Article 1." Persons who take part in such a *levée en masse* need only respect the last two conditions: they "shall be regarded as belligerents if they carry arms openly and if they respect the laws and customs of war".

The reference to 'militia and volunteer corps' and the *levée en masse* reflects nineteenth-century practice, notably that of the Franco-German War of 1870. These categories have lost most practical significance. The opposite is the case with the category of resistance fighters in occupied territory, a category not mentioned in the Regulations because, as we saw in Section 2.1, in 1899 no agreement had been reached on the question of whether such persons should be recognised as combatants or, alternatively, could be regarded – and summarily executed – as *franc-tireurs*.

For resistance fighters whose lives are spared it makes considerable difference whether they are put on trial for their warlike activities or, rather, are treated as prisoners of war who are not liable to punishment for the mere fact of their participation in hostilities. In 1949, the latter solution was obtained but only in respect of 'resistance movements' that fulfil all four of the above conditions (Art. 4 of the Prisoners of War Convention; see also Section 3.4.1). Had this rule been in force at the time of the Second World War, the *maquisards* of the French Forces of the Interior and the resistance army of Marshal Tito in Yugoslavia might have met these conditions, but most other resistance movements in European countries under German occupation would still have failed to fulfil their terms.

It may be recalled here that in 1899 the Martens clause had been inserted in the preamble to the Hague Convention on Land Warfare, precisely with a view to forestalling the argument that since the treatment of captured resistance fighters was an "unforeseen case" on which a "written undertaking" had not been achieved, the case was therefore "left to the arbitrary judgment of military commanders" (see Section 2.1).

Two more points: one is that in the last quarter of the twentieth century a tendency has arisen to interpret in particular the second and third conditions in a fairly liberal manner – in conformity with the practice of the regular armed forces, whose members were no longer marching into battle dressed in conspicuous uniforms, any more than they brandished their rifles or hand grenades without need. The other point concerns the position of resistance fighters and other irregular fighters who are refused treatment as prisoners of war: are they 'unlawful combatants', whether merely in a descriptive sense or by way of formal qualification? And in either case, does this label affect the way they should be treated, be it under Convention III or IV?

The latter question became urgent in the post-9/11 years, in what was called the fight against international terrorism. Much has been said and written about it, in particular in consequence of the policy pursued for some time by the United States to deny captured persons suspected of belonging to or supporting the Al Qaeda network treatment as prisoners of war. Here it may suffice to note that issues concerning the application of the Geneva Conventions to a particular person can only arise if this person is captured in, or in relation to, a situation that may properly be regarded as an (international or internal) armed conflict. Terrorist activities planned or committed outside the framework of an armed conflict do not fall within the scope of the law of armed conflict.

3.3.2   Means of warfare

The Hague Regulations provide several rules and principles on means of warfare. The starting point is formulated in Article 22: "The right of belligerents to adopt means of injuring the enemy is not unlimited." One step lower on the scale of abstraction figures the prohibition to employ "arms, projectiles, or material calculated to cause unnecessary suffering" (Art. 23(e)). In this formula, 'unnecessary' signifies a level of suffering caused by a particular means of warfare that is not justified by its military utility, either because such utility is entirely lacking or at best negligible, or because in weighing utility against suffering the scale dips to the latter side. The principle is still too abstract, however, to warrant immediate result. Apart from cases where states expressly agree to forbid the use of a specified weapon (as they did at St Petersburg in 1868 with respect to the explosive or inflammable projectiles weighing less than 400 grammes) states do not lightly decide to discard a weapon, once introduced into their arsenals, on the claim that it causes unnecessary suffering.

As for the St Petersburg Declaration, subsequent technical developments and state practice have made the prohibition on use of the light explosive or inflammable projectiles lose much of its significance. Other prohibitory rules, dating from the period of the Hague Peace Conferences, concern the employment of dum-dum bullets, and of poison and poisoned weapons.

Declaration IV, 3 of 1899, which prohibits the use of dum-dum bullets, defines these as "bullets which expand or flatten easily in the human body, such as bullets with a hard envelope which does not entirely cover the core or is pierced with incisions". The rationale underlying this prohibition is that bullets meeting the description are apt to produce effects comparable to those of the light explosive or inflammable projectiles prohibited in 1868; in the human body, they cause injuries far graver than those normally caused by an ordinary bullet and not in effect necessary to put an adversary out of combat. Thus, the prohibition represents a clear instance of application of the rule forbidding the use of weapons causing 'unnecessary suffering'.

The prohibition on the use of poison or poisoned weapons embodied in Article 23(a) of the Hague Regulations is of mainly historical interest. Of greater interest was for long years the Geneva Gas Protocol of 1925, which proclaimed that "the use in war of asphyxiating, poisonous or other gases, and of all analogous liquids, materials or devices, has been justly condemned by the general opinion of the civilised world", and added the agreement of the contracting states "to extend this prohibition to the use of bacteriological methods of warfare". The Protocol always suffered from (1) a low number of ratifications, (2) the frequently made reservation that the Protocol would cease to be binding from the moment any adverse party used gas, and (3) problems of interpretation, in particular, whether its terms covered tear gas and herbicides. The United States in particular never accepted that this would be the case. When in 1975 the President finally ratified the Protocol, he maintained this traditional US stance. At the same time, he renounced, "as a matter of national policy", the "first use of herbicides in war" (except in or around military bases and installations) and the "first use of riot control agents in war except in defensive military modes to save lives". A subsequent Executive Order elaborated and clarified the exceptions to some degree. One example of use of 'riot control agents' (i.e. tear gas) exempted from the 'voluntary' renunciation was use against rioting inmates of a prisoner-of-war camp – a use which is surely closer to normal police use of tear gas than to warlike use, and which need not entail the risk of retaliation by the enemy and the consequent possible suspension of the entire prohibition on use of chemical weapons.

The 1925 Gas Protocol for all practical purposes lost its relevance with the adoption, first, in 1972, of the Convention on bacteriological (biological) and toxin weapons, and then in 1993 of the Convention on Chemical Weapons. These Conventions, both widely accepted, prohibit not only the use but also the possession, production, etc. of these weapons, in the case of the Chemical Weapons Convention in terms that meet the US objections. (See further Section 5.1.2c.)

While the above principles and rules on the use of weapons are either of general application in all warfare or apply more specifically to the conduct of war on land, mention should be made of one rule laid down in the 1907 Hague Convention VIII Relative to the Laying of Automatic Submarine Contact Mines (which serves to restrict, rather than prohibit, the use of such mines and of torpedoes). Article 2 prohibits "to lay automatic contact mines off the coast and ports of the enemy, with the sole object of intercepting commercial shipping". The International Court of Justice (ICJ) has applied this rule in its Judgment of 1986 in the case of *Nicaragua* v. *the United States*, holding that by laying such mines off the coast of Nicaragua the United States had violated this provision.

This concludes the discussion of the pre-1977 prohibitions or restrictions on use of specific weapons. Use of various modern, and often criticised, explosive and incendiary weapons such as napalm and 'fragmentation bombs' was not expressly prohibited, and neither was the wartime use of nuclear weapons. The problems posed by the existence and possible use of nuclear weapons are broached later in this chapter. The post-1977 restrictions on the use of certain modern 'conventional' means of warfare are discussed in Section 5.1.1.

3.3.3 Methods of warfare

Article 23(b) of the Hague Regulations prohibits "To kill or wound treacherously individuals belonging to the hostile nation or army". At the same time, "ruses of war ... are considered permissible" (Art. 24). As far as they go, these rules are unassailably correct. The problem lies in determining what constitutes a ruse of war and what a treacherous mode of acting. Article 23(f) provides some examples of the latter: "improper use of a flag of truce, of the national flag or of the military insignia and uniform of the enemy, as well as the distinctive badges of the Geneva Convention". (The flag of truce is a white flag, used to protect a negotiator or messenger; the "distinctive badge of the Geneva Convention" is the armlet with a red cross or a red crescent on a white ground.) For the rest, one might find a general guideline in what was noted by Kant some two centuries ago and subsequently repeated by Lieber in the Instructions for the Armies of the United States: treacherous is all such conduct that undermines the basis of trust which is indispensable for a return to peace. Even so, the difficulty of resolving the question in concrete instances remained. (As we shall see, the matter was taken up again at the Conference that drafted the Protocols of 1977; Section 4.1.4b.)

The Regulations also prohibit, not so much on account of their treacherous character as because of the cruelty and lowered standard of civilisation they betray: "To kill or wound an enemy who, having laid down his arms, or no longer having means of defence, has surrendered at discretion" (Art. 23(c)); "To declare that no quarter will be given" – meaning that no prisoners shall be taken (Art. 23(d)); and "pillage of a town or place, even when taken by assault" (Art. 28).

With respect to the rules on surrender and quarter it should be pointed out that these are not simply the same as saying that prisoners of war must not be wantonly killed: while they do include that prohibition, they also, and more importantly, aim to bridge the gap that may lie between the moment a combatant becomes *hors de combat* (by laying down their arms or from any other cause) and the moment they are taken prisoner.

3.3.4   *Military objectives and protection of the civilian population*

"The only legitimate object which states should endeavour to accomplish during war" is, in the words of the St Petersburg Declaration, "to weaken the military forces of the enemy". One evident method to achieve this goal is by eliminating those 'objects' that may be regarded as 'military objectives' in the strict sense, such as units of the enemy armed forces, their armoured cars and mobile artillery, and military installations such as fixed gun emplacements and munitions depots. That all such objects represent legitimate military objectives is beyond question.

Another useful method is by denying the enemy the acquisition or production of weapons, munitions and any other objects necessary for the continuation of military operations. This may be done without violence by cutting off the supply of these goods or of the raw materials required for their production (by blockades, or measures of economic warfare). It may also be done forcibly, by making the factories involved in the production of these goods the target of military operations. In theory, such operations can be carried out by artillery, either acting in close support of ground forces, or, independent of the infantry and cavalry but dependent on its own firing range, by long-distance bombardment.

Around 1900, when the Hague Regulations were drafted, such long-distance operations were beyond the capacity of the land artillery. This fired its guns, rather, in support of ground troops, to ward off an enemy assault or, in an offensive operation, to breach the fortifications of a place under siege. The Hague Regulations are accordingly silent on long-distance bombardment. Article 25 prohibits the "attack or bombardment" of undefended towns, and Article 27 provides for the sparing, as far as possible, of certain buildings (churches, museums, hospitals, etc.) in the event of sieges and bombardments of defended places, provided the buildings are not being used for military purposes at the time.

In contrast, warships could come close to coastal places beyond the reach of the army and target objects within those places. Article 2 of the 1907 Hague Convention on naval bombardment reflects this capability: it lists among the objects open to bombardment even when situated within an undefended locality, not only "military works, military or naval establishments, depots of arms or war *matériel* … and the ships of war in the harbour" (evident military objectives), but also "workshops or plants which could be utilised for the needs of the hostile fleet or army".

The tail end of this Article could already give rise to the question of which industries could be regarded as 'military objectives', and which others not. This question became urgent when it became apparent that the air arm – which started its development not long after the Hague Peace Conferences – would be capable of acting, not only in close support of ground forces, but in independent operations far beyond battle areas on the ground. The question could be asked in respect of many other objects as well: bridges, railroad yards, road intersections, etc.; and, apart from its military interest, the issue was of vital importance because of the enhanced risks for the civilian population ensuing from such an extension of the concept of 'military objective'.

As noted before, the Regulations did not address this question, and the 1923 Hague Rules on Aerial Warfare remained a non-binding document. Taking up the subject in the 1950s, the ICRC would suggest that governments accept a list (to be adjusted periodically, if necessary) enumerating the categories of objects that could be regarded as military objectives; but its attempts remained unsuccessful. Without such an agreed, clear-cut dividing line between lawful military objectives and other objects, the only yardstick of sorts was that each and every object could be regarded as a military objective if in the circumstances its elimination could be expected to significantly "weaken the military forces of the enemy", thus representing a clear military advantage to the attacker. This standard amounted to much the same thing as the principle of military economy, according to which the objects that qualify first and foremost as targets of attack are those whose destruction may be expected to have the greatest and most immediate effect on the military powers of the adversary.

Apart from this general and obviously very vague standard, certain principles of target selection could be discerned in the existing written law, notably, in Article 25 of the Regulations, which prohibits the attack or bombardment of undefended towns; in Article 26, which obliges commanding officers to do whatever they can to warn the authorities before commencing the bombardment of a defended locality (except in cases of assault); in the comparable rules in Articles 2 and 6 of the Hague Convention on naval bombardment; and, even though temporary in character, in the prohibition in the 1907 Declaration (XIV) of launching projectiles or explosives from balloons "or by other new methods of a similar nature". With hindsight, one might even wish to read into these provisions such notions as a duty of target identification prior to attack, the prohibition of area bombardment (meaning the blind bombardment of a built-up area that harbours some isolated military objectives), or the principle that an attack on a military objective must not cause damage to the civilian population out of all proportion to the military advantage gained.

Be this as it may, subsequent developments in the techniques of warfare exposed the simple treaty provisions of 1899 and 1907 as totally insufficient to provide the civilian populations of countries at war with anything like adequate protection against the dangers arising from military operations. The situation was aggravated by the attempts, made on both sides in the Second World War, to justify air operations that were probably unlawful in principle – such as the wholesale bombardment of enemy cities – as reprisals against earlier unlawful acts committed by the enemy.

It may be repeated that after the war, the International Tribunals of Nuremberg and Tokyo expressly held that the pre-existing treaty rules on land warfare had been in force as customary law. Particular importance also attaches to the two resolutions referred to earlier in Section 2.4: Resolution XXVIII of the 20th International Conference of the Red Cross (Vienna, 1965) and UNGA Resolution 2444 (XXIII) (1968). They reaffirm some "principles for observance by all governmental and other authorities responsible for action in armed conflicts", two of which may be quoted again:

(b) that it is prohibited to launch attacks against the civilian populations as such;
(c) that distinction must be made at all times between persons taking part in the hostilities and members of the civilian population to the effect that the latter be spared as much as possible.

While these resolutions may be said to have reaffirmed the validity of the principle of protection of the civilian population against the dangers of war, it was left to the Diplomatic Conference of 1974–7 to achieve clarity on the precise prohibitions and restrictions states were prepared to accept in this regard, including the issue of recourse to reprisals. For further discussion on this development see Chapter 4.

Other specific pre-1977 rules prohibiting the targeting of certain localities or objects, such as hospitals, transports of wounded persons, safety zones recognised by the belligerent parties and protected cultural property, are discussed below in the relevant sections of this chapter.

3.3.5 Nuclear weapons

The use, in 1945, of 'atomic bombs' over Hiroshima and Nagasaki, and the subsequent development and threatened use of nuclear weapons, has led to a great many questions of politics, international relations and international law. We shall mostly confine ourselves here to the specific field of the law of armed conflict as it existed prior to 1977.

A controversial question has always been whether and to what extent the traditional rules and principles on use of weapons and protection of the civilian population could be regarded as applicable to the use – as opposed to any other aspects of the possession – of nuclear weapons. Those who denied the application of the rules essentially rested their case on two arguments: the weapons were new, and they were of a different order from other weapons.

The argument of the novelty of nuclear weapons was flawed from the outset. Rules and principles on use of weapons of war did not come into being on the implicit understanding that they would be limited to existing weapons, and they have always been regarded as applicable to the use of all kinds of new weapons without exception.

Are nuclear weapons different? Even the two bombs of 1945 were horrendously destructive, both instantly and in their long-term effects. Since these have remained the only instances of actual use of nuclear weapons, the discussion focused from the outset on the deterrent effect attributed to the possession and peace-time deployment of nuclear weapons rather than on their use. Central to this discussion was the so-called 'counter-city strategy', i.e. the threat of use of (megaton) nuclear weapons against enemy cities. Arguing that this threat was indispensable to the maintenance of peace and therefore could not be unlawful, the advocates of this view concluded that the wartime use of nuclear weapons should also be kept out of the scope of the existing law.

No matter what one may think of the legality of such a threat to destroy entire cities, uttered in peacetime and intended to preserve peace, there was never much room for doubt that if deterrence failed and an armed conflict broke out, the actual realisation of a threatened counter-city strategy, with the destruction beyond comprehension it would entail, could not be justified with a simple reference to the 'different character' of nuclear weapons. As the law stood, therefore, execution of the strategy could at best, if at all, be justified as a measure of reprisal against a comparable earlier wrong.

Other conceivable, more 'military' uses of (smaller) nuclear weapons, against military objectives such as concentrations of enemy armed forces, missile launching pads or other very important military objectives, offered even less support to those who wished to deny the applicability of the existing law. Any such military use of nuclear weapons would have to be tested against the rules and principles in force as general standards for the military use of all weapons of war, including those relating to the protection of the civilian population.

In conclusion, application of the pre-1977 rules of Hague law to the possible wartime use of nuclear weapons does not warrant the conclusion that any such use would have been prohibited in all circumstances. The limits of permissible use of weapons were sufficiently vague and flexible to leave open at least the theoretical possibility of a use of nuclear weapons that would not overstep these limits. (For the situation after the adoption and entry into force of Protocol I of 1977, see Section 4.1.5i, and for the 1996 Advisory Opinion of the ICJ, Section 5.3.2a.)

3.3.6   Cultural property

The principle underlying the 1954 Hague Convention for the Protection of Cultural Property in the Event of Armed Conflict, to the effect that cultural objects must be spared as far as possible, may safely be stated to have general validity. It already finds expression in Article 27 of the 1907 Hague Regulations, on sieges and bombardments, and in Article 5 of the 1907 Hague Convention on naval bombardment. In either case, protection of the cultural objects in question is subject to the condition that "they are not being used at the time for military purposes", and the presence of the objects must be indicated by distinctive signs.

The 1954 Convention elaborates the principle into a detailed system of protection. Article 1 provides a definition of 'cultural property', which contains the following elements:

(a) "movable or immovable property of great importance to the cultural heritage of every people", such as monuments, works of art, manuscripts, books and scientific collections;

(b) "buildings whose main and effective purpose is to preserve or exhibit the movable cultural property" defined under (a), such as libraries and museums, and refuges intended to shelter the objects in question in the event of armed conflict; and

(c) "centres containing a large amount of cultural property" as defined under (a) and (b).

Protection can be general or special. The lower standard of general protection is composed of two elements: safeguard and respect (Art. 2). Elaborating the element of 'safeguard', Article 3 requires states to prepare in time of peace for the safeguarding of cultural property within their territory against the foreseeable effects of an armed conflict, for instance, by constructing refuges, making preparations for transport of the property to a safe place, or (as provided in Article 6) marking cultural property with a distinctive emblem. Article 16 describes the emblem as "a shield, pointed below, per saltire blue and white"; this means, in common language: "a shield consisting of a royal-blue square, one of the angles of which forms the point of the shield, and of a royal-blue triangle above the square, the space on either side being taken up by a white triangle".

Making this type of peace-time preparation, in the Netherlands shields fitting the description are attached to a great variety of buildings, usually somewhere near their entrances. Unfortunately, the shields have very modest dimensions (about 10 centimetres high), so that one must be rather observant to notice them at all. This leaves one wondering what the protective value of such a shield may be in the event of armed conflict.

Article 4 obliges contracting states to 'respect' cultural property, both within their own territory and in that of other contracting states. In either case, they must refrain from "any use of the property and its immediate surroundings or of the appliances in use for its protection for purposes which are likely to expose it to destruction or damage in the event of armed conflict". As far as a state's own territory is concerned, the first part of the sentence may be read as implying an obligation to refrain from such use even in time of peace. Either obligation "may be waived only in cases where military necessity imperatively requires such a waiver".

Article 4 also obliges contracting states "to prohibit, prevent and, if necessary, put a stop to" acts such as theft or vandalism directed against cultural property, and it prohibits "acts of reprisal" against such property. Then, importantly, Article 19 provides that in an internal armed conflict as well, "each party to the conflict shall be bound to apply, as a minimum, the provisions of the present Convention which relate to respect for cultural property".

'General protection' clearly amounts to very limited protection. More complete protection may be expected of a system of 'special protection'; but such a system obviously must be of limited application. Article 8 accordingly restricts the possibility of placing objects under special protection to "a limited number of refuges intended to shelter movable cultural property in the event of armed conflict, centres containing monuments and other immovable cultural property of very great importance"; and, in order to qualify, such an object must be situated at an adequate distance from any important military objective or (in the case of a refuge) "be so constructed that, in all probability, it will not be damaged by bombs"; and the object must not under any circumstance be "used for military purposes".

As provided in Article 8, an object is brought under special protection by its entry in the International Register of Cultural Property under Special Protection. The Register is kept by the Director-General of UNESCO. Requests for registration may be objected to by other contracting states, on the ground that the object either does not qualify as cultural property at all, or does not comply with the conditions mentioned in Article 8.

'Special protection' applies from the moment of registration of an object. It entails the obligation on contracting states to "ensure the immunity" of the object, by refraining from "any act of hostility" directed against the object as well as (with one exception that does not need to be mentioned here) "from any use of such property or its surroundings for military purposes" (Art. 9). While this 'immunity' already goes further than the safeguard and respect of general protection, it is reinforced by the requirement that the object shall be marked with the distinctive emblem "repeated three times in a triangular formation (one shield below)" as well as by control on the part of UNESCO during the armed conflict (Arts. 10, 16).

Another distinctive feature of the system of special protection lies in the rules on 'withdrawal of immunity'. According to Article 11, this may come about in two types of circumstance. One is violation by a contracting state of its obligations under Article 9: this releases the other party from its obligation to "ensure the immunity" of the object; even so, "whenever possible", it "shall first request the cessation of such violation within a reasonable time".

The other circumstance is 'unavoidable military necessity' – apparently a more stringent requirement than the 'imperative military necessity' of the rules on general protection. The effect of 'unavoidable military necessity' applies "only for such time as that necessity continues", and the necessity can only be established "by the officer commanding a force the equivalent of a division in size or larger". The party withdrawing immunity is moreover obliged to inform the Commissioner-General for Cultural Property, "in writing, stating the reasons". (The Commissioner-General for Cultural Property is a person chosen by the parties concerned or appointed by the President of the International Court of Justice, from an international list of qualified persons nominated by the contracting states.)

Both systems of general and special protection have shown important shortcomings in practice. To mention just one, the rules on special protection are hard to implement in densely populated and highly industrialised regions. As mentioned before, the resulting desire to thoroughly amend the Convention has recently culminated in the adoption of a new instrument that is discussed in Section 5.2.3.

3.4   Geneva

The 1949 Geneva Conventions contain both common and specific provisions. It was also noted that they apply in their totality in international armed conflicts, whereas common Article 3 specifically applies in internal armed conflicts. The present section is accordingly organised as follows: first, the notion of 'protected persons' as defined in Conventions I–III and IV, respectively (Section 3.4.1), and some aspects of the principle of protection underlying the Conventions (Section 3.4.2); then, the substantive parts of each Convention separately (Section 3.4.3 to 3.4.6); and, finally, common Article 3 (Section 3.4.7).

3.4.1   Protected persons

The law of Geneva serves to protect persons who, as a consequence of an armed conflict, are in the power of a party to the conflict of which they are not nationals – it does not, in other words, protect against the violence of war itself. It may be recalled that Geneva-type protection was granted for the first time in 1864, to "the wounded in armies in the field". Since 1949 it extends to all categories of persons listed as protected persons in the four Geneva Conventions of that year:

- Convention I for the Amelioration of the Condition of the Wounded and Sick in Armed Forces in the Field (the First or Red Cross Convention);

- Convention II for the Amelioration of the Condition of Wounded, Sick and Shipwrecked Members of Armed Forces at Sea (the Second or Sea Red Cross Convention);
- Convention III Relative to the Treatment of Prisoners of War (the Third or Prisoners of War Convention); and
- Convention IV Relative to the Protection of Civilian Persons in Time of War (the Fourth or Civilians Convention).

Conventions I–III relate to combatants who have fallen into enemy hands (and some related groups). In particular, Conventions I and II protect combatants who are wounded, sick or shipwrecked, and Convention III provides general rules concerning the status, protection and treatment of prisoners of war, whether healthy or wounded.

For the complete catalogue of persons protected under Conventions I–III, the reader is referred to Article 4 of the Third Convention. The following list is drawn from that article:

1. members of the armed forces of a party to the conflict, even if the government or authority to whom they profess allegiance is not recognised by the adversary;
2. members of other militias or volunteer corps, including organised resistance movements, which belong to a party to the conflict and operate in or outside their own territory, even if this is occupied; provided that the group they belong to fulfils the four conditions of Article 1 of the Hague Regulations that are repeated in the relevant articles of the Conventions:
   (a) to be commanded by a person responsible for his subordinates;
   (b) to have a fixed distinctive sign recognisable at a distance;
   (c) to carry arms openly;
   (d) to conduct their operations in accordance with the laws and customs of war;
3. participants in a *levée en masse*, provided they carry arms openly and respect the laws and customs of war;
4. persons who accompany the armed forces without actually being members thereof, such as duly accredited war correspondents and members of welfare services;
5. crew members of the merchant marine and the crews of civil aircraft of the parties to the conflict.

Persons belonging to categories 1–3 are all 'combatants' proper who, once captured by the enemy, may be detained as prisoners of war for the duration of the hostilities. Persons falling under categories 4 and 5 are civilians; yet they are captured in a situation indicating their close (though in principle non-combatant) cooperation with the enemy armed forces or war effort. Although the capturing party may decide to simply let these persons go, it is entitled to detain them, whether for a limited time or for the duration of the armed conflict. If it does detain them, it is obliged to treat them as prisoners of war.

The Fourth Convention protects persons "who, at a given moment and in any manner whatsoever, find themselves, in case of a conflict or occupation, in the hands of a Party to the conflict or Occupying Power of which they are not nationals". Excluded from this broad definition are, for instance, nationals of a neutral state on the territory of a party to the conflict and nationals of a co-belligerent, as long as "the State of which they are nationals has normal diplomatic representation in the State in whose hands they are"; and, of course, all those who are protected by Conventions I–III (Art. 4).

A first point to emphasise here is the limited scope of the Civilians Convention: in spite of its sweeping title, it is neither intended to protect civilians from the dangers of warfare – such as air bombardment – to which they may be exposed in their own territory, nor does it offer them protection against the acts of their proper state. The protection extends essentially to civilians in the power of the adversary – except for Part II, which, as we shall see later, applies to the whole of the populations of the countries in conflict.

Another point: as may be evident, the crucial question whether a person falls under the scope of Conventions I–III or of Convention IV, is not always readily answered. Who is to provide this answer? And how should the person concerned (say, the resistance fighter in occupied territory) be treated in the meantime? Article 5 of the Prisoners of War Convention provides this answer: "Should any doubt arise as to whether persons, having committed a belligerent act and having fallen into the hands of the enemy, belong to one of the categories enumerated in Article 4, such persons shall enjoy the protection of the present Convention until such time as their status has been determined by a competent tribunal." This rule, applied for instance by the United States in the Vietnam war and by Israel in the Middle East, removes the risk of arbitrary decision on the part of individual commanders and creates at least the possibility of a duly considered decision. It may be noted that a negative decision, to the effect that a person does not fall under one of the categories of Article 4, implies that this person falls under the protection of Convention IV.

3.4.2   Principle of protection

The system of protection of the Geneva Conventions rests on the fundamental principle that protected persons must be respected and protected
in all circumstances, and must be treated humanely, without any adverse
distinction founded on sex, race, nationality, religion, political opinions
or any other similar criteria (Articles 12 of Conventions I and II, 16 of
Convention III and 27 of Convention IV).

'Respect' and 'protection' are complementary notions. 'Respect', a pas-
sive element, indicates an obligation not to harm, expose to suffering
or kill a protected person; 'protection', as the active element, signifies a
duty to ward off dangers and prevent harm. The third element involved
in the principle, that of 'humane' treatment, relates to the attitude that
should govern all aspects of the treatment of protected persons; this attitude should aim to ensure to these persons an existence worthy of human
beings, in spite of – and with full recognition of – the harsh circumstances
of their present situation. The prohibition of discrimination adds a last
essential element that must be taken into account in respect of all three
other main elements.

Starting from these fundamental notions, the some four hundred, in
part highly detailed, articles of the Conventions provide an elaborate
system of rules for the protection of the various categories of protected
persons. Of this abundant body of law, no more than the main lines are
presented here. The common articles relating to implementation and
sanctions are dealt with in Section 3.5.

3.4.3   First Convention

Article 12 provides that the wounded and sick shall be treated and cared
for "by the Party to the conflict in whose power they may be", adding that
"only urgent medical reasons will authorise priority in the order of treatment to be administered". The article prohibits any "attempts upon their
lives, or violence to their persons" and, in particular, to murder or exter-
minate the wounded and sick, to subject them to torture or biological
experiments, wilfully to leave them without medical assistance and care,
or to create conditions exposing them to contagion or infection.

Parties to the conflict are required to take all possible measures, especially after an engagement, "to search for and collect the wounded and
sick" (Art. 15). Any particulars that may assist in the identification of every
single wounded, sick or dead person must be recorded as soon as possible

and the information forwarded to the national information bureau that each party to the conflict is obliged to establish at the outset of the hostilities. This in turn transmits the information to "the Power on which these persons depend", through the intermediary of a Central Prisoners of War Agency (Art. 16) – in practice, the Central Tracing Agency of the ICRC, located in Geneva (see further Sections 3.4.5 and 5.3.9b).

The parties are also required to do their utmost to search for and identify the dead; last wills and other articles "of an intrinsic or sentimental value" must be collected and an honourable interment of the dead ensured, cremation being allowed solely "for imperative reasons of hygiene or for motives based on the religion of the deceased" (Arts. 15–17). At the outset of hostilities each party must organise an Official Graves Registration Service (Art. 17); the work of this service, which consists of the registration, maintenance and marking of the graves (or, as the case may be, of the ashes) serves "to allow subsequent exhumations and to ensure the identification of bodies, whatever the site of the graves, and the possible transportation to the home country".

Besides the official authorities, individual persons may also concern themselves in the fate of the wounded and sick and, admitting them into their houses, take up their care. Ever since the Convention of 1864, the principle has been firmly established that none of the parties to the conflict may censure private individuals for such activities: on the contrary, the authorities should encourage this. Article 18 of the First Convention expressly reaffirms this role of the population. At the same time, it emphasises that the civilian population too must respect the wounded and sick, and must "abstain from offering them violence".

For the rest, care of the wounded and sick is the primary responsibility of the military medical services. Their function actually is a double one: on the one hand, to contribute to the numerical and fighting strength of their own armed forces and, on the other, to provide medical aid to combatants, whether friend or foe, who are in need of care as a consequence of the armed conflict. As stated before, priority in medical aid may only be determined on the basis of urgent medical reasons and not, therefore, on the grounds that a combatant belongs to one's own party.

So as to enable them to perform their tasks, protection also extends to the military medical services themselves, together with the fixed establishments and mobile units (field and other hospitals and ambulances) at their disposal. Article 24 provides that the permanent medical and administrative personnel of the military medical services (doctors, nurses, stretcher bearers and so on), as well as chaplains attached to the armed forces "shall be respected and protected in all circumstances". When they fall into enemy hands, they may be retained "only in so far as the state of health, the spiritual needs and the number of prisoners of war require" (and without becoming prisoners of war; Art. 28). With respect to auxiliary personnel trained to perform similar functions, such as nurses, Article 25 provides that they "shall likewise be respected and protected if they are carrying out these duties at the time when they come into contact with the enemy or fall into his hands". In the latter event they "shall be prisoners of war, but shall be employed on their medical duties in so far as the need arises" (Art. 29).

Personnel of the parties' national Red Cross or Red Crescent Societies, when employed on the same duties as the personnel of the military medical services mentioned in Article 24, enjoy the same protection as that personnel, provided they are subject to military laws and regulations (Art. 26). A recognised Society of a neutral country that wishes to lend the assistance of its medical personnel and units to a party to the conflict needs both the previous consent of its own government, as well as the authorisation of the party concerned; the personnel and units assigned to this task are placed under the control of that party. The neutral government must notify its consent to the adverse party as well (Art. 27). If members of this personnel fall into the hands of the latter party, they may not be detained at all and must, in principle, be given permission "to return to their country or, if this is not possible, to the territory of the party to the conflict in whose service they were, as soon as a route for their return is open and military considerations permit" (Art. 32).

Fixed establishments and mobile medical units of the military medical services such as (field) hospitals and ambulances may not be attacked (Art. 19). But neither may they be "used to commit, outside their humanitarian duties, acts harmful to the enemy" (Art. 21).

Article 23 provides for the establishment of 'hospital zones and localities' to protect the wounded and sick and the personnel entrusted with their care from the effects of war. To be effective, such a measure requires express recognition by the adverse party.

Among the rules in the Convention on the protection of transports of wounded and sick or of medical equipment, those concerning medical aircraft deserve particular attention. The rules in question, laid down in Article 36, are so stringent as to render the effective use of such aircraft virtually impossible: the aircraft must be "exclusively employed for the removal of wounded and sick and for the transport of medical personnel and equipment"; each and every detail about their flight (altitude, time and route) must have been "specifically agreed upon between the belligerents concerned"; they may not fly over enemy or enemy-occupied territory, and they must "obey every summons to land". In formulating these restrictive rules the fear of abuse of medical aircraft, notably for purposes of observation from the air, prevailed over all other considerations.

Although the above system of protection – of personnel and equipment, hospitals and ambulances, and transports – does not depend for its legal force on any outward signs, its practical effect depends in no slight measure on the use of, and respect for, the distinctive emblem, that is, the red cross or red crescent on a white ground. Articles 38–44 prescribe in detail how the emblem must be displayed. Article 38 also mentions the red lion and sun on a white ground, an emblem used in the past by Iran. Israel from its creation in 1948 has employed the Magen David Adom, or Red Shield of David, on a white ground. While this emblem was not internationally recognised in 1949 and therefore is not mentioned in the Convention, it was often respected in practice. As will be explained in Section 5.2.5, a third emblem, the 'red crystal', was created in 2005 to help resolve the problem of states such as Israel that do not wish to use the red cross or the red crescent.

A last point concerns reprisals: these are categorically prohibited "against the wounded, sick, personnel, buildings or equipment protected by the Convention" (Art. 46). This is to say that a party to the conflict cannot claim the right to set aside rules of the Convention in order to induce the adverse party to return to an attitude of respect for the law of armed conflict.

3.4.4 Second Convention

Copying the text of Article 12 of the First Convention, Article 12 of the Second Convention includes the shipwrecked at sea among the categories of protected persons, and it specifies that "the term 'shipwreck' means shipwreck from any cause and includes forced landings at sea by or from aircraft".

Events at sea may result in a greater variety of situations than are likely to occur on land: shipwrecked persons may be picked up by warships, hospital ships, merchant vessels, yachts or any other craft, sailing under a belligerent or neutral flag, and they may be put ashore in a belligerent or neutral port. Only one of the many resultant special provisions is mentioned here. This is the rule, laid down in Article 14, that a belligerent warship has the right to demand that the wounded, sick or shipwrecked on board military or other hospital ships, merchant vessels, yachts, etc. "shall be surrendered, whatever their nationality"; this, as far as the wounded and sick are concerned, under the double condition that they "are in a fit state to be moved and that the warship can provide adequate facilities for necessary medical treatment". By doing this, the warship may capture enemy combatants who are found on board the other vessel, and make them prisoners of war.

Hospital ships have an important place in the Second Convention. Article 22 defines them as "ships built or equipped ... specially and solely with a view to assisting the wounded, sick and shipwrecked, to treating them and to transporting them"; the ships thus combine the functions of a hospital and medical transport.

The Convention distinguishes between 'military' hospital ships (which are not warships) and hospital ships utilised by Red Cross or Red Crescent Societies or other private institutions or persons. All these ships "may in no circumstances be attacked or captured, but shall at all times be respected and protected", provided a number of conditions are fulfilled. The most important condition is "that their names and descriptions have been notified to the Parties to the conflict ten days before those ships are employed". The description must include a ship's "registered gross tonnage, the length from stem to stern and the number of masts and funnels". As an additional requirement, non-military hospital ships must have been granted an official commission by "the Party to the conflict on which they depend" or, in the case of hospital ships under a neutral flag, have received the previous consent of their own government and the authorisation of the party to the conflict under whose control they will exercise their functions (Arts. 22–4).

Article 43 provides that hospital ships must be painted white, with the distinctive emblem (red cross or red crescent) painted in dark red, as large as possible and "so placed as to afford the greatest possible visibility from the sea and from the air". By day, in good weather conditions and within optical range, the ships will thus be sufficiently recognisable as hospital vessels; in less favourable conditions, other means of identification will have to be utilised.

As distinct from medical aircraft, hospital ships are free in principle to perform their functions anywhere and all times; yet, in doing so they "shall in no wise hamper the movements of the combatants", and any actions they undertake during or shortly after an engagement will be at their own risk (Art. 30). The parties to the conflict moreover can drastically restrict the ostensible freedom of action of hospital ships in a number of ways. Article 31 recognises their right to control and search the ships, and to "refuse assistance from these vessels, order them off, make them take a certain course, control the use of their wireless and other means of communication, and even detain them for a period not exceeding seven days from the time of interception, if the gravity of the circumstances so requires".

Article 27 provides that under the same conditions as those applicable to hospital vessels, "small craft employed by the state or by the officially recognised lifeboat institutions for coastal rescue operations [shall be respected and protected] so far as operational requirements permit". Protection is also extended "so far as possible to fixed coastal installations used exclusively by these craft for their humanitarian missions".

As with the First Convention, the Second Convention prohibits reprisals against the persons and objects it is designed to protect (Art. 47).

3.4.5 Third Convention

Combatants who fall into enemy hands are prisoners of war from the moment of capture. Who is responsible for their treatment: the capturer or the state? Article 12 of the Third Convention states the principle: "Prisoners of war are in the hands of the enemy Power, but not of the individuals or military units who have captured them." This implies the responsibility of the detaining power for everything that happens to them – a responsibility of the state that does not detract in any way from the responsibility of individual persons that may arise from violations of the Convention.

Article 13 provides that "[p]risoners of war must at all times be humanely treated", and it prohibits "any unlawful act or omission … causing death or seriously endangering the health of a prisoner of war". Prisoners of war obviously may not be arbitrarily killed: indeed, they must be protected, "particularly against acts of violence or intimidation and against insults and public curiosity"; and reprisals directed against prisoners of war are prohibited. In addition, they "are entitled in all circumstances to respect for their persons and their honour" (Art. 14).

To the authorities of the detaining power, prisoners of war are mainly of interest as potential sources of information. In order to secure this information they may interrogate them, use kind words and create a congenial atmosphere to make them talk, listen in on their conversations and so on. In contrast, the authorities are not allowed to have recourse to "physical or mental torture" or "any other form of coercion". The only information every prisoner of war is obliged to give is "his surname, first names and rank, date of birth, and army, regimental, personal or serial number, or failing this, equivalent information" (Art. 17).

Prisoners of war captured in a combat zone must be evacuated, as soon as possible and if their condition permits, to camps situated outside the danger area, where they may be kept interned at the expense of the detaining power (Arts. 15, 19, 21). Every such prisoner-of-war camp "shall be put under the immediate authority of a responsible commissioned officer belonging to the regular armed forces of the Detaining Power". This officer, who, under the direction of their government bears responsibility for the application of the Convention in the camp, must not only possess a copy of the Convention but also "ensure that its provisions are known to the camp staff and the guard" (Art. 39). The text of the Convention must moreover "be posted, in the prisoners' own language, in places where all may read them" (Art. 41).

There is nothing in international law that renders it unlawful for a prisoner of war to attempt to escape. The camp authorities may take measures to prevent such attempts, but the means open to them are not unlimited: Article 42 provides that weapons may be used against prisoners of war only as "an extreme measure, which shall always be preceded by warnings appropriate to the circumstances". An attempt at escape that remains abortive exposes the prisoner of war to nothing more than disciplinary punishment (Art. 92).

The detention of prisoners of war lasts in principle until the "cessation of active hostilities", after which they "shall be released and repatriated without delay" (Art. 118 – a provision that has given rise to serious difficulties in practice, for instance, after the Korean War, when numerous North Korean prisoners in American hands refused to be repatriated to their communist homeland).

Detention may come to an earlier conclusion by a number of causes. A first obvious cause is death during capture (Art. 120). Second, prisoners who are seriously wounded or seriously sick must be sent back to their own country or accommodated in a neutral country as soon as they are fit to travel (Art. 109). In less serious cases but where the release of prisoners of war "may contribute to the improvement of their state of health", the detaining power may offer to release them partially or wholly "on parole or promise, in so far as is allowed by the laws of the Power on which they depend" (Art. 21).

The complete release on parole or promise, which enables prisoners of war to return to their own country, need not be confined to the case of probable improvement of their state of health but may be offered on other grounds as well. One condition will normally be that the released prisoner shall no longer take an active part in hostilities for the duration of the armed conflict. Article 21 provides that prisoners of war who accept release on parole or promise are honour-bound to observe the conditions scrupulously, this both towards the enemy and to their own authorities; the latter authorities, for their part, are bound "neither to require nor to accept" from them "any service incompatible with the parole or promise given"; always according to Article 21.

As the laws of a number of countries do not allow their military personnel to accept such an offer, or make this permissible only in exceptional situations, the complete release on parole or promise is a rare occurrence. In practice, greater relevance may attach to the possibility of partial release, that is, freedom of movement for a limited period and for a specific purpose. As suggested in Article 21, a prisoner's state of health may profit greatly by a temporary freedom to move outside the premises of the camp.

One method, not mentioned in the Convention, by which the detention of prisoners of war may be terminated, is their exchange as a result of an express agreement between parties to the conflict. Agreements to this effect are often brought about and executed in the course of an armed conflict, usually through the intermediation of the ICRC.

Other matters elaborated in the Third Convention concern the living conditions of the prisoners of war: their quarters, food and clothing; hygiene and medical care; religious, intellectual and physical activities; and so on. Article 49 permits the detaining power to "utilise the labour of prisoners of war who are physically fit". While detaining powers have often done this simply to benefit from additional workforce, the article specifies that a policy of putting prisoners to work should serve in particular to maintain them "in a good state of physical and mental health". Officers, however, "may in no circumstances be compelled to work" (but may accept, or ask for, work if they so desire), whereas non-commissioned officers "shall only be required to do supervisory work".

Article 50 specifies the types of work prisoners of war may be compelled to do. In drawing up the list the drafters of the Convention, although well aware that any form of labour of prisoners ultimately may be to the benefit of the detaining power, drew the line at activities that contribute all too directly to the war effort. Thus, while compelling prisoners of war to carry out "public works and building operations which have no military character or purpose" is permitted, compelling them to carry out the same works having a military character or purpose is not.

Expressly excluded from the classes of permissible labour is work in the metallurgical, machine and chemical industries (Art. 50). This brings to mind the discussion in Section 3.3.4, of the notion of 'military objective' and its extension to certain industrial objects once long-distance air bombardment had become a real possibility. It should be pointed out that the specific reference to these industries cannot lead to the conclusion that every metallurgical, machine or chemical plant constitutes a legitimate military objective: as stated above, in order for a given object to qualify as a military objective its elimination must in the circumstances contribute to weakening the military forces of the enemy and thus represent a clear military advantage to the attacker. No matter how vague, this yardstick is decidedly narrower than the one applied in Article 50 preventing prisoners of war from carrying out types of work that would bring them too close to making a material contribution to the enemy war effort.

Another important point is that only volunteers may be employed on unhealthy or dangerous labour, such as the removal of mines (Art. 52).

Prisoners of war are permitted to maintain relations with the exterior. Thus, Article 70 provides that they shall be enabled to inform their relatives of their capture, state of health, transfer to a hospital or to another camp, and so on. An annex to the Convention provides the model of a 'capture card' to be used for this purpose. Besides these capture cards, prisoners of war must also "be allowed to send and receive letters and cards", although the detaining power is empowered to limit the numbers of these if it finds this necessary (Art. 71). Another right of prisoners of war, mentioned in Article 72, is "to receive by post or by any other means individual parcels or collective shipments" of all sorts (such as the well-known Red Cross parcels). Again, Article 78 recognises the right of prisoners of war to address requests and complaints regarding their conditions of captivity (e.g. the labour they are compelled to do) to the military authorities of the detaining power as well as to the representatives of the supervisory institutions provided in the Convention. (See also Section 3.5.2.)

Apart from these rights of communication of the prisoners of war themselves, the detaining power is obliged to maintain from the outset of the armed conflict an information bureau where all information about the prisoners of war is collected (Art. 122). The Bureau must also forward all such information, both to the states concerned and to the 'Central Prisoners of War Information Agency' provided in Article 123 and with the task "to collect all the information it may obtain through official or private channels respecting prisoners of war, and to transmit it as rapidly as possible to the country of origin of the prisoners of war or to the Power on which they depend". Article 140 of the Fourth Convention provides for the creation of a similar office, the Central Information Agency, for information about detained or interned civilians; the two offices, maintained by the ICRC, are in fact combined into one: the Central Tracing Agency. (See also Sections 3.4.6f and 5.3.9b.)

According to Article 82, prisoners of war are "subject to the laws, regulations and orders in force in the armed forces of the Detaining Power"; the provision adds that this power "shall be justified in taking judicial or disciplinary measures in respect of any offence committed by a prisoner of war against such laws, regulations or orders". In doing so, it must respect the specific rules on "penal and disciplinary sanctions" laid down in the Convention. Articles 82 *et seq.* provide detailed rules concerning such matters as: the competent authority (the same as is competent to deal with comparable offences committed by members of its own armed forces), applicable procedures, permissible penalties and the execution of punishments, all of this with an eye to guaranteeing a fair trial and a just punishment.

The text of Article 82 does not preclude the detaining power from putting a prisoner of war on trial for an offence committed prior to capture, notably, for an act that may qualify as a war crime. Indeed, its power in this respect is implicitly recognised in Article 85, which provides that a prisoner, when "prosecuted under the laws of the Detaining Power" for such an act "shall retain, even if convicted, the benefits of the present Convention". The provision aims to prevent a repetition of the practice followed by the Allied powers after the Second World War with respect to war criminals of the Axis powers. The Soviet Union and other states of the then communist bloc made a reservation to Article 85, to the effect that they would not be bound by the obligation "to extend the application of the Convention to prisoners of war who have been convicted under the law of the Detaining Power, in accordance with the principles of the Nuremberg trial, for war crimes and crimes against humanity, it being understood that persons convicted of such crimes must be subject to the conditions obtaining in the country in question for those who undergo their punishment". A number of other states have protested against this reservation, or, as in the case of the United States, rejected it. As of the time of writing, only Russia still maintains the reservation.

3.4.6   Fourth Convention

The two substantive parts of the Fourth or Civilians Convention deal with two entirely different situations: Part II aims to provide 'general protection' of populations against certain consequences of war, whereas Part III deals with the 'status and treatment' of persons who fall under the definition of 'protected persons'. The latter part is subdivided into five sections: I – Provisions Common to the Territories of the Parties to the Conflict and to Occupied Territories; II – Aliens in the Territory of a Party to the Conflict; III – Occupied Territories; IV – Regulations for the Treatment of Internees (who may be aliens in the territory of a party to the conflict or persons in occupied territory); and V – Information Bureaux and Central Agency. We divide the present section along the same lines.

3.4.6a   General protection of populations against certain consequences of war

Covering "the whole of the populations of the countries in conflict" without discrimination, the provisions of Part II "are intended to alleviate the sufferings caused by war" (Art. 13). Yet they were not written with an eye to providing general protection of civilian populations against the effects of hostilities: this effort had to wait for the Protocols of 1977. Rather, Part II offers specific forms of protection or assistance to specified categories of persons.

Provision is made, first, for the establishment of two types of protective zones: 'hospital and safety zones and localities' (Art. 14) and 'neutralised zones' (Art. 15). Hospital and safety zones and localities are meant "to protect from the effects of war, wounded, sick and aged persons, children under fifteen, expectant mothers and mothers of children under seven": categories of persons, in other words, who are not expected to make a material contribution to the war effort. For such 'zones and localities' to become effective requires their recognition by the adversary, if possible by the conclusion of an express agreement to that effect between the belligerents (cf. also the hospital zones and localities of the First Convention).

The drafters of Article 14 visualised the hospital and safety zones as fairly large areas, situated at a considerable distance from any battle area. To this day, the concept has remained a mere theoretical possibility: history provides no examples of the establishment of such zones, and the idea appears extremely difficult to realise in any densely populated and highly industrialised region – precisely the regions whose populations might most need this kind of protection.

The neutralised zones of Article 15, designed to be established in regions of actual fighting, are "intended to shelter from the effects of war the following persons, without distinction: (a) wounded and sick combatants or non-combatants; (b) civilian persons who take no part in hostilities, and who, while they reside in the zones, perform no work of a military character". Here too, an agreement between the belligerents is required and the article specifies that such agreements must be concluded in writing. Both the term 'neutralised' and the description of the persons admitted for shelter reflect the essentially undefended character of these zones. (See Section 4.1.5j for subsequent developments.) A limited number of instances of the establishment of such neutralised zones have occurred in practice, usually through the intermediation of the ICRC.

Categories of especially vulnerable persons granted some form of protection in the remaining provisions of Part II include the wounded and sick, the infirm, aged persons, children and maternity cases. Duly recognised civilian hospitals with their staff, as well as land, sea or air transports of wounded and sick civilians, the infirm or maternity cases are entitled to the same type of respect and protection as Conventions I and II provide to their military counterparts (Art. 18 *et seq.*). The protection of hospitals obviously cannot amount to absolute immunity even from incidental damage. Recognising this, Article 18 provides that "[i]n view of the dangers to which hospitals may be exposed by being close to military objectives, it is recommended that such hospitals be situated as far as possible from such objectives".

The experience of the naval blockades of both world wars inspired Article 23, obliging each contracting party to "allow the free passage of all consignments of medical and hospital stores and objects necessary for religious worship intended only for civilians" of another contracting party, "even if the latter is its adversary"; and likewise of "all consignments of essential foodstuffs, clothing and tonics intended for children under fifteen, expectant mothers and maternity cases". The party allowing free passage may require sufficient guarantees and measures of supervision to ensure that the consignments will go to these categories of civilians. Note that Article 23 does not encompass the whole of the population: the contracting states in 1949 were not prepared to extend the protection against starvation as a result of a blockade beyond the categories of especially vulnerable people enumerated in the article.

Equally important, in view of the experiences of numerous armed conflicts, are the provisions of Part II relating to measures for the protection of children under fifteen "who are orphaned or are separated from their families as a result of the war" (Art. 24); the exchange of family news (Art. 25); and the restoration of contact between members of dispersed families (Art. 26). An important role is attributed in this regard to the Central Information Agency for protected persons, whose creation "in a neutral country" is provided for in Article 140. The article indicates that the Agency may be the same as the one provided for in the Third Convention. In practice, the Central Tracing Agency operated in Geneva by the ICRC performs its functions for civilians and combatants alike. The national Red Cross and Red Crescent Societies likewise contribute greatly to the implementation of these articles.

3.4.6b   Provisions common to the territory of parties to the conflict and to occupied territory

Article 4 of the Fourth Convention defines 'protected persons' as those persons who find themselves "in the hands of a Party to the conflict or Occupying Power of which they are not nationals" and who are protected by one of the other Conventions. The article also excludes "nationals of a State which is not bound by the Convention" (presently no longer relevant), nationals of a neutral state who find themselves in the territory of a belligerent state, and nationals of a co-belligerent state, the latter two as long as their state "has normal diplomatic representation in the State in whose hands they are". (See also the discussion in Section 3.4.1 on the categories of civilians protected by the Fourth Convention.)

The common provisions of Part III, Section I deal with the respect due to fundamental rights of the human person, and of women in particular (specifically prohibiting "rape, enforced prostitution, or any form of indecent assault"; Arts. 27, 28); the responsibility of a party to the conflict for the treatment of protected persons in its hands (Art. 29); and the right of protected persons to apply to supervisory bodies and relief organisations (Art. 30). Prohibited forms of ill-treatment include "physical or moral coercion ... in particular to obtain information" (Art. 31), as well as "any measure of such a character as to cause the physical suffering or extermination of protected persons". Measures in the latter category include "murder, torture, corporal punishments, mutilation and medical or scientific experiments not necessitated by the medical treatment of a protected person", and "any other measures of brutality whether applied by civilian or military agents" (Art. 32).

Article 33 prohibits punishment for an offence someone has not personally committed, as well as collective penalties, "reprisals against protected persons and their property" and any other "measures of intimidation or terrorism". Article 34, finally, making short work of the notorious practice of taking and eventually killing hostages, simply and radically prohibits any "taking of hostages".

3.4.6c   Aliens in the territory of a party to the conflict

Article 35 lays down the right of those aliens who are protected persons (that is, first of all, enemy nationals) "to leave the territory … unless their departure is contrary to the national interests of the State". If permission is refused they are "entitled to have such refusal reconsidered by an appropriate court or administrative board".

Protected persons who do not leave the territory retain a number of fundamental rights, for example: to receive relief and medical attention, to practise their religion, and to move from "an area particularly exposed to the dangers of war … to the same extent as the nationals of the state concerned" (Art. 38). They must be granted the opportunity to support themselves; alternatively, the state is obliged to ensure their support and that of their dependants (Art. 39). Enemy nationals "may only be compelled to do work which is normally necessary to ensure the feeding, sheltering, clothing, transport and health of human beings and which is not directly related to the conduct of military operations" (Art. 40). It should be noted that the article does not exclude all work connected with the war effort.

If the security of a party to the conflict makes such a measure absolutely necessary, this party may intern protected persons in its territory or place them in assigned residence. On the other hand, a protected person may also voluntarily demand internment, for instance, to seek protection from a hostile environment (Arts. 41, 42).

The above system of protection of enemy nationals and other protected persons in the territory of a party to the conflict is subject to an important proviso: Article 5 provides that if the state concerned "is satisfied that an individual protected person is definitely suspected of or engaged in activities hostile to the security of the State, such individual person shall not be entitled to claim such rights and privileges under the present Convention as would, if exercised in the favour of such individual person, be prejudicial to the security of such State". One right that immediately comes to mind is that of communication: with one's family, a lawyer, etc.

The threefold repetition of 'individual' in the quoted text emphasises the point that Article 5 may never be applied as a collective measure. This means, for instance, that collective internment of persons of a particular nationality is prohibited: each internee must be shown to be individually suspected of activities hostile to the security of the state. The article specifies that any person submitted to this special regime must "nevertheless be treated with humanity"; in case of trial they must be given a "fair and regular trial" in conformity with the rules laid down in the Convention; and the special regime must come to an end "at the earliest date consistent with the security of the State".

3.4.6d   Occupied territory

Rules relating to occupied territory were already found in the Hague Regulations on Land Warfare. Article 42 states the principle that for a territory to be "considered occupied", it must be "actually placed under the authority of the hostile army"; and the occupation "extends only to the territory where such authority has been established and can be exercised". Article 43 derives from this situation of fact a twofold obligation: on the one hand, the occupying power "shall take all the measures in his power to restore, and ensure, as far as possible, public order and safety"; and on the other, in doing so it must respect, "unless absolutely prevented, the laws in force in the country".

The Regulations contain provisions on such diverse matters as the collection of taxes, requisition of property and services, and the fate of movable and immovable property belonging to the state. We pass over these specific provisions in silence. A general remark is that in modern society the degree to which state organs influence, and even participate directly in, economic and social affairs is immeasurably greater than in the days when the Regulations were drafted. An occupying power cannot fail to find itself confronted with the consequences of these deep societal changes and the increased role of the state.

The provisions of the Fourth Convention, written at a time when these changes were well on their way, reflect this trend. Part III, Section III opens with an important statement of principle: it is forbidden to deprive protected persons in occupied territory, "in any case or in any manner whatsoever", of the benefits of the Convention, whether by a change in the institutions of the territory, an agreement between the local authorities and the occupying power, or complete or partial annexation of the territory (Art. 47).

Measures specifically prohibited "regardless of their motive" include the forcible transfer of individual persons or groups, as well as deportations from the occupied territory to any other country. The only exception concerns the evacuation of a given area: this is permissible "if the security of the population or imperative military reasons so demand" (Art. 49).

Article 51 provides that protected persons over the age of 18 may be compelled to work, although only in the occupied territory where they are located and "only on work which is necessary either for the needs of the army of occupation, or for the public utility services, or for the feeding, sheltering, clothing, transportation or health of the population of the occupied country". The construction of fortifications, artillery emplacements, etc. does not fall under this permissible labour: such work is not "necessary for the needs of the army of occupation" but, rather, serves for (future) military operations of the occupying power.

In principle, the institutions and public officials in the territory continue to function as before. As they owe the occupying power no duty of allegiance, each new regulation or instruction emanating from that authority may confront them with the question of whether they can go on cooperating in the execution of these orders – a question that may become very awkward, for instance, for the police force. Article 54 of the Convention accordingly recognises the right of public officials and judges to "abstain from fulfilling their functions for reasons of conscience". In such an event, the occupying power may not alter their status, or apply sanctions or take measures of coercion or discrimination against them: at most, it may remove them from their posts.

The occupying power must devote special care to the well-being of children (Art. 50). It shall "to the fullest extent of the means available to it" ensure the food and medical supplies of the population (Art. 55), as well as public health and hygiene in the territory (Art. 56). Article 57 limits the power of the occupant to requisition civilian hospitals to "cases of urgent necessity for the care of military wounded and sick", and then only temporarily and "on condition that suitable arrangements are made in due time for the care and treatment of the patients and for the needs of the civilian population for hospital accommodation". Also, the occupant "shall permit ministers of religion to give spiritual assistance to the members of their religious communities" (Art. 58).

Articles 59–61 deal with collective relief actions that other states or "impartial humanitarian organisations such as the International Committee of the Red Cross" may undertake to assist an inadequately supplied population. The occupying power is obliged to agree to such schemes and to facilitate them, under the conditions set out in the cited articles. Apart from such collective relief, protected persons in occupied territory may also receive individual relief consignments: Article 62 makes this right subject only to "imperative reasons of security". In the same vein, the occupying power is obliged, subject to "temporary and exceptional measures imposed for urgent reasons of security", to permit national Red Cross or Red Crescent Societies "to pursue their activities in accordance with Red Cross principles, as defined by the International Red Cross Conferences". Other relief societies, as well as existing civil defence organisations, must also be permitted to carry on their work under the same conditions (Art. 63).

One important aspect of the obligation of an occupying power to "restore, and ensure, as far as possible, public order and safety" concerns its relation to the penal laws in force in the territory prior to the occupation. The principle is that these remain in force, but the occupant may repeal or suspend them "in cases where they constitute a threat to its security or an obstacle to the application of the present Convention", for instance, when a law renders every form of work for the occupying power an offence. Similarly, the existing tribunals continue in principle "to function in respect of all offences covered by the said laws" (all of this in Art. 64).

At the same time, Article 64 also recognises the power of the occupying power to enact regulations "essential to enable [it] to fulfil its obligations under the present Convention, to maintain the orderly government of the territory, and to ensure the security of [itself], of the members and property of the occupying forces or administration, and likewise of the establishments and lines of communication used by them". Any penal provisions so enacted must be properly "published and brought to the knowledge of the inhabitants in their own language" and cannot have retroactive effect (Art. 65). Obviously, acts in contravention of such regulations will have to be dealt with by the occupant's courts. Article 66 provides that these must be "properly constituted, non-political military courts"; the courts of first instance must "sit in the occupied territory", and courts of appeal "shall preferably sit" in the same territory.

Articles 67 *et seq.* lay down the standards these courts must meet in their administration of criminal justice. Besides rules of procedure, particular importance attaches to the rules relating to permissible punishments. Internment or simple imprisonment is the heaviest punishment for an offence "solely intended to harm the Occupying Power" but that "does not constitute an attempt on the life or limb of members of the occupying forces or administration, nor a grave collective danger, nor seriously damage the property of the occupying forces or administration or the installations used by them" (Art. 68).

Article 68 also limits the power of the occupant to impose the death penalty, first, to particularly grave crimes, viz., espionage, "serious acts of sabotage against the military installations of the Occupying Power" and "intentional offences which have caused the death of one or more persons". A further condition is "that such offences were punishable by death under the law of the occupied territory in force before the occupation began". The death penalty can only be pronounced against an offender who was not under the age of 18 at the time of the offence, and "the attention of the court [must have] been particularly called to the fact that since the accused is not a national of the Occupying Power, he is not bound to it by any duty of allegiance".

Section III closes with some provisions on the safety measures an occupying power may consider necessary, "for imperative reasons of security", with regard to protected persons. Article 78 limits the occupier's powers in this regard: "it may, at the most, subject them to assigned residence or to internment". Such a decision is moreover subject to appeal and, if upheld, to periodical review.

Here again, the effect of the above rules on permissible forms of punishment and safety measures is affected to no slight degree by Article 5. Paragraph 2 thereof provides that "[w]here in occupied territory an individual protected person is detained as a spy or saboteur, or as a person under definite suspicion of activity hostile to the security of the Occupying Power", they may be denied the "rights of communication under the present Convention" if this is considered necessary on grounds of "absolute military security". Even then, they must be treated with humanity and, if put on trial, must be given a "fair and regular trial" in conformity with the rules laid down in the Convention; and the special regime must come to an end "at the earliest date consistent with the security of the State" (Art. 5(3)).

With respect to armed resistance in occupied territory, it was noted earlier that resistance fighters qualify as 'protected persons' when they are found not to meet the conditions for prisoner-of-war status spelled out in the Third Convention (see Section 3.3.1). While entitled to treatment as civilians, they are obviously liable to being placed under the special security regime of Article 5 and, provided 'absolute necessity' so requires, deprived of their rights of communication under the Convention. They may moreover be punished for any acts of armed resistance they committed prior to capture. At the same time, in any criminal proceedings against them they are, like any other accused, entitled to such protections as are provided by the rules guaranteeing a fair trial.

A final note of comment on the regime of occupation as reflected in the Hague Regulations and Convention IV is that it evidently was not written with an eye to situations of prolonged occupation like the one that has existed for many years in the Middle East, with Israel occupying the West Bank and the Gaza Strip. Apart from all other problems that arose, and continue to arise, from this situation, Israel in 2002 started building a wall in the West Bank that separates Israeli and Palestinian populations. In reaction, the UN General Assembly in 2003 asked the International Court of Justice to give its opinion on the legal consequences arising from the construction of the wall. For the Advisory Opinion the Court delivered in 2004, see Section 5.3.2b.

3.4.6e   Internment

Section IV contains "Regulations for the Treatment of Internees", whether within the territory of a party to the conflict or in occupied territory (Arts. 79 *et seq.*). It may suffice to note here that the regime laid down in these articles is very similar to the regime for the internment of prisoners of war laid down in the Third Convention.

3.4.6f   Information bureaux and Tracing Agency

Section V of Part III deals with the establishment and functioning of national information bureaux (Art. 136) and a Central Information Agency (Art. 140). As noted in Section 3.4.5, the Agency of Article 140 and the comparable Agency of Article 123 of the Prisoners of War Convention have been combined into the Central Tracing Agency, organised and maintained by the ICRC.

3.4.7   *Common Article 3*

Article 3 common to the Conventions of 1949, as the only article especially written for situations of internal armed conflict, has been described as a 'mini-convention', or a 'convention within the conventions'. Given that in present times a majority of armed conflicts fall within this category, the article has assumed an importance the drafters could hardly have foreseen.

Article 3 presupposes a situation of armed conflict occurring between at least two parties within the territory of a state; it speaks of "armed forces" and "members" thereof, and it provides rules that parties to the armed conflict are "bound to apply, as a minimum". Yet, and although it does refer to "persons taking no active part in hostilities", it does not provide the persons who are actively engaged in hostilities, no matter on which side, with anything like the combatant or prisoner-of-war status of international armed conflict. From the point of view of international humanitarian law (as opposed to domestic law) persons taking an active part in hostilities are just that, whether they belong to the regular armed forces or to a non-state armed group.

One particular difficulty is that non-state armed groups are not and, indeed, cannot become parties to the Conventions. They may use this as an argument to deny any obligation to respect the principles set forth in the article. On the other hand, an argument encouraging them to adopt a more positive attitude towards the law is that respect of their obligations under Article 3 may help improving their 'image', in the country as in the eyes of the outside world, and thus may work to their advantage.

Another aspect of the same problem is that governments are rarely willing to recognise insurgents as an official 'party to the conflict', or even as a separate entity. They may therefore wish to avoid any statement officially acknowledging that Article 3 is applicable. In an attempt to meet this objection, the article stipulates that application of its provisions "shall not affect the legal status of the Parties to the conflict" (para. 4). Evidently, this form of words cannot prevent the potential effect the application of the article may have, or be perceived to have, on the *political* status of the insurgents.

A government faced with this dilemma might realise that while a refusal to recognise the application of Article 3 may serve to show that it withholds political status from the insurgents, such a refusal in the face of obvious facts may at the same time do serious damage to its own 'image', again, both in the eyes of its own population and in those of the outside world. For, as we shall see, the rules contained in Article 3 are minimum standards in the most literal sense of the term; standards, in other words, no respectable government could disregard for any length of time without losing its aura of respectability.

It should be noted that Article 3 is applicable in *all* conflicts not of an international character that occur in the territory of a state. These include not only conflicts involving the government armed forces fighting against a non-state armed group but also conflicts between such groups without involvement of the government armed forces. (For a discussion of the more limited scope of application of the Second Additional Protocol see Section 4.2.1.)

Article 3 prescribes the humane treatment, without discrimination, of all those who take no active part in the hostilities, including members of armed forces (regular or otherwise) who "have laid down their arms" or are *hors de combat* as a consequence of "sickness, wounds, detention, or any other cause". With regard to all these persons, "the following acts are and shall remain prohibited at any time and in any place whatsoever:

(a) violence to life and person, in particular murder of all kinds, mutilation, cruel treatment and torture;
(b) taking of hostages;
(c) outrages upon personal dignity, in particular humiliating and degrading treatment;
(d) the passing of sentences and the carrying out of executions without previous judgment pronounced by a regularly constituted court, affording all the judicial guarantees which are recognised as indispensable by civilised peoples" (para. 1(1)).

It may be noted that the above rules on humane treatment are no different than the comparable rules in human rights law, except for the fact that the obligation to respect the rules lies on all parties to the conflict and not, as in human rights law, solely on the government.

As regards humanitarian assistance, Article 3 requires no more than that "the wounded and sick shall be collected and cared for" (para. 1(2)). Matters such as registration, information, or the status of medical personnel, hospitals and ambulances, are not mentioned at all.

The third paragraph encourages the parties to the conflict "to bring into force, by means of special agreements, all or part of the other provisions" of the Conventions. The parties may actually be prepared to do this when they have a shared interest, for instance, in organising an exchange of prisoners who are a burden on their hands. The conclusion of such agreements will often come about through the intermediation of the ICRC. (For the role of the ICRC in situations of internal armed conflict, see also Section 3.5.2.)

3.5   Implementation and enforcement

This section discusses the instruments and mechanisms for implementation and enforcement that existed under the pre-1977 rules for the promotion of respect for humanitarian law: instruction and education (Section 3.5.1), the activities of protecting powers and humanitarian agencies (Section 3.5.2), and collective and individual responsibility for violations (Sections 3.5.3, 3.5.4).

3.5.1   Instruction and education

To promote implementation of humanitarian law, instruction and education are crucial. The actual implementation of the law in a situation of armed conflict depends on a multitude of individual persons at all levels of society: one could hardly expect that its rules will be respected and, for instance, soldiers will always recognise as unlawful an order wantonly to kill prisoners of war or unarmed civilians, if adequate information has not been disseminated in advance and on the widest possible scale.

This line of thought was reflected as long ago as 1899 in the Hague Convention on Land Warfare: Article 1 provides that the contracting states "shall issue instructions to their armed land forces" in conformity with the annexed Regulations. The point is brought out with even greater force in the Geneva Conventions of 1949. Articles 47, 48, 127 and 144 of the four Conventions, respectively, require the contracting states, "in time of peace as in time of war", to disseminate the text of the Conventions "as widely as possible in their respective countries", and "in particular, to include the study thereof in their programmes of military and, if possible, civil instruction", so that the principles of the law embodied in the Conventions may become known to the entire population.

A similar obligation is found in Article 25 of the 1954 Hague Convention on cultural property.

With respect to these explicit treaty obligations, many states parties fall far short of expectations. While instruction to the armed forces may not be wholly lacking, education of the civilian population often leaves much to be desired. In this deplorable situation, the ICRC, the International Federation of Red Cross and Red Crescent Societies and national societies exert considerable effort to fill the gap. Yet this activity 'by substitution' cannot absolve the authorities of their treaty obligations, nor indeed of their responsibility for the consequences of non-performance on this score.

3.5.2   Protecting powers and other humanitarian agencies

Outside supervision as a means to improve the implementation of the law of armed conflict developed in the pre-1949 era mainly within the framework of the law of Geneva. It grew out of practice: in the event of severance of diplomatic relations between states A and B, A could ask state C to act as protector of its interests and those of its nationals in respect of – and with the agreement of – state B. If an armed conflict then broke out between

A and B, it was almost natural for C to continue to protect the interests of A's nationals, who in their relations to B suddenly found themselves in the position of 'enemy nationals', 'internees' or 'prisoners of war'. This practice subsequently was incorporated in the Geneva Conventions, first of 1929 and then of 1949, as the system of protecting powers. Although last widely applied during the Second World War (with the neutral states Sweden and Switzerland acting as protecting powers for numerous parties on both sides of the conflict), the system persists mainly as 'law on the books' and therefore deserves to be presented here.

The four Geneva Conventions prescribe that they "shall be applied with the co-operation and under the scrutiny of the Protecting Power whose duty it is to safeguard the interests of the Parties to the conflict" (Arts. 8 of Conventions I–III, 9 of Convention IV). To this end, the protecting powers may use their diplomatic or consular staff, or they may appoint special delegates (who require the approval of the party to the conflict where they are to carry out their duties). The parties to the conflict must "facilitate to the greatest extent possible the task" of these representatives or delegates, and these are in turn obliged not to exceed their mission: in particular, they always must "take account of the imperative necessities of security of the state wherein they carry out their duties".

The function of protecting powers in practice assumed the character of management of interests and mediation. When information came to light, for instance, that prisoners of war were suffering from bad housing conditions or a lack of food, were compelled to carry out forbidden types of work, were not allowed to send and receive mail, or were maltreated in any other manner, a protecting power could seek an improvement of the situation. At the same time, it was never the function of protecting powers to act as a sort of public prosecutor, investigating and exposing violations of the Conventions.

Article 9 of Conventions I–III and Article 10 of Convention IV emphasise that the provisions of the Conventions "constitute no obstacle to the humanitarian activities which the International Committee of the Red Cross or any other impartial humanitarian organisation may, subject to the consent of the party to the conflict concerned, undertake for the protection of [protected persons] and for their relief". The express reference to the ICRC amounts to an official recognition of its customary right of initiative in matters of humanitarian protection and assistance.

Article 10 of Conventions I–III and Article 11 of Convention IV address the (now common) situation where no protecting powers are functioning because agreement on the appointment of such powers has not been forthcoming. In this situation, contracting parties may "agree to entrust to an organisation which offers all guarantees of impartiality and efficacy the duties incumbent on the Protecting Powers" (para. 1). When this fails (as has always been the case) a detaining power must "request a neutral State, or such an organisation, to undertake the functions" of a protecting power (para. 2). While this would not require the agreement of the adverse party, to find such a state or organisation prepared to accept, in the absence of the adverse party's consent, the functions of a protecting power proved as much of a stumbling block as it did in the previous situations.

As a last resort, paragraph 3 requires the detaining power to request or accept, always "subject to the provisions of this article", "the offer of the services of a humanitarian organisation" such as the ICRC, to "assume the humanitarian functions assumed by Protecting Powers" under the Conventions. Note that the reference to the 'detaining power' would limit the scope of protection under this paragraph to protected persons who one way or another find themselves in detention. Apart from this, even this provision failed to work: the detaining power could disregard its obligation to request the services of the ICRC or other humanitarian organisation, and the ICRC could hardly be expected to "offer its services" without first having ascertained that these are indeed welcome.

The protecting powers system applies only to the law of Geneva (with the exception of common Article 3). Nothing comparable to this system developed for the law of the Hague, and The Hague Conventions of 1899 and 1907 are silent on the matter. The exception is the 1954 Hague Convention on the protection of cultural property: this contains a system, comparable to that of the Geneva Conventions, of cooperation and assistance in the application of the Convention and the annexed Regulations. The system includes the (theoretical) cooperation of protecting powers and assigns a (practically more important) role to UNESCO.

While all this may appear, and is, very disappointing, it should be noted with gratitude that the ICRC has, ever since its creation in 1863, been performing supervisory functions in innumerable cases, including internal armed conflicts, and to the benefit of millions of prisoners of war, internees and other protected persons, sometimes side by side with the delegates of protecting powers and, more often, in their absence. Recognising this practice, Article 126 of the Third Convention and Article 143 of the Fourth Convention accord the delegates of the ICRC the same prerogatives as those accorded delegates of protecting powers for the purpose of visiting prisoners of war, civilian detainees and internees, and interviewing them without witnesses. These visits, which represent an important aspect of the protective role of the ICRC, have the purely humanitarian purpose of preserving the physical and moral integrity of detainees, preventing any abuse, and ensuring that detainees enjoy the decent material and psychological conditions of detention they are entitled to by law.

As regards internal armed conflict in particular, common Article 3(2) provides that "[a]n impartial humanitarian body, such as the International Committee of the Red Cross, may offer its services to the Parties to the conflict". Although not formulated as a formal mandate, it serves to preclude any accusation that by offering its services, the ICRC is interfering in the domestic affairs of the state involved. Its functioning as an incontestably impartial and humanitarian organisation finds further support in the incorporation of its mandate in the Statutes of the International Red Cross and Red Crescent Movement, a document recognised by the states parties to the Conventions. (On the structure and functioning of the International Red Cross and Red Crescent Movement, see Section 5.3.9a.)

In the course of its activities the ICRC often encounters instances of serious violations of the Conventions, and exceptionally, when confidential dialogue with the party concerned has not brought about the desired results, the ICRC may have recourse to a public denunciation, in general terms, of the practices involved. The ICRC does not, however, engage in the tracing and exposure of those individually responsible for such violations: it regards such functions as irreconcilable with its humanitarian mandate of protection and assistance. (The matter of criminal repression of violations of the law of armed conflict is broached in Section 3.5.4, and as far as recent developments are concerned, in Sections 4.3.4 and 5.3.)

3.5.3   Collective responsibility

Violations of the law of war may give rise to a variety of reactions, both against the person or persons believed to be individually responsible for the acts, as well as against the collectivity (the state, another party to the conflict, a village) to which these persons are assumed to be linked, whether as members or otherwise. The reactions may be instant or delayed; come from individual persons or from collectivities such as the adverse party, third states, or an international body such as the Security Council; and, not least important, be lawful or unlawful.

Among entities apt to be held responsible for violations of the law of war, the state party to the conflict is the first to come to mind. Its responsibility "for all acts committed by persons forming part of its armed forces" was recognised as long ago as 1907, in a provision the Second Hague Peace Conference wrote into Article 3 of the Hague Convention on Land Warfare. This specific case of responsibility is part of a state's general responsibility for internationally unlawful acts that are attributable to it. Thus, apart from violations committed by its armed forces, its responsibility extends to violations of the law of armed conflict committed by other state agents (the police, the guards of a prisoner-of-war camp), and even to possible wrongful conduct of civilians.

Collective responsibility obtains in situations of internal armed conflict as well, first of all to the territorial state if it is engaged in the conflict. Then, as noted before, common Article 3 of the 1949 Geneva Conventions also governs the position of organised non-state armed groups fighting against other similar groups or against the armed forces of the state. Even though they cannot become party to the Conventions, these groups are generally regarded as bound by the applicable rules of international humanitarian law and may be held responsible for the conduct of their members, whether by opposing parties or the outside world. Yet, accountability should not in the first place be expected as a result of the traditional state-centred methods of reciprocity, reprisal and compensation, dealt with hereafter. More success may be achieved through various forms of outside pressure.

In the opening paragraph of this section, reference was also made to a village, which might be held collectively responsible for violations committed within or close to it. The difference between this and the state or non-state armed group is obvious: while those entities were all parties to the conflict, the village, normally speaking, is not. We shall outline this difference, and the legal consequences thereof, later in this section.

3.5.3a   Reciprocity

The first and most primitive manifestation of the idea of collective responsibility of a state or other party to the conflict arises when the adverse party, confronted with the violation of one or more rules, considers itself no longer bound to respect the rule or rules in question. Such a reaction amounts to a rigorous application of the principle of negative reciprocity. For the 1949 Geneva Conventions the operation of this crude principle is excluded by the provision in common Article 1 that the contracting states are bound to respect the Conventions "in all circumstances".

While it may be questioned whether this provision could be a hundred per cent effective even in the context of the law of Geneva, the situation is different in respect of the pre-1977 law of The Hague. The treaties concerned do not expressly exclude negative reciprocity, and it may be doubted whether an unconditional exclusion would be always appropriate here. Doubt appears particularly justified in a situation where the violation of given rules may give the guilty party a clear military advantage. One may think here of rules prohibiting or restricting the use of militarily significant weapons. As noted earlier, the ban on use of chemical weapons was long regarded as being subject to reciprocity. This probably was in accordance with their military significance: it seems indeed hard to accept that a belligerent state should simply resign itself to the adverse effects it would be made to suffer from its opponent's use of chemical weapons when it had the capacity to retaliate in kind and thus restore the military balance.

Reciprocity may also represent a positive factor, though, when respect of the law by one state entails respect by the other. This positive aspect may again be demonstrated with the example of chemical weapons: while both sides in the Second World War possessed chemical weapons, neither side actually started using them.

In the Geneva Conventions, a form of positive reciprocity has been given a prominent place in common Article 2(3). This envisions the situation where some parties to the conflict are parties to the Conventions, while another party to the conflict is not. The paragraph provides that "if the latter accepts and applies the provisions" of the Conventions, the former parties shall be bound to apply the Conventions even in relation to that party. As noted earlier, this situation cannot arise today, given that all existing states are party to the Conventions.

3.5.3b   Reprisals

Belligerent reprisals are acts that wilfully violate given rules of the law of armed conflict, resorted to by a party to the conflict in reaction to conduct on the part of the adverse party that is perceived to reflect a policy of violation of the same or other rules of that body of law. Required is that all efforts have failed to induce the adverse party to discontinue its policy and respect the law (requirement of 'subsidiarity'). A reprisal must not inflict damage disproportionate to that done by the illegal act that prompted it, and must be terminated as soon as the adverse party discontinues the incriminated policy. Another restriction, advocated by some experts before the Second World War, was that the reprisal must not amount to an inhumane act.

Under the customary law of armed conflict of that pre-Second World War period, belligerent reprisals belonged to a state's arsenal of permissible measures of law enforcement. They often had an escalating effect, however, and they would usually affect persons other than the individuals responsible for the initial violation. For these reasons, the right of recourse to belligerent reprisals was increasingly restricted. Thus, as mentioned before, reprisals against protected persons and property were expressly prohibited in all four Geneva Conventions of 1949 and in the Hague Convention of 1954 on cultural property.

On the other hand, no such prohibition was found in the Hague Conventions of 1899 and 1907, nor in the 1925 Geneva Gas Protocol. This led to uncertainty, for instance, whether air bombardment of a civilian population could be justified as a reprisal; what, for instance, of the inhumane character of such a measure? Strangely enough, some experts of the period who defended this element as a requirement for a valid reprisal, nonetheless held that reprisals against a civilian population were admissible.

In the course of the Second World War, both sides on the European theatre carried out large-scale bombardments against built-up areas in enemy territory, accidentally or more often intentionally striking at areas without military objectives. The parties generally attempted to justify this policy with the argument of reprisal, without taking too much trouble to claim compliance with the requirements of subsidiarity and proportionality. As a belated reaction to this practice, the UN General Assembly in 1970 adopted Resolution 2675 (XXV) "affirming" as one of the "basic principles for the protection of civilian populations in armed conflicts", that "[c]ivilian populations, or individual members thereof, should not be the object of reprisals". Taken by itself, this affirmation was not enough to effectively take away the existing uncertainty on this point of law. (See also Section 4.1.5h.)

It may be noted that reprisals as a legal instrument have remained unknown in the practice of the internal armed conflicts of our times. (See also Section 3.5.3e on collective punishment.)

3.5.3c   Compensation

As yet another conceivable outcome of collective responsibility, a party to the conflict may have to pay compensation for the damage caused by conduct for which it is held responsible. In 1907, the duty for states to pay such compensation was expressly included in The Hague Convention on Land Warfare. According to Article 3 (which, as mentioned in the introduction to this section, holds the state responsible for "all acts committed by persons forming part of its armed forces"), a belligerent party that is responsible for a violation of the rules laid down in the Regulations "shall, if the case demands, be liable to pay compensation".

While Article 12 of Convention III and Article 29 of Convention IV cite the responsibility of the state for the treatment given persons protected under these Conventions "irrespective of the individual responsibilities that may exist", they do not refer to the possible financial implications of this form of state responsibility (but see below in relation to Articles 51, 52, 131 and 148 of Conventions I–IV, respectively).

In the practice of the period, the liability of states to pay compensation for violations of the law of armed conflict has had mixed results at best. One road towards post-war payment involved the conclusion of a lump-sum agreement, usually as part of a peace treaty that burdened the vanquished state with the obligation to pay the victor state an amount of money, ostensibly by way of reparation for losses suffered by the latter party as a result of the war. The amount was bound to remain far below the actual losses suffered on that side. More important, it was not likely to be determined by, nor even necessarily brought in direct ratio to, the damage specifically inflicted by acts violating the law of armed conflict – nor did the victorious party pay compensation for the similar damage done to interests of the vanquished party that resulted from violations of the law committed under the victor's responsibility.

Lump-sum agreements may contain a clause waiving any further claims, whether of the victorious state or its nationals, against the vanquished state for damages arising out of the war. The effect of this is uncertain. Special arrangements apart, individuals have no access to the international plane to bring their claims against a state of which they are not nationals. They may, on the other hand, have access to the domestic courts of the responsible state and attempt to seek compensation for the violations they suffered. Cases of this sort have been brought before Japanese courts by persons who as prisoners of war, civilian detainees or inhabitants of occupied territory had suffered damages at the hands of the Japanese armed forces in the course of the Second World War. (On these cases, see also Section 5.3.8.)

A remarkable situation arose in the aftermath of the Second World War in the Far East. It concerned damage incurred by nationals of Japan, the vanquished state, through acts of the United States. The peace treaty between these countries provides that Japan would assume responsibility for any claims by its nationals against the USA. Japanese nationals brought a case before the Tokyo District Court, arguing that the use by the USA of atomic bombs against Hiroshima and Nagasaki had constituted a wrongful act; that by concluding the peace treaty Japan had waived its nationals' right to seek compensation from the USA in respect of such wrongful acts, and that, accordingly, the Japanese Government was liable to pay damages (the *Shimoda* case). The Court held that the use of the atomic bombs had indeed been unlawful. Yet, in order to avoid awarding the claimed damages against the Japanese Government, while conceding that individuals might be the subjects of rights under international law in situations where a right to claim had been expressly granted to them, such as in mixed arbitral tribunals, the Court argued that they were ordinarily precluded from seeking redress for a violation of international law before a domestic court.

The *Shimoda* case demonstrates the strange consequences that may arise from such a shifting of liability to pay compensation on to the vanquished party. The 1949 Geneva Conventions exclude the possibility of such a shift in responsibility in the criminal sphere, at any rate as far as grave breaches are concerned. The relevant articles provide that "[n]o High Contracting Power shall be allowed to absolve itself or any other High Contracting Party of any liability incurred by itself or by another High Contracting Party in respect of [such] breaches" (Articles 51, 52, 131 and 148 of Conventions I–IV, respectively).

It may be mentioned that more recently, non-state parties to an internal armed conflict have been known to recognise responsibility for particular violations committed by members of their armed groups, and even to pay compensation to the victims for the injury and damage resulting from the acts. It should be added that these were rare occasions indeed.

3.5.3d External pressure

As may be apparent from the foregoing, the main relevance of the various traditional manifestations of 'collective' responsibility lies in their deterrent effect. The realisation that any infringement of the law of armed conflict gives rise to the responsibility of the state party concerned (and, hence, may give rise to an immediate response based on the principle of negative reciprocity or to belligerent reprisals, or, in the long run, may result in that state party having to pay damages after the war) may provide the authorities with an additional incentive to respect, and ensure respect for, this body of law. External pressure may significantly reinforce this effect.

External pressure frequently stems from public opinion, inspired by reports and comments of non-governmental organisations such as Human Rights Watch and Amnesty International, and the media. It may also take the form of (discreet or public) representations by third parties: governments, or regional or universal intergovernmental organisations and the ICRC. After all, as members of the international community of states and in many instances as parties to the body of treaty or customary law that is being infringed, it is their shared interest to see the law respected. Article 1 common to the 1949 Geneva Conventions gives expression to this idea when it states that all contracting states "undertake to respect and to ensure respect" for the Conventions "in all circumstances". In the words of the International Court of Justice, "such an obligation does not derive only from the Conventions themselves, but from the general principles of humanitarian law to which the Conventions merely give specific expression" (*Nicaragua* v. *United States of America*, Judgment on the Merits, 1986).

3.5.3e   Collective punishment

As noted in the introduction to this chapter, the phrase 'collective responsibility' is also occasionally used in the sense of holding a community (a village, a town) collectively responsible for acts committed by one or more individuals in their midst. This type of 'responsibility' has frequently resulted in vicious acts of retaliation against the inhabitants of such villages or towns, for instance, in reaction to acts of armed resistance against an occupying power. In present-day internal armed conflicts, a similar inclination may often be noticed, with local communities being subjected to harsh measures on the suspicion that activities in support of the other party have been carried out by members of the community.

For international armed conflicts, Article 33 of the Fourth Convention expressly prohibits this form of repression: "No protected person may be punished for an offence he or she has not personally committed. Collective penalties and likewise all measures of intimidation or of terrorism are prohibited." As regards situations of internal armed conflict, the only relevant rule is the provision in common Article 3 that prohibits the taking of hostages – and, a fortiori, the wanton execution of such persons. For the rest, the general principle of common Article 3 requiring humane treatment for all persons taking no active part in the hostilities, and the specific prohibitions of "violence to life and person, in particular murder of all kinds, mutilation, cruel treatment and torture" and of "outrages upon personal dignity, in particular humiliating and degrading treatment" provide the remaining solid ground to hold retaliatory acts of the type dealt with here, not only utterly despicable, but unjustifiable.

3.5.4   Individual responsibility

As with 'collective responsibility' for violations of the law of armed conflict, the notion of individual liability for war crimes is of fluctuating import. As far as practical application goes, its major achievement for a long time remained the massive, though obviously one-sided, post-Second World War prosecution and trial of the war criminals of the Axis powers.

The Hague Conventions of 1899 and 1907 on Land Warfare are silent on the matter of individual criminal liability for violations of the annexed Regulations. This is not to say that such individual liability would have been against the intention of the contracting states: on the contrary, the competence of states to punish their nationals or those of the enemy for the war crimes they might have committed had long developed into an accepted part of customary law, so much so that there was no need for express confirmation by treaty. Obviously, a competence to deal with particular crimes is an entirely different matter than an obligation to do so. As regards war crimes, no general obligation of this order existed at the time of the Hague Peace Conferences, and neither was it created by the Conventions on Land Warfare of 1899 and 1907.

Yet, the idea was not unknown: the Geneva Wounded and Sick Convention of 1906 was the first to include an obligation upon states to take legislative measures for the repression of certain infractions, and the next year, at the Second Hague Peace Conference, a similar provision was incorporated in the Hague Convention (X) for the Adaptation to Maritime Warfare of the Principles of the Geneva Convention. The idea was developed somewhat further in the Geneva Wounded and Sick Convention of 1929. Yet the Prisoners of War Convention adopted by the same Conference remained silent on the matter.

Finally, in 1949, elaborate provisions on penal sanctions and the prosecution of offenders were introduced in all four Geneva Conventions. The provisions distinguish between two levels of violation: 'grave breaches' and other, presumably less grave violations.

As provided by Articles 49, 50, 129 and 146 of Conventions I–IV, respectively, each contracting state must ensure that its legislation provides "effective penal sanctions for persons committing, or ordering to be committed, any of the grave breaches" defined in the Conventions. It is also "under the obligation to search for persons alleged to have committed, or to have ordered to be committed, such grave breaches", and it must "bring such persons, regardless of their nationality, before its own courts", unless it prefers to "hand [them] over for trial" to another con-tracting state that has made out a prima facie case. The reference in these provisions to 'persons' without further qualification as to their national-ity or that of the victims of the breaches or of the place where these were committed, is generally accepted to amount to an application of the prin-ciple of universal jurisdiction, meaning that states have jurisdiction over grave breaches irrespective of the place of the act or the nationality of the perpetrator.

The acts that constitute grave breaches are enumerated in each Convention (Arts. 50, 51, 130 and 147 of Conventions I–IV, respect-ively). The definitions comprise acts "committed against persons or property protected by the Convention", such as wilful killing, torture or inhumane treatment, wilfully causing great suffering or serious injury to body or health, unlawful deportation and the taking of hos-tages. The express reference to "persons or property protected by the Convention" implies that in every single instance it must be shown that the victim was a protected person as defined in the relevant article of the Convention. The problem is greatest in respect of Convention IV, with its complicated definition of 'protected persons' in Article 4 (see above, Sections 3.1, 3.4.6b). It may be noted here that the Yugoslavia Tribunal has held that a difference in ethnic origin could satisfy the requirement of a 'different nationality'.

The 'other' violations of Articles 49, 50, 129 and 146 are broadly described as "all acts contrary to the provisions of the [Conventions] other than the grave breaches" defined earlier. The obligations of contracting states with regard to these other infractions are limited to taking "measures neces-sary for [their] suppression". This may be a disciplinary correction or any other suitable measure including criminal prosecution.

Two points deserve to be made. The first is that neither the grave breaches nor the other violations are characterised as 'war crimes': in 1949 the term was expressly avoided, for political reasons related to the position of the communist bloc with regard to the treatment of post-Second World War prisoners of war convicted as 'war criminals'. The second point is the total silence on the possibility of international adju-dication of violations of the Geneva Conventions, this notwithstanding the experience of the two International Military Tribunals, and in stark contrast with the position adopted one year earlier in the Convention on the Prevention and Punishment of the Crime of Genocide; Article VI of that Convention expressly reserves the possibility of trial by a competent 'international penal tribunal'. Admittedly, that provision may have been accepted with 'tongue in cheek' by states that expected not to see such a tribunal any time soon.

The practical effect of the above provisions has long been negligible. Few states enacted legislation specifically providing penal sanctions for the perpetrators of grave breaches as defined in the Conventions. In the Netherlands, for instance, the legislature long confined itself to making any act amounting to a violation of the laws and customs of war punishable as a war crime; and while the law made the penalty dependent on the measure of injury inflicted by the crime, the various levels of gravity had nothing to do with the definitions of grave breaches in the Conventions. In addition, many states regarded their existing criminal law (often the military law) as entirely adequate to cope with the prosecution of grave breaches, and other states did not even take the trouble of answering the periodic requests for information sent out by the ICRC.

Matters were no better in respect of the obligations of investigation and prosecution. Since the entry into force of the Conventions, in October 1950, few actions of this type were undertaken against suspects other than a state's nationals, and even this rarely.

The Hague Convention of 1954 for the Protection of Cultural Property in the Event of Armed Conflict contains a much simpler provision on sanctions. Article 28 obliges contracting states to "take, within the framework of their ordinary criminal legislation, all necessary steps to prosecute and impose penal or disciplinary sanctions upon those persons, of whatever nationality, who commit or order to be committed a breach of the present Convention".

4

The Protocols of 1977

As related towards the end of Chapter 2, the Diplomatic Conference on the Reaffirmation and Development of International Humanitarian Law Applicable in Armed Conflicts, or CDDH, on 8 June 1977 adopted the text of two Protocols Additional to the Geneva Conventions of 12 August 1949. One (Protocol I) is applicable in international armed conflicts; the other (Protocol II), in non-international armed conflicts.

The Conference adopted the Protocols 'by consensus', that is, without formal vote. This does not mean to say that every single provision was equally acceptable to all delegations: far from it. Statements made at the end of the Conference left no doubt that a number of delegations maintained serious misgivings about certain provisions of Protocol I, and some delegations even about Protocol II in its entirety. It may be noted with satisfaction, therefore, that an important number of states have subsequently seen fit to ratify or accede to the Protocols.

It is also worthy of note that a good part of the provisions of Protocol I, and perhaps even some of those of Protocol II, represent rules of pre-existing customary international law or have subsequently been recognised as such. With respect to these customary provisions, it might be deemed immaterial whether a state ratifies or accedes to the Protocols or not. In practice, a non-ratifying state such as the United States tends to recognise as binding those rules of Protocol I it regards as customary. Yet ratification or accession remains important, not merely with regard to those provisions that were undoubtedly new and have not yet become customary, but also in view of the many provisions that introduce a more precise or elaborate formulation of what previously was recognised as a rather vague and broad customary rule, such as the precept that civilian populations must be "spared as much as possible".

Only states parties to the Geneva Conventions of 1949 can become parties to the Protocols. As of August 2010, 170 states are party to Protocol I and 165 to Protocol II.

In this chapter, attention is first given to Protocol I, as the most elaborate and detailed of the two (Section 4.1), and then to Protocol II (Section 4.2). Topics are discussed more or less in the same order as in Chapter 3, with such deviations from that scheme as result from the 'confluence of the currents of The Hague, Geneva and New York' effected in the Protocols.

4.1 Protocol I

4.1.1 Character of the law

The preamble reaffirms that the provisions of the Conventions and the Protocol "must be fully applied in all circumstances to all persons who are protected by those instruments, without any adverse distinction based on the nature or origin of the armed conflict or on the causes espoused by or attributed to the Parties to the conflict". This language is designed to place beyond doubt that all the parties to an international armed conflict are obliged mutually to observe the rules of humanitarian law, no matter which party is regarded, or regards itself as the attacker or the defender, and irrespective of any claims of 'just cause'.

The reaffirmation is important because under the terms of the Charter of the United Nations, the inter-state use of force (and, indeed, any "threat or use of force against the territorial integrity or political independence of any State, or in any other manner inconsistent with the Purposes of the United Nations") is prohibited, whereas recourse to individual or collective self-defence against an armed attack remains permissible. While this distinction between the attacker (or, in the worst case, the aggressor) and the defending side has effects, as it should, in certain areas of international law, it would be unacceptable and go against the very purposes of the law of armed conflict if the distinction were permitted to result in differences in the obligations of the parties to the conflict under that particular body of law.

Yet, the opposite effect would be equally unacceptable: that is, if the notion of equality of belligerent parties were transplanted to those areas of international law where the distinction between attacker and defender has rightly led to a difference in legal position. In order to preclude such an unwarranted effect the preamble also specifies that nothing in the Protocol or in the Conventions "can be construed as legitimising or authorising any act of aggression or any other use of force inconsistent with the Charter of the United Nations".

Like the 1949 Conventions, Protocol I also obliges the parties "to respect and to ensure respect for [its provisions] in all circumstances" (Art. 1(1)). Here too, it is not open to doubt that in drawing up the various provisions of Protocol I the authors have taken the factor of 'military necessity' into account. Hence, deviations from the rules cannot be justified with an appeal to military necessity, unless a given rule expressly admits such an appeal.

Article 1(2), repeating in slightly modernised terms the Martens clause of 1899, places beyond doubt that 'military necessity' in the sense of unfettered military discretion does not automatically prevail in situations that are not explicitly governed by any rule in the Protocol or other treaties:

> In cases not covered by this Protocol or by other international agreements, civilians and combatants remain under the protection and authority of the principles of international law derived from established custom, from the principles of humanity and from the dictates of public conscience.

4.1.2   Scope of application

Protocol I applies in the same situations of international armed conflict and occupation as the 1949 Conventions (Art. 1(3)). Paragraph 4 declares that these situations include wars of national liberation. The paragraph defines these as:

> armed conflicts in which peoples are fighting against colonial domination and alien occupation and against racist régimes in the exercise of their right of self-determination, as enshrined in the Charter of the United Nations and the Declaration on Principles of International Law concerning Friendly Relations and Cooperation among States in accordance with the Charter of the United Nations [adopted by the UN General Assembly as an annex to its Resolution 2625 (XXV) of 24 October 1970].

This formula purports to bring within the range of international armed conflicts (and, hence, within the scope of application of the Geneva Conventions and Protocol I) those 'wars of national liberation' the UN General Assembly was already treating as such, in the framework of the decolonisation process. The references to "colonial domination", "alien occupation" and "racist régimes", as well as to the "right of self-determination", are designed to limit the scope of the provision: it was not the intention of the drafters that henceforth any conflict a group of self-styled 'freedom fighters' designates as a 'war of liberation' would thereby automatically fall within the category of international armed conflicts Even so, the wording of the paragraph is rather elastic. Several states, both in Western Europe and elsewhere, accordingly feared from the outset that

Article 1(4) might offer an opening to separatist movements, or movements violently opposing the existing social order, to label their actions as a 'war of national liberation' and in that manner at least score some political advantage.

Article 1(4) also presents the difficulty that peoples fighting "in the exercise of their right of self-determination" cannot become parties to the Conventions or the Protocol. In an attempt to remove this obstacle, Article 96(3) of the Protocol provides that the authority representing such a people may address a unilateral declaration to the Depositary (the Swiss Government) stating that it undertakes to apply the Conventions and the Protocol. The paragraph requires that the war is fought "against a High Contracting Party"; a declaration under Article 96(3) can therefore only have effect if the state against which the war is waged is itself a party to the Protocol (and, hence, to the Conventions). The effect of such a declaration is to make the Conventions and the Protocol applicable in that armed conflict and therefore equally binding upon all parties to the conflict.

It should be emphasised that Article 1(4) can only have its intended effect if both conditions are met: the state concerned must be a party to the Protocol, and the authority representing the people must undertake to apply the Conventions and the Protocol by means of a declaration addressed to the Depositary. Also worthy of note is the provision in Article 4 that "application of the Conventions and of this Protocol … shall not affect the legal status of the Parties to the conflict".

In practice, no case has occurred since the entry into force of the Protocol, of an armed conflict that met the conditions of Article 1(4) with the state involved being a party to the Protocol and the authorities representing the people making the declaration of Article 96(3). On the other hand, leaders of rebellious movements have occasionally claimed that they were fighting a war of national liberation. Such statements did not have the effect of making the Conventions and Protocol I applicable to the situation.

A general comment may be repeated here that was already made in Section 3.1, namely, that international judicial bodies have their own power to determine whether the Conventions and Protocol I are, or were, applicable to a given situation of international violence.

4.1.3   Combatant and prisoner-of-war status

How to recognise a combatant? In the past, there was no great difficulty as far as the regular armies were concerned: they marched proudly in their magnificent uniforms, with swords and shields – and somewhat later, the long rifle – on prominent display. Even now, on ceremonial occasions, one may witness such a splendid show of colours. Both in the past and in more recent times, however, there were also other situations in which groups of people took part in the fighting without distinguishing themselves quite so clearly from the rest of the population: resistance fighters in occupied territory, 'liberation fighters' taking part in the decolonisation wars and in our days all kinds of irregular fighters. Should they all be recognised as combatants and, upon capture, as prisoners of war? The attempt to find a solution to this riddle had failed completely in 1899, and in 1949 a sort of solution was accepted that was satisfactory only to the regular armies, leaving the irregulars mostly out in the cold.

The negotiators of Protocol I tried their hand at the conundrum again, and the result of their endeavours, as embodied in Section II of Part III of the Protocol, is summarised in the next paragraphs. Their main concern can best be shown, however, by quoting part of Article 48 that opens the next part of the Protocol (Civilian Population):

> In order to ensure respect for and protection of the civilian population ... the Parties to the conflict shall at all times distinguish between the civilian population and combatants ...

Indeed, in the whole of Protocol I, and no matter what the importance of many other provisions, this may be its most cardinal provision. It was the most difficult to elaborate, and remains the most difficult to apply and interpret.

4.1.3a   Qualification as 'armed force' and 'combatant': general rules

As a first step towards solving the problem, Article 43 gives an entirely novel definition of 'armed forces' and 'combatants'. According to paragraph 1:

> The armed forces of a party to the conflict consist of all organised armed forces, groups and units which are under a command responsible to that Party for the conduct of its subordinates, even if that Party is represented by a government or an authority not recognised by an adverse Party. Such armed forces shall be subject to an internal disciplinary system which, *inter alia*, shall enforce compliance with the rules of international law applicable in armed conflict.

This definition makes no distinction between the (regular) armed forces of the state and (irregular) armed forces of a resistance or liberation movement, or other similar non-state armed forces. One implication is that 'regular' armed forces – that is, those that are not a 'militia or volunteer corps' – for the first time are submitted to express requirements.

For all 'armed forces', these requirements may be summed up as: a measure of organisation, a responsible command, and an internal disciplinary system designed notably to ensure compliance with the written and unwritten rules of armed conflict. Compared with the traditional requirements of the Hague Regulations, the most striking difference is that qualification as an armed force is no longer made dependent on its members having a uniform or carrying arms openly at all times as a means of distinguishing the members of the armed force from the civilian population.

This brings us to the second, and more complicated, part of the solution sought in 1977 to the age-old problem of protection of the civilian population in a situation of irregular warfare. The solution was sought in the context, not – as in the past – of the notion of 'armed force' but in terms of the rights and obligations of its individual members. Setting out their rights first, Article 43(2) specifies that they all "are combatants, that is to say, they have the right to participate directly in hostilities". (Excepted are "medical personnel and chaplains covered by Article 33 of the Third Convention", as non-combatant members of the armed forces.)

This status and this right are directly linked with the right of combatants to "be a prisoner of war" when they fall into the power of an adverse party (Art. 44(1)). As a matter of course, individual combatants are "obliged to comply with the rules of international law applicable in armed conflict" and bear individual responsibility for any violations they might commit. Article 44(2) emphasises that, one exception apart, such violations by individuals "shall not deprive a combatant of his right to be a combatant or, if he falls into the power of an adverse party, of his right to be a prisoner of war": those rights are inherent in membership of the armed force. The exception is announced in the closing phrase of the quoted sentence: "except as provided in paragraph 3 and 4".

4.1.3b   The individual obligation of combatants to distinguish themselves from civilians

Article 44(3) begins by laying upon individual combatants the obligation to distinguish themselves from civilians:

> In order to promote the protection of the civilian population from the effects of hostilities, combatants are obliged to distinguish themselves

> from the civilian population when they are engaged in an attack or in a
> military operation preparatory to an attack.

This provision closely resembles the text, quoted above, of Article 48: in
that Article the obligation is addressed to the parties to the conflict; here,
it is translated into an obligation resting upon individual combatants. On
the other hand, combatants do not need to so distinguish themselves at
all times: it suffices for them to do this whenever they are engaged in "an
attack or in a military operation preparatory to an attack". This may still
cover a considerable length of time, beginning quite a while before the
assault is finally launched.

But even the preparation of typical guerrilla activities such as an
ambush or a hit-and-run action may begin days, if not weeks, before the
final operation. Can persons engaged in armed resistance in occupied territory, or in a war of national liberation or other type of irregular warfare,
be expected to survive if they are to distinguish themselves from civilians
throughout that period? Can, conversely, civilians hope to survive if the
irregular fighters in their area never distinguish themselves as such?

4.1.3c   Exception to the general rule of distinction

In a valiant attempt to solve this last bit of the problem, the second sentence
of Article 44(3), "recognising that there are situations in armed conflicts
where, owing to the nature of the hostilities an armed combatant cannot
so distinguish himself", declares that "he shall retain his status as a combatant, provided that, in such situations, he carries his arms openly":

(a) during each military engagement; and
(b) during such time as he is visible to the adversary while he is engaged in
     a military deployment preceding the launching of an attack in which
     he is to participate.

If, on the contrary, our combatant falls into the power of the adversary
"while failing to meet the requirements set forth in the second sentence of
paragraph 3", he "shall forfeit his right to be a prisoner of war" (Art. 44(4)).
Yet, this severe consequence is mitigated by the provision in the same
paragraph that "he shall, nevertheless, be given protections equivalent in
all respects to those accorded to prisoners of war by the Third Convention
and by this Protocol". These 'equivalent' protections apply even "in the
case where such a person is tried and punished for any offences he has
committed" – such as the offence of taking part in an attack or ambush
while posturing as a civilian, which may be punishable as an act of perfidy
(see Section 4.1.4). Even apart from these 'equivalent protections', there

is also, by virtue of Article 45(3), entitlement to "the protection of Article 75 of this Protocol", which provides fundamental guarantees for persons in the power of a party to the conflict not benefiting from a more favourable protection under the Conventions or the Protocol. (See further, in Section 4.1.8.)

Of interest to the resistance fighter in occupied territory is the rule in Article 45(3) providing that unless held as a spy, he "shall also be entitled, notwithstanding Article 5 of the Fourth Convention, to his rights of communication under that Convention". This at least prevents the occupying power from keeping him totally incommunicado.

Article 44(5) specifies that combatants (in the broad sense as defined in Articles 43 and 44) who fall "into the power of an adverse party while not engaged in an attack or in a military operation preparatory to an attack" retain their "rights to be a combatant and a prisoner of war" irrespective of their prior activities (for which they may or may not be punishable, perhaps, again, for an act of perfidy).

Finally, Article 44(7) emphasises that the article "is not intended to change the generally accepted practice of States with respect to the wearing of the uniform by combatants assigned to the regular, uniformed armed units of a Party to the conflict".

This set of rules and exceptions reflects a compromise between those who demanded that irregular fighters be accorded the status of combatants without being obliged to distinguish themselves from civilians, and those on the other side who strongly opposed any exceptions in favour of irregular fighters, whether in normal or difficult situations. The compromise goes a long way towards meeting the interests of both parties: the 'irregulars' are recognised as combatants in principle and lose this status only in exceptional cases, and the other party is given the possibility, precisely in such exceptional cases, of trying and punishing the prisoners caught 'redhanded' as persons without status and, hence, without evoking the protests and retaliatory actions the wartime trial of prisoners of war has sometimes occasioned.

It should be noted that several states upon ratification of the Protocol have specified that they regarded the new rules as applicable only in wars of national liberation (by now, for all practical purposes a thing of the past) and in situations of occupation of enemy territory. For some other states, and notably for the United States and Israel, the new rules have played an important role in their decision not to become party to Protocol I. The United States in particular has argued that the practice in the Vietnam War of treating captured Vietcong fighters as prisoners of war in spite of their failure to distinguish themselves from the population, was a matter of policy and not of legal obligation. Apart from this, it appears that in the years following the adoption and entry into force of Protocol I, implementation of the new rules in situations of actual hostilities has not made any progress.

4.1.3d   Espionage

Part III, Section II, of Protocol I contains rules addressing two special situations. One concerns the "member of the armed forces of a Party to the conflict who falls into the power of an adverse Party while engaging in espionage". Article 46(1) states the general rule: such a person "shall not have the right to the status of prisoner of war and may be treated as a spy". Paragraphs 2–4 provide refinements to this general rule. Paragraph 3 is of particular relevance to the resistance fighter in occupied territory:

> A member of the armed forces of a Party to the conflict who is a resident of territory occupied by an adverse Party and who, on behalf of the Party on which he depends, gathers or attempts to gather information of military value within that territory shall not be considered as engaging in espionage unless he does so through an act of false pretences or deliberately in a clandestine manner. Moreover, such a resident shall not lose his right to the status of prisoner of war and may not be treated as a spy unless he is captured while engaging in espionage.

To give an example, resistance fighters in occupied territory who, dressed as civilians but without having recourse to false pretences or a clandestine mode of acting, attempt to gather information of military value, do not forfeit their status as combatants. If they do make use of such forbidden methods (for instance, by wearing a uniform of the occupying forces) and are caught in the course of an attempt to gather the 'information of military value' they are after, they forfeit their right to the status of prisoner of war. In that case, however, Article 45(3) will apply: such persons will enjoy the minimum protection of Article 75. Yet, in this case the occupying power will be entitled, by virtue of Article 5 of Convention IV, to deny them (just like any other spy) their rights of communication under that Convention.

If our resistance fighter is caught in the process of transmitting information of military value, they must be treated as a prisoner of war; it is then immaterial whether they gathered the information with the aid of false pretences or a clandestine manner, or otherwise.

It should be noted that the provision is equally applicable and offers the same protection to members of the regular armed forces engaged in espionage.

4.1.3e Mercenaries

The other special situation is that of the mercenary. Article 47(1) provides that such a person "shall not have the right to be a combatant or a prisoner of war". It was notably the group of African states who fought for acceptance of this exception, which in Western eyes goes against the basic idea that the right to be a prisoner of war should not be made dependent on the motives, no matter how objectionable, that prompt a person to take part in hostilities. Yet, the potentially disastrous effects of paragraph 1 are largely neutralised by paragraph 2, according to which a person will qualify as a mercenary only if they fulfil a cumulative list of conditions; one of these conditions is that they are "not a member of the armed forces of a Party to the conflict" – always in the broad sense of Article 43.

The effect of the definition is that the exception of Article 47 applies only to members of an entirely independent mercenary army that is not (in terms of Article 43(1)) "under a command responsible to [a Party to a conflict] for the conduct of its subordinates". Viewed thus, Article 47 does not even amount to a genuine exception, since under the terms of Article 43 such an army is not counted among the "armed forces of a Party to a conflict".

4.1.3f   Treatment in case of doubt about status

In sum, the new rules on 'armed forces', 'combatants' and 'prisoners of war' constitute an important improvement over the old rules of the Hague Regulations on Land Warfare of 1899 and the Third Convention of 1949. The new rules may, however, easily lead to a situation where the status of a "person who takes part in hostilities and falls into the power of an adverse Party" is not immediately evident upon capture. There may be doubt whether the person is a member of an 'organised armed force, group or unit', or whether the group they belong to meets the requirements of Article 43. Does the prisoner wear a uniform or is there anything else identifying them as a member of an armed force? Are they a fighter to whom the exception of Article 44(3) and (4) applies? Or that of Article 46 on spies? Must they be regarded as a mercenary?

With respect to all such questions, Article 45(1) begins by creating a presumption of prisoner-of-war status in favour of any "person who takes part in hostilities and falls into the power of an adverse Party … if he claims the status of prisoner of war, or if he appears to be entitled to such status, or if the Party on which he depends claims such status on his behalf by notification to the Detaining Power or to the Protecting Power".

The second sentence, reaffirming the rule on 'doubt' set out in Article 5(2) of the Third Convention, provides that:

> Should any doubt arise as to whether any such person is entitled to the status as prisoner of war, he shall continue to have such status and, therefore, to be protected by the Third Convention and this Protocol until such time as his status has been determined by a competent tribunal.

Article 45(2) makes provision for the event that a person who has fallen into the hands of an adverse party but is *not* held as a prisoner of war, claims that status the very moment they are put on trial for "an offence arising out of the hostilities". Even in that case "he shall have the right to assert his entitlement to prisoner-of-war status before a judicial tribunal and to have that question adjudicated", whenever procedurally possible, "before the trial for the offence". Representatives of the protecting power "shall be entitled to attend the proceedings … unless, exceptionally, the proceedings are held *in camera* in the interest of State security" – a circumstance the detaining power must notify the protecting power about. In practice, the ICRC often attends such proceedings.

4.1.4   Methods and means of warfare

4.1.4a   Basic rules

Part III, Section I, of Protocol I gathers under this heading topics that in Chapter 3 were dealt with under the separate headings of 'means of warfare' and 'methods'. The merging is apparent in Article 35 ("Basic rules"), which repeats two existing principles of the law of The Hague and adds one new principle, each time adding the term 'methods' to the classical limitations on 'means' of warfare:

1. In any armed conflict, the right of the Parties to the conflict to choose methods or means of warfare is not unlimited.
2. It is prohibited to employ weapons, projectiles and material and methods of warfare of a nature to cause superfluous injury or unnecessary suffering.
3. It is prohibited to employ methods or means of warfare which are intended, or may be expected, to cause widespread, long-term and severe damage to the natural environment.

Apart from the addition of 'methods', the reaffirmation of the first two principles adds nothing new, and their elaboration into internationally accepted prohibitions or restrictions on use of specific conventional weapons (such as incendiary weapons, mines and booby traps), although under discussion at the CDDH, had to wait for another occasion (see Section 5.1). As regards the newly added third principle, inspired mainly by the large-scale measures of deforestation carried out by the American armed forces in the course of the war in Vietnam, its terms and, in particular, the words qualifying the concept of 'damage to the natural environment', are too vague and restrictive for much to be expected of a concrete application of this 'basic rule'. Indeed, at the CDDH, the term 'long-term' was interpreted as signifying several decades; and for a method or means of warfare to fall under the prohibition its use must be accompanied by an intention or expectation to cause the required damage. Here too, an express prohibition on use of defoliants and herbicides (or general recognition that the prohibition in the Geneva Protocol of 1925 covers the use of such chemical agents) would obviously have been more effective. But again, that was not on the agenda of the CDDH.

The Conference could, and did, tackle the matter of means or methods from another angle. As noted in Section 3.3.2, once integrated into arsenals, a weapon is not lightly discarded on the mere assertion that it causes unnecessary suffering. It is therefore important to forestall the introduction of means or methods of warfare that might have that effect. Addressing this issue, Article 36 provides that "[i]n the study, development, acquisition or adoption of a new weapon, means or method of warfare" each state party to the Protocol is required "to determine whether its employment would, in some or all circumstances, be prohibited" by any applicable rule of international law.

Several states have introduced procedures for such a unilateral evaluation. There remains the difficulty that the effects of new means or methods of warfare in actual battle conditions often are insufficiently known – and for obvious reasons cannot be experimentally tested. Yet the obligation in Article 36 makes a useful contribution to the goal of prohibiting excessively injurious means and methods of warfare.

The introduction of 'methods' into the text of Article 35 has not inspired the CDDH to take up a subject that has since become topical, viz., the issue of 'targeted killing': the attack, often from the air and with manned or unmanned armed vehicles, on chosen individuals. This method in practice raises a host of questions, on target selection, verification of information, damage assessment, etc. More important is the question whether targeted killing is justifiable if other methods of eliminating the chosen individual might have been available. Here, the ancient principle that "the right of the Parties to the conflict to choose methods or means of warfare

is not unlimited", may gain practical significance. (See also Section 1.1 on
the character of the law of war and Section 4.1.4d on quarter.)

A final comment on the 'basic rules' is that their inclusion in Article 35
does not imply any intention on the part of the drafters to pass judgment
on the legality or illegality of the employment of nuclear weapons. The
consensus at the CDDH was that it had not been convoked to bring the
problems surrounding the existence and possible use of nuclear weapons
to a solution, and more specifically, that any *new* rules it adopted (such
as the principle of environmental protection in Article 35(3)) were not
laid down with a view to the use of nuclear weapons. This question is discussed further in Section 4.1.5i.

4.1.4b   Perfidy and ruses of war

Article 37(1) provides a modified version of the prohibition in Article 23(b)
of the Hague Regulations, to "kill or wound treacherously individuals
belonging to the hostile nation or army". Its first sentence prohibits "to
kill, injure or capture an adversary by resort to perfidy". (It will be noted
that capture has been added to the list.) While the Hague Regulations left
the notion of 'treachery' undefined, the second sentence of Article 37(1)
seeks to define 'perfidy' in terms so concrete and precise as to permit its
application in a legal setting (for instance, by a court), as follows:

> Acts inviting the confidence of an adversary to lead him to believe that he
> is entitled to, or is obliged to accord, protection under the rules of inter-
> national law applicable in armed conflict, with intent to betray that confi-
> dence, shall constitute perfidy.

Two points are worthy of note here. One is the construction of the paragraph. Although the "acts inviting confidence ... with intent to betray it"
are stated to "constitute perfidy", carrying out such acts is not enough
to constitute a crime. Rather, the acts are a qualifying element which,
together with the material element, the actual killing, injuring or capturing of the adversary, constitutes the act of 'perfidious killing' (etc.).

The other point is that the definition of 'perfidy' does not simply refer to
'confidence' in a general sense: the confidence experienced by the adversary must specifically relate to a belief that they are entitled to "protection under the rules of international law applicable in armed conflict".
A betrayal of confidence not related to this form of legal protection does
not amount to perfidy in the sense of Article 37. In particular, this second,
limiting element in the definition of perfidy tends to convert the abstract
term into a sufficiently concrete concept. Filling in the picture with

further detail, the article provides the following four examples of perfidy (paragraph 1):

(a) the feigning of an intent to negotiate under a flag of truce or of a surrender;
(b) the feigning of an incapacitation by wounds or sickness;
(c) the feigning of civilian, non-combatant status; and
(d) the feigning of protected status by the use of signs, emblems or uniforms of the United Nations or of neutral or other States not Parties to the conflict.

Example (c) brings to mind the obligation of combatants to distinguish themselves from the civilian population. As noted in that context, Article 44(3) makes an exception for "situations in armed conflicts where, owing to the nature of the hostilities an armed combatant cannot so distinguish himself". In order to exclude all possible misunderstandings, the last sentence of this paragraph specifies that "[a]cts which comply with the requirements of this paragraph shall not be considered as perfidious within the meaning of Article 37, paragraph 1 (c)".

The opposite of the prohibited act of perfidy was in 1899, as it is today, the permissible ruse of war. Article 37(2) reaffirms in its first sentence the rule of Article 24 of the Hague Regulations: "Ruses of war are not prohibited." As explained in the second sentence, ruses, like acts of perfidy, "are intended to mislead an adversary or to induce him to act recklessly". Yet, unlike such perfidious acts, they "infringe no rule of international law applicable in armed conflict" and neither do they "invite the confidence of an adversary with respect to protection under the law". Here again, some examples of ruses complete the provision: "the use of camouflage, decoys, mock operations and misinformation".

A concrete example may shed some further light on the distinction between acts of perfidy and ruses of war. A combatant on the battlefield may feign death to avoid capture and, either, rejoin their own forces or get behind the enemy lines. This is misleading rather than perfidious conduct: it is a ruse of war. But if the combatant feigns death with intent to kill or injure an adversary, who then approaches them on the assumption that they are wounded and in need of help, this brings the case within the notion of perfidy in Article 37(1)(b). Even then, the combatant feigning death with intent to kill or injure becomes guilty of a violation of Article 37(1) only if they actually kill or injure the adversary, or attempt to do so. For, it is worth repeating, the article does not prohibit perfidy per se but, rather, "to kill, injure or capture an adversary by resort to perfidy".

4.1.4c　Emblems, flags and uniforms

Article 38 prohibits, inter alia, the improper use of the red cross or red crescent, of the flag of truce (being a white flag, indicating a readiness to negotiate) and of the emblem of the United Nations. Then, while Article 39(1) prohibits "to make use in an armed conflict of the flags or military emblems, insignia or uniforms of neutral or other States not Parties to the conflict", Article 39(2) does not prohibit the use of the enemy uniform outright but spells out in which situations the use is prohibited:

> It is prohibited to make use of the flags or military emblems, insignia or uniforms of adverse Parties while engaging in attacks or in order to shield, favour, protect or impede military operations.

The first two paragraphs of Article 39 do not address the special situation of spies, who obviously cherish the use of a neutral or enemy uniform as one of their favoured methods for acquiring the information they are after. While spies, if caught redhanded, are liable to be punished for their acts of espionage, it is generally recognised that their use of such uniforms does not of itself constitute an encroachment of any rule of international law. Article 39(3) expressly confirms this fact.

The same paragraph also provides that "[n]othing in this article or in Article 37, paragraph 1 (d), shall affect the existing generally recognised rules of international law applicable to ... the use of flags in the conduct of armed conflict at sea". This language refers to the ancient practice of approaching the adversary under cover of a false flag, warships only being obliged to display their true flag immediately before opening fire (the 'oath to the flag'). It is doubted even in naval circles whether this practice should be maintained as a legitimate method of waging naval warfare today. However, like other questions specifically belonging to the realm of warfare at sea, this question was not on the agenda of the Diplomatic Conference, a fact duly reflected by the quoted clause.

4.1.4d　Quarter

Articles 40–2 elaborate in greater detail the two prohibitions contained in Article 23(c) and (d) of the Hague Regulations: to "kill or wound an enemy who, having laid down his arms, or having no longer means of defence, has surrendered at discretion", and to "declare that no quarter will be given". Article 40 clarifies and adds greater precision to the rule on quarter:

> It is prohibited to order that there shall be no survivors, to threaten an adversary therewith or to conduct hostilities on this basis.

Article 41 substitutes the surrender at discretion of the Hague Regulations with protection of an enemy *hors de combat*. The basic rule is formulated in paragraph 1:

> A person who is recognised or who, in the circumstances, should be recognised to be *hors de combat* shall not be made the object of attack.

It should be noted that in this formula, "should be recognised" is mentioned next to, and on the same footing as, "is recognised". For a soldier to avoid liability for a violation of Article 41 it is not sufficient to say: "I did not see it": it must be shown that neither would an average, normally attentive soldier have noticed that this adversary was *hors the combat*.

Article 41(2) specifies that a person is *hors de combat* if:

(a) he is in the power of an adverse party;
(b) he clearly expresses an intention to surrender; or
(c) he has been rendered unconscious or is otherwise incapacitated by wounds or sickness, and therefore is incapable of defending himself;

> provided that in any of these cases he abstains from any hostile act and does not attempt to escape.

The case under (a) may seem to be a matter of course: from the moment a combatant falls into enemy hands they are, and enjoy the protection of, a prisoner of war (Third Convention, Arts. 4, 13). Yet, the express reference to this case is important for two reasons. One lies in the concluding phrase of the paragraph: captured combatants who attempt to use violence against their captors or to escape, effectively discontinue their status of being *hors de combat* and therefore, in the words of the first paragraph, may once again "be made the object of attack".

The second reason is connected with the converse situation: rather than captured combatants who attempt to use violence against their captors, it is the patrol that captured them and, instead of evacuating them to the rear (which it regards as too burdensome in the circumstances), would prefer to kill them and thus be relieved of the burden of their presence. Article 41, paragraphs (1) and (2)(a) implicitly exclude this way out of the problem. For good measure, paragraph 3 indicates the behaviour to be followed when "persons entitled to protection as prisoners of war have fallen into the power of an adverse Party under unusual conditions of combat which prevent their evacuation": "they shall be released and all feasible precautions shall be taken to ensure their safety". It may be commented that while this may be the ideal solution, it may not in all cases be a realistic one.

Admittedly, no treaty rule lays down in express terms that an enemy cannot be killed if they could be taken prisoner instead. But neither is there solid ground for the assertion that an enemy "has surrendered" (and, hence, can no longer be killed) only from the moment their capture has been formally completed. If not against the terms, the argument goes against the spirit of Article 23(c–d) and, indeed, against the very notion of humanitarian law as the body of law aiming to protect human life and ward off unnecessary human suffering; or, in terms of the Martens clause, against the notion of "the protection and the rule of the principles of the law of nations, as they result from the usages established among civilized peoples, from the laws of humanity, and the dictates of the public conscience". (On 'targeted killing', see Section 4.1.4a.)

As regards the cases mentioned under (b) and (c), we may point to their relationship with perfidy: whenever a person by merely feigning to be in one of these situations makes an adversary believe that he is obliged to accord them protection, and then attempts to "kill, injure or capture" that adversary, they not only lose their privileged status as a person *hors de combat* but are guilty of perfidy as well.

4.1.4e   Occupants of an aircraft in distress

Article 42, finally, deals with a situation close to that of being *hors de combat*: that of occupants of an aircraft in distress. Paragraph 1 provides that no person parachuting from such an aircraft "shall be made the object of attack during his descent". It is immaterial whether such persons may be expected to land in territory controlled by their own party or by an adverse party; in the former case, their helplessness during the descent is taken to prevail over the argument that they may soon be taking an active part in hostilities again.

In the event of the parachutist "reaching the ground in territory controlled by an adverse Party", Article 42(2) stipulates that he "shall be given an opportunity to surrender before being made the object of attack, unless it is apparent that he is engaging in a hostile act".

Paragraph 3 specifies that "[a]irborne troops are not protected by this Article". Such troops may, in other words, be made the object of attack even while they are descending by parachute from an aircraft in distress. Once they have reached the ground in territory controlled by the adverse party, the normal rules apply: being combatants, they may be attacked and defend themselves against the attack; they may also themselves attack the enemy; finally, in terms of Article 41(2)(a), they may "clearly express their intention to surrender" and thus bring themselves under the protection of that article.

4.1.5   Protection of the civilian population

As summarily as the Hague Regulations on Land Warfare had dealt with the subject of protection of the civilian population, so detailed and thoroughly thought out are the rules on this subject in Protocol I. Section (I) of Part IV (Civilian Population) devoted to the "General Protection against Effects of Hostilities" contains twenty elaborate articles. The cardinal importance of this issue was apparent earlier in the present chapter, when both the continued entitlement to combatant and prisoner-of-war status and, in one case, the notion of perfidy were found to be dependent on compliance with the obligation of combatants to distinguish themselves from civilians (Sections 4.1.3, 4.1.4).

It may be noted that Part IV of the Protocol comprises two more sections: II, on "Relief in Favour of the Civilian Population", and III, on "Treatment of Persons in the Power of a Party to the Conflict".

4.1.5a   Basic rule and field of application

Article 48, opening Section I (General Protection against Effects of Hostilities), sets forth the "basic rule of distinction". Its crucial importance has already been emphasised and its text quoted in part, in the opening paragraphs of Section 4.1.3 on "combatant and prisoner-of-war status". Yet, as the keystone of the whole set of interconnected provisions on protection of the civilian population, it deserves to be quoted again, this time in full:

> In order to ensure respect for and protection of the civilian population and civilian objects, the Parties to the conflict shall at all times distinguish between the civilian population and combatants and between civilian objects and military objectives and accordingly shall direct their operations only against military objectives.

As with the distinction between combatants and civilians (who may and may not, respectively, be attacked), distinction must also be made in military operations between objects that, as military objectives, may be attacked and civilian objects that must not be attacked. Articles 50 to 52 elaborate this principle. Before that, Article 49 defines the term 'attacks', as well as the territorial scope of these provisions and their relation to other existing rules on protection of civilians and civilian objects.

Article 49(1) defines 'attacks' as "acts of violence against the adversary, whether in offence or in defence". It should be explained that 'acts of violence' mean acts of warfare involving the use of violent means: the term covers the rifle shot and the exploding bomb, not the act of taking someone prisoner (even though the latter act may also involve the use of force). The concluding words, "whether in offence or in defence", put beyond doubt that the party to the conflict that, either in the conflict as a whole or in respect of a given military operation, finds itself on the defending side, is nonetheless obliged to carry out its "acts of violence against the adversary" in conformity with the rules for the protection of the civilian population.

Elaborating this point, Article 49(2) specifies that the provisions relating to attacks "apply to all attacks in whatever territory conducted, including the national territory belonging to a Party to the conflict but under the control of an adverse Party". By virtue of this provision, if the territory of a state is invaded and its armed forces carry out attacks against the invading forces, whether in defence of the remainder of the territory or in an attempt to push the enemy back, they must do this with full respect of the rules in question. The rule applies equally to armed resistance units that carry out attacks on the occupying forces. In such circumstances, the obligation of 'respect and protection' covers not only the enemy civilian population but a state's own population as well.

While this may extend the scope of application of the protective rules compared to the Geneva Conventions (which do not afford protection to a state's own population), Article 49(3) in another respect restricts the scope of the rules, notably, to the civilian population on land. The first sentence provides that "[t]he provisions of this Section apply to any land, sea or air warfare which may affect the civilian population, individual civilians or civilian objects on land". With respect to attacks from the sea or the air in particular, the second sentence states that the provisions in question "apply to all attacks from the sea or from the air against objectives on land" (but "do not otherwise affect the rules of international law applicable in armed conflict at sea or in the air"). While the bracketed phrase shows once again that the CDDH avoided the specifics of naval and air warfare, the reader may be assured that the impact, in particular, of actions from the air was foremost in the minds of the delegates drafting the rules on protection of the civilian population against the effects of hostilities.

Finally, reminding us that rules on the protection of the civilian population may be found elsewhere as well, Article 49(4) states that the provisions of Part IV, Section I, "are additional to … other rules of international law relating to the protection of civilians and civilian objects on land, at sea or in the air against the effects of hostilities".

4.1.5b   Civilians and combatants

According to Article 50(1) "a civilian is any person who does not belong to one of the categories of persons referred to in Article 4A(1), (2), (3) and (6) of the Third Convention and in Article 43 of this Protocol". In brief, a civilian is any person who does not belong to the category of combatants. The latter category is defined with all possible precision in the quoted articles. Yet, in the course of a military operation, doubt may arise as to whether a given person is a combatant or a civilian.

The second sentence of Article 50(1) prescribes how to act in a situation where the status of a person is uncertain: "In case of doubt whether a person is a civilian, that person shall be considered to be a civilian." In practical terms, this means that a combatant may only open fire on persons of uncertain status or who find themselves in a location that puts their status into doubt (say, in a terrain where civilians are not expected) if he is convinced that they are enemy combatants, or, taking into account the loss of protection civilians suffer when they take a direct part in hostilities, persons who are doing that. This rule applies in all circumstances, whether in daylight or in the dark of the night, and for attacks from the air as much as for the foot soldier.

From the definition of 'civilians' follows that of the 'civilian population': this "comprises all persons who are civilians" (Art. 50(2)).

In practice, civilians and combatants are not always strictly separated. One need only think of common situations such as the town harbouring, besides the civilian inhabitants, units of armed forces, or the stream of refugees intermingled with an army retreating in disorder. Tackling this problem from the perspective of definition of the civilian population, Article 50(3) provides that "[t]he presence within the civilian population of individuals who do not come within the definition of civilians does not deprive the population of its civilian character". The question remains what effect a significant presence of such 'non-civilians' will have on the protection of the civilian population: if the "individuals who do not come within the definition of civilians" are combatants, they cannot be attacked if in the circumstances ruling at the time, this must be expected to entail excessive losses or injuries among the civilian population.

This brings us back to the very reasons underlying the distinction: while combatants have the right to participate directly in hostilities and may therefore be the object of attempts on the part of the enemy to disable them, civilians lack the right of direct participation but, on the other hand, in the words of Article 51(1), "enjoy general protection against dangers arising from military operations". It stands to reason that realisation of this idea of 'general protection' depends on the degree to which civilians are keeping separate from combatant activities, whether geographically or in a material sense.

4.1.5c   Civilians and direct participation in hostilities

Under Article 51(3) civilians lose their entitlement to protection "for such time as they take a direct part in hostilities", a form of words which implies that for the time of their direct participation such civilians may be made the object of attack. It may be obvious that the requirement of 'direct' participation excludes indirect participation, and 'hostilities' is narrower than the general war effort. However, interpretation of these terms in the myriad different situations that may occur in practice has proved difficult, and agreement was not always forthcoming. In this situation, the ICRC in 2003 undertook a deep-probing study into the matter. After several rounds of discussion with outside experts, it published its findings in 2009 in a document entitled "Interpretive Guidance on the Notion of Direct Participation in Hostilities under International Humanitarian Law".

Out of the many aspects discussed in the Interpretive Guidance, it may suffice to summarise here the following argument in the part entitled "The concept of direct participation in hostilities": for an act to constitute 'direct participation' it must be likely to do harm to the adverse party's 'military operations or military capacity' or, in the absence of such military harm, to kill, wound or destroy persons or objects that are protected against attack. The harm need not actually materialise: the objective likelihood of its occurrence suffices. The harm may arise either from the act itself or from a military operation of which the act 'constitutes an integral part'. And the act must be designed to be in support of one party to the conflict and against the other.

It may be clear that translation into practice of this notion of 'direct participation' may not always be easy. In effect, the main problem in determining whether a situation amounts to direct participation is one of perspective, distance and time: the soldier involved in an ongoing battle situation will be able to take into consideration but a fraction of the elements a court sitting over an incident ten years hence may be inclined to bring into play. Again, the army or air force general commanding the operation may have access to more information than the soldier in the field – but may not always be able to check its reliability. In sum, both at the time of action and after the event, the test of direct participation in hostilities must be one of reasonableness.

Likely cases of acts constituting direct participation in hostilities would be: firing at enemy soldiers, throwing a Molotov cocktail at an enemy tank, blowing up a bridge carrying enemy war materiel, or electronic interference with enemy military communications or computer networks. In respect of other activities, opinions may differ on whether they amount to direct participation.

One particularly delicate case concerns the 'human shield'. The term is actually used to cover a wide variety of situations, ranging from combatants seeking shelter amidst a column of civilian refugees (who thus are unwittingly used as shields) to civilians whose presence on a bridge or other military objective impedes an attack on the target. In the first case, it is not likely that anyone would regard the refugees as direct participants in hostilities.

The situation on the bridge is a different matter: while to some, this amounts to direct participation (with the effect that the civilians need not be taken into account in a proportionality calculus), others emphasise their status as civilians in the first place and advocate that this element be entered at least into the balance of necessity versus humanity. Should the verdict depend on whether the civilians are acting at their own risk and peril or were forced to take up their position? Again, and as noted a moment ago, while in retrospect one may wish to draw this distinction, for the attacker 'on the spot' (that is, in practice, high up in the air or in an air operations command post far from the scene) the distinction probably is imperceptible or to all intents and purposes unverifiable. In the end, and assuming that all feasible precautions, including giving due warning, have been taken, the decision whether or not to push forward with the attack may hinge on a weighing of necessity versus publicity.

Civilians who, having carried out acts of direct participation in hostilities, fall into enemy hands may be tried and punished for their activities. They are in that case not entitled to protection as prisoners of war, nor even to the 'equivalent protection' specified in Article 44(4). This does not imply that they are devoid of all rights: by virtue of Article 45(3) they retain the right to protection in accordance with Article 75 of this Protocol; see further Section 4.1.8.

The 'time of direct participation' encompasses both the time during which the civilian is approaching the chosen target with a view to carrying out a hostile act and the time needed to withdraw from the scene after the act. Whether a civilian may be regarded as directly participating in hostilities (and, therefore, liable to be attacked) even at the stage of preparatory measures will depend on circumstances, and, with that, on (reliable) information.

While the above discussion centred mainly on the fate of individual civilians, the problem of direct participation has become aggravated by the introduction and rapid development of private military and security companies. On many theatres of war, such companies are nowadays carrying out multiple tasks that bring them close to the actual conduct of war, or even right into it. In this last case, the participants are plainly taking a direct part in hostilities. In other cases, the assessment will have to be made in each separate instance whether the limit between direct and indirect (or non-)participation has been respected.

In conclusion, it may be noted that the notion of direct participation in hostilities is a great deal narrower than that of making a contribution to the war effort. Especially in the Second World War (but not only at that time) the thesis was repeatedly heard that any contribution to the war effort was sufficient ground for civilians to lose their right to protection against the effects of military operations. 'Contributing to the war effort' was interpreted as covering such activities as working in the arms industry, the transport of arms or munitions to an arsenal far from the theatre of military operations, or the construction of military fortifications in defence of the home territory. It is equally certain, however, that such activities do not amount to a direct participation in hostilities. It deserves some emphasis that with the adoption of Article 51(3) the arguments made in the Second World War have lost any basis they might have had in the past.

On the topic of direct participation in hostilities, see also Section 5.2.2 on the recently published HPCR Manual on Air and Missile Warfare.

4.1.5d   Civilian objects and military objectives

The reasons underlying the distinction between civilian objects and military objectives are quite similar to those underlying the distinction between civilians and combatants: military objectives effectively contribute to military action and may therefore be attacked, whereas civilian objects do not make such a contribution and hence may not be attacked. Article 52(1) lays down the prohibition of attacks on civilian objects and then defines these objects, as in the case of civilians, in negative terms: "Civilian objects are all objects which are not military objectives as defined in paragraph 2." Paragraph 2, second sentence, defines military objectives:

> In so far as objects are concerned, military objectives are limited to those objects which by their nature, location, purpose or use make an effective contribution to military action and whose total or partial destruction, capture or neutralisation, in the circumstances ruling at the time, offers a definite military advantage.

Civilian objects, in other words, are objects that do not "by their nature, location, purpose or use make an effective contribution to military action, and whose total or partial destruction, capture or neutralisation, in the circumstances ruling at the time", does not offer "a definite military advantage".

Typically, military objects such as a tank or armoured vehicle, an artillery emplacement, an arms depot or a military airfield may be presumed to be military objectives. On the other hand, an object such as "a place of worship, a house or other dwelling or a school" is "normally dedicated to civilian purposes". Article 52(3) states that in case of doubt whether such an object "is being used to make an effective contribution to military action, it shall be presumed not to be so used". Note that the list is not exclusive: the criterion is whether an object may be regarded as "normally dedicated to civilian purposes". Note also that such an object too may actually be used in such a way (for instance, as military quarters or a command post or munitions depot) that it contributes effectively to military action. It may then be regarded as a military objective and attacked, provided always that the condition requiring that its destruction must offer a "definite military advantage in the circumstances ruling at the time" is also met. The presumption obviously applies only in case of doubt.

There remain all sorts of objects that fall under neither presumption. Objects such as a road, bridge or railway line, (parts of) a sea port, a power-generating facility, any industrial plant, or a means of transport, may or may not come within the terms of a military objective. They will do so when they meet the dual criteria that they not only (normally by their location or use) make "an effective contribution to military action" but that their "total or partial destruction, capture or neutralisation, in the circumstances ruling at the time, offers a definite military advantage".

The above definition of military objectives purports to curb the tendency, apparent in the past, to regard virtually every object as a military objective. Instead of an abstract definition one might perhaps prefer a list specifying the objects a belligerent party may regard as military objectives – as the ICRC did in the 1950s (see Section 3.3.4). However, the examples given above may suffice to demonstrate the impracticability of this solution. The question of whether an object such as a truck, a bridge or a school represents a military objective depends entirely on the concrete situation. A list of objects qualifying as military objectives that does not include such objects is unacceptable from a military point of view; to include them in the list without any restrictions is equally unacceptable from the point of view of protection of the civilian population: the general definition couched in abstract terms is the only realistically available solution to a vexed problem.

This leads to a last comment. As noted in the section on 'direct participation', civilians who are employed in the arms industry do not thereby lose their protection 'as civilians'. But obviously, this does not imply that by virtue of their presence, the factory where they are working acquires protection as a 'civilian object'. Decisive is whether an object "makes an effective contribution to military action", and the key words 'military action', even though less vague and narrower than 'the war effort', doubtless encompass more than the hostilities proper. Staying with the examples given a moment ago, the arms industry, or the transport of weapons and munitions, obviously make a contribution to military action that is not merely 'effective' but, indeed, indispensable.

It bears repeating that for an object to represent a military objective, Article 52(2) requires that its "total or partial destruction, capture or neutralisation, in the circumstances ruling at the time, offers a definite military advantage". When the object in question is an arms factory, this requirement is easily fulfilled. The question is therefore once again: what protection, if any, can a 'protected' civilian expect when he or she finds themselves in the vicinity of, or even within, a non-protected object?

To find an answer to this question we next examine the rules elaborating the notion of "general protection of the civilian population against dangers arising from military operations".

4.1.5e   Two main lines of protection

As mentioned in Section 2.4 ('Confluence'), Resolution XXVIII of the 20th International Conference of the Red Cross (Vienna, 1965) stated four basic principles of the law of armed conflict. In 1968 the UN General Assembly endorsed three of these principles with the adoption of Resolution 2444 (XXIII). Two of these principles are of immediate concern to the question of protection of the civilian population and are therefore quoted here once again:

> That it is prohibited to launch attacks against the civilian population as such;
>> That distinction must be made at all times between persons taking part in the hostilities and members of the civilian population to the effect that the latter be spared as much as possible.

Protocol I seeks to protect the civilian population along the two lines set out in this text. The first line is reflected in identical terms in Article 51(2) ("The civilian population as such, as well as individual civilians, shall not be the object of attack") and Article 52(1) ("Civilian objects shall not be the object of attack"). The second is reaffirmed in Article 57(1): "In the conduct of military operations, constant care shall be taken to spare the civilian population, civilians and civilian objects." It bears repeating, moreover, that Article 48 already lays an obligation on the parties to the conflict to "direct their operations only against military objectives".

4.1.5f Prohibition of attacks against the civilian population and civilian objects

Article 51 elaborates the prohibition to make the civilian population or individual civilians the object of attack.

Paragraph 2, second sentence, specifies that "[a]cts or threats of violence the primary purpose of which is to spread terror among the civilian population are prohibited". This addition to the basic rule confirms once and for all the illegality of the so-called terror bombardment, any similar act of spreading terror among the civilian population, and even the threat of such acts. A frequently heard argument in defence of this type of warfare is that the actions are aimed at breaking the morale of the civilian population and, with that, the will of the authorities to continue the war. In rare cases this may actually have happened, but most often the method was ineffective. Apart from this practical consideration, the argument is at odds with the principle, already expressed in 1868 in the Declaration of St Petersburg, that "the only legitimate object which States should endeavour to accomplish during war is to weaken the *military forces* of the enemy". Put differently, the method amounts to a flat denial of the distinction between civilians and combatants, and actually draws the entire population into the armed conflict.

Another matter altogether is the attack on an area of civilian habitation, carried out because it is presumed to contain military objectives.

As a practical matter, such an attack may assume the shape either of so-called 'carpet-bombing' or area bombardment, or of precision attacks on the military objectives.

Taking up one aspect of the matter, Article 51(4) outlaws blind or 'indiscriminate' attacks, and defines these as follows:

> Indiscriminate attacks are:
> (a) those which are not directed against a specific military objective;
> (b) those which employ a method or means of combat which cannot be directed at a specific military objective; or
> (c) those which employ a method or means of combat the effects of which cannot be limited as required by this Protocol;
>
> and consequently, in each such case, are of a nature to strike military objectives and civilians or civilian objects without distinction.

Article 51(5) provides definitions of two types of attack that, "among others", must be "considered as indiscriminate". The first type, the area bombardment, is defined under (a):

> an attack by bombardment by any methods or means which treats as a single military objective a number of clearly separated and distinct military objectives located in a city, town, village or other area containing a similar concentration of civilians or civilian objects.

The reference in this definition to other areas "containing a similar concentration of civilians or civilian objects" is designed to cover such objects as a refugee camp, a column of refugees on a road and so on.

The other type of attack that is "considered as indiscriminate" is one that may be expected to cause excessive damage among the civilian population. It is defined in Article 51(5)(b):

> an attack which may be expected to cause incidental loss of civilian life, injury to civilians, damage to civilian objects, or a combination thereof, which would be excessive in relation to the concrete and direct military advantage anticipated.

This type of attack represents a borderline case in more than one respect. First, a line is drawn between attacks causing excessive damage to civilians and civilian objects and other attacks causing damage that is not considered excessive. Second, the definition covers attacks that do not necessarily fall under the definition in Article 51(4) of indiscriminate attacks: an attack may meet the description in paragraph 5(b) even though it is "directed at a specific military objective" and the method and means of combat employed are capable in principle of being so directed and of being "limited as required by this Protocol", an example being a planned precision bombardment carried out with insufficient precision.

Viewed thus, the situation addressed by Article 51(5)(b) may be said to belong under the heading of "carrying out one's attacks on military objectives in such a manner as to spare the civilian population as much as possible", rather than under the present heading of "refraining from attacks against the civilian population". This case is accordingly dealt with in Section 4.1.5h on 'Precautionary measures'. To avoid any misunderstanding, though, one point should be placed beyond doubt straightaway. The mere fact that an attack does not cause excessive damage to the civilian population and, hence, is not an attack "to be considered as indiscriminate" in the sense of Article 51(5)(b), is not enough to justify the conclusion that the attack meets all the requirements laid down in the Protocol for the protection of the civilian population.

Article 51(6) prohibits "attacks against the civilian population or civilians by way of reprisals". We shall deal with this rule, together with comparable prohibitions in Articles 52–6, in Section 4.3.3b.

Article 51(7) prohibits parties to a conflict from utilising the "presence or movements of the civilian population or individual civilians" to "render certain points or areas immune from military operations, in particular in attempts to shield military objectives from attacks or to shield, favour or impede military operations". Parties also must not "direct the movement of the civilian population or individual civilians in order to attempt to shield military objectives from attacks or to shield military operations". Like the rule in Article 51(5)(b), these prohibitions are narrowly connected with the obligations of the parties to take precautionary measures for the protection of the civilian population, and will accordingly be discussed under that heading.

The connection is explicitly made in Article 51(8), providing that any violation of the prohibitions set out in the preceding paragraph "shall not release the Parties to the conflict from their legal obligations with respect to the civilian population and civilians, including the obligation to take the precautionary measures provided for in Article 57".

After the discussion in Section 4.1.5d, of the notion of 'civilian object' and how to distinguish it from military objectives, followed by the discussion in the present section of the 'protection of the civilian population' (which more than once included references to civilian objects as well), the only point that remains to be made on the 'general protection of civilian objects' is the statement in the first sentence of Article 52(1) that "[c]ivilian objects shall not be the object of attack or of reprisals". As noted, reprisals are discussed in Section 4.3.3b.

4.1.5g   Prohibition to attack specified objects

Article 53, the first of the provisions in Protocol I designed to protect specified objects, deals with cultural objects and places of worship. Without detracting from the more detailed and precise obligations of states parties to the Hague Convention of 1954, it prohibits:

(a) to commit any acts of hostility directed against the historic monuments, works of art or places of worship which constitute the cultural or spiritual heritage of peoples;
(b) to use such objects in support of the military effort;
(c) to make such objects the object of reprisals.

These few broad strokes evidently cannot equal the Hague Convention as an instrument for the protection of cultural property. Therefore, states that have not ratified or acceded to the Hague Convention might wish to reconsider their position in this respect. They also, as noted before, have the option to become party to the 1999 Second Protocol to that Convention.

Article 54 prohibits the use of methods of warfare designed to endanger the survival of the civilian population. Paragraph 1 states the principle that "[s]tarvation of civilians as a method of warfare is prohibited".

Paragraphs 2–4 provide detailed prescriptions serving to ensure that a long series of "objects indispensable to the survival of the civilian population" shall not be "attacked, destroyed, removed or rendered useless" for the "specific purpose of denying them for their sustenance value to the civilian population or to the adverse Party", provided the adverse party does not use the objects concerned "as sustenance solely for the members of its armed forces" or otherwise "in direct support of military action". Paragraph 2 lists the following examples of objects indispensable to the survival of the civilian population: "foodstuffs, agricultural areas for the production of foodstuffs, crops, livestock, drinking water installations and supplies and irrigation works". The terms 'specific', 'solely' and 'direct' in these provisions are obviously problematic, with opposed parties tending to read situations differently.

Article 54(5) adds to this complicated set of rules for the prohibition of a 'scorched earth' policy the following exception:

> In recognition of the vital requirements of any Party to the conflict in the defence of its national territory against invasion, derogation from

the prohibitions contained in paragraph 2 may be made by a Party to the conflict … within such territory under its own control where required by imperative military necessity.

The above exception is solely available to the state defending its own territory. When an occupation army is forced to retreat, it cannot invoke the exception in justification of a 'scorched earth' policy.

As a matter of historical interest, we note the practice often followed by the Netherlands in the past, of inundating significant parts of its territory in order to halt, or at all events to impede, the progress of an invading army. A law of 1896, which so far has not been revoked, identifies the authorities empowered to order an inundation and makes provision for the payment of damages. Although without utility today, establishing such 'waterlines' would not run counter to Article 54: while depriving the invading forces of "agricultural areas for the production of foodstuffs", this would not be done "for their sustenance value … to the adverse Party".

The principle underlying the prohibition in Article 35(3) on use of methods and means of warfare "which are intended, or may be expected, to cause such damage to the natural environment" is stated in positive terms in the first sentence of Article 55(1) ("Protection of the natural environment"): "Care shall be taken in warfare to protect the natural environment against widespread, long-term and severe damage." The second sentence repeats the prohibition, adding a clause that brings the provision among the rules ensuring the protection of the civilian population: "and thereby to prejudice the health or survival of the population".

Article 56, on "Protection of works and installations containing dangerous forces", is as complex and detailed as Article 55 is general and broadly phrased. The works and installations in question are exhaustively listed in Article 56(1) as "dams, dykes and nuclear electrical generating stations". While under the terms of Article 52(2) such objects may or may not be military objectives, Article 56(1) provides that in either case, they "shall not be made the object of attack … if such attack may cause the release of dangerous forces and consequent severe losses among the civilian population". The article also prohibits attacks on "other military objectives located at or in the vicinity of these works or installations" if those attacks give rise to the same risks.

The special protection of these objects ceases whenever the conditions set forth in Article 56(2) obtain. General conditions, applicable to all three classes of object, are that the object in question must be used "in regular, significant and direct support of military operations", and the attack must be "the only feasible way to terminate such support". With respect to dams and dykes in particular, Article 56(2)(a) adds the further condition that the object "is used for other than its normal function".

The report on the negotiations that resulted in the adoption of the latter phrase places on record that the term 'normal function' means "the function of holding back, or being ready to hold back, water". As long as an outer or inner dyke serves no other purpose, it will not lose its protection. Even if, say, an inner dyke carries a main road and thus has an important traffic function that may at first sight even seem to preponderate over its 'normal' function of "being ready to hold back water", this does not result in a loss of protection, not even if the traffic includes occasional military transport: protection ceases only if the traffic on the dyke is "in regular, significant and direct support of military operations", and "attack is the only feasible way to terminate such support".

All things considered, it may be concluded that although the above solution of a delicate problem provides no watertight guarantee, say, for the many Dutch or Vietnamese dykes, it does provide them with a high level of protection.

Whenever one of the objects mentioned in Article 56 loses its special protection and hence may be made the object of attack, the rules on general protection of the civilian population continue to apply. Article 56(3) specifies that these rules include "the precautionary measures provided for in Article 57", and it adds that in such a case "all practical precautions shall be taken to avoid the release of the dangerous forces". This latter obligation appears to rest on both parties, obviously to the extent that either party is in a position to take such precautions.

Article 56(5) broaches a topic that is bound to arise in any discussion of special protection of given objects or persons: viz., the question of whether measures taken for the defence of such objects or persons affect their protected position. As this is a question of precautionary measures, it shall be discussed under that heading.

Article 56(6) urges interested parties "to conclude further agreements among themselves to provide additional protection for objects containing dangerous forces".

One way to achieve additional protection is by marking the protected objects, thereby facilitating their identification. Article 56(7) makes provision for this option: "Parties to the conflict may mark [the objects] with a special sign consisting of a group of three bright orange circles placed on the same axis." An annex to Protocol I provides a picture of the sign and specific indications about the right way to use it. The sign appears more suitable for the identification of nuclear power stations and dams than for a system of dykes spreading, as in the case of the Netherlands, widely over the country. Be this as it may, its use is not obligatory, and Article 56(7) specifies that "[t]he absence of such marking in no way relieves any Party to the conflict of its obligations under this Article".

4.1.5h   Precautionary measures

Chapter IV ('Precautionary Measures') of the first Section of Part IV comprises two articles. One, Article 57, deals with precautions "in attack", that is, precautions to be taken by the attacker. The other, Article 58, deals with precautions "against the effects of attack", that is, precautions parties should take against the possible effects of attacks on military objectives under their control.

As mentioned before, Article 57(1) lays down the principle that "[i]n the conduct of military operations, constant care shall be taken to spare the civilian population, civilians and civilian objects". This should be taken literally: total avoidance of damage to the civilian population is the standard that combatants should seek to achieve in all cases.

Article 57(2)(a) is addressed to "those who plan or decide upon an attack". In the event of a major military operation this will be the commanding general with his staff; in case of a minor action, say, of a few soldiers on patrol or a small group of guerrilla fighters it will be the leader (or the collective leadership) of the unit. These persons have a threefold obligation:

 (i) they must "do everything feasible to verify" that the chosen target is a military objective and may be attacked as such;
(ii) they must "take all feasible precautions in the choice of means and methods of attack with a view to avoiding, and in any event to minimising, incidental loss of civilian life, injury to civilians and damage to civilian objects";
(iii) they must "refrain from deciding to launch" a planned attack whenever it "may be expected to cause" such loss, injury or damage in a measure "which would be excessive in relation to the concrete and direct military advantage anticipated".

Article 57(2)(b) deals with the next phase: the decision to attack has been taken but the attack has not yet been carried out. In this interval between decision and execution it may become apparent that the chosen target is not a military objective or may not be attacked (because it is under special protection), or that the attack, if carried out, would cause excessive damage. In either such case, the attack "shall be cancelled or suspended".

The above, slightly abbreviated complex of provisions gives rise to several difficult problems of appreciation. The first question is whether the chosen target actually is a military objective (the school with some armoured vehicles in the courtyard) and, if so, whether it is nevertheless still protected from attack (the machine-gun nest at the foot of the dyke). Those involved in the attack must be aware of these questions for the entire duration of the military operation, that is, both at the planning and decision-making stages and in the phase of execution. For it may easily happen that the person or unit charged with carrying out the attack finds that the target no longer qualifies as a military objective (the armoured vehicles have left the courtyard) or now risks entailing excessive collateral damage (a munitions truck meanwhile surrounded by a column of refugees).

The requirement in Article 57(2)(a)(i) of doing "everything feasible to verify" that the target may actually be attacked raises the question of available means of verification. In this respect, much has changed since Protocol I was adopted. On this, see also Section 5.2.2 on air and missile warfare.

Article 57(2)(a)(ii) poses a practical problem: the attacker does not always have the luxury of a "choice of means and methods of attack". If a choice is actually available, they must choose the munitions capable of neutralising the machine-gun nest without doing damage to the dyke, rather than employing a heavy bomb that destroys both. More complex problems of choice arise at higher levels of command: whether to use a 'smart bomb' when the weapon is expensive and supply limited, or whether to attack from the air rather than with ground forces. Both these questions too will be taken up again in Section 5.2.2 on air and missile warfare.

It should be noted that the primary obligation in this sub-paragraph is to "avoid" damage to the civilian population; the goal of "minimising" such damage will come into play only when total avoidance is not feasible.

Even minimised damage may be considerable, even excessive. This brings us back, first, to Article 51(5)(b) providing, as we saw earlier, that an attack which may be expected to cause excessive damage in relation to the concrete and direct military advantage anticipated is "to be considered as indiscriminate". Article 57(2)(a)(ii) and 2(b), in terms identical to those of Article 51(5)(b), draws the line that attackers must never overstep: they must discriminate and therefore must refrain from deciding or carrying out an attack that may be expected to cause such excessive damage in relation to the concrete and direct military advantage anticipated.

These paragraphs unmistakably may confront the persons concerned with extremely difficult problems. What exactly is the "concrete and direct military advantage anticipated"; what the "incidental loss of civilian life, injury to civilians or damage to civilian objects" that may in effect be expected; and, most difficult of all, what is the ratio between these two? A subtle weighing process cannot be expected here: the attacker is obliged to refrain from the attack only if the disproportion between the two sides in the equation "becomes apparent". Yet the decision is not entirely left to the subjective judgment of the attacker: decisive is whether a normally alert attacker who is reasonably well informed and who, moreover, makes reasonable use of the available information could have expected the excessive damage among the civilian population.

The above provisions are so intricate, both in language and in train of thought, that full implementation may probably be expected only at higher levels of command. For the small unit on patrol, or guerrilla unit, respect of the principles underlying the detailed provisions may (and must) be expected: that civilians and civilian objects are not made the object of attack; that needlessly heavy weapons are not used against military objectives; that an attack is not carried out when no reasonable person could doubt the strictly limited military significance of the chosen target as compared to the severe damage the attack may be expected to cause among the civilian population. It should also be taken into consideration that the small unit may not have a wide choice of methods and means of combat at its disposal and, moreover, may be limited in more than one way (lack of time, lack of sophisticated information-gathering equipment) in its capacity to evaluate all relevant aspects of the situation. In the end, therefore, what it boils down to is that even such a small unit must be thoroughly aware, in carrying out its task, of the implications of its basic obligation to spare the civilian population as much as possible.

At higher levels of command, where a choice between various operations and modes of execution is often possible and where a constant stream of information is supposed to guarantee at all times a reliable picture of the situation, the above prescriptions apply without reserve. Decisive here is not so much a particular level of command as, rather, the combination, within a given time frame, of freedom of choice of ways and means and availability of information.

The next provision, Article 57(2)(c), repeating in somewhat modernised terms a rule found already in Article 26 of the Hague Regulations, requires that "effective warning shall be given of attacks which may affect the civilian population, unless circumstances do not permit".

Article 57(3) indicates yet another way of minimising the risks for the civilian population: not, this time, by selecting a particular method or means of attack, but by selecting among several military objectives offering a similar military advantage, the objective "the attack on which may be expected to cause the least danger to civilian lives and to civilian objects". The rule seems impeccable from a theoretical point of view; in practice, too much should not be expected from it, as the situation where a variety of military objectives may be attacked with similar military advantage is not particularly common.

Article 57(4) provides a rare occasion where the Protocol deals in so many words with the "conduct of military operations at sea or in the air". In such events, each party to the conflict "shall, in conformity with its rights and duties under the rules of international law applicable in armed conflict, take all reasonable precautions to avoid losses of civilian lives and damage to civilian objects". The statement is redundant and does not noticeably contribute to the 'reaffirmation and development' of the law of war at sea or in the air. As noted in Section 2.4, naval and air warfare have since been expertly reformulated, respectively, in the 1994 San Remo Manual on International Law Applicable to Armed Conflicts at Sea and the 2009 HPCR Manual on International Law Applicable in Air and Missile Warfare (see Sections 5.2.1 and 5.2.2).

Several of the above provisions of Article 57 are subtly phrased and could, by their subtlety, give rise to the misunderstanding that an attack that does not cause excessive damage to the civilian population is entirely permissible. To avoid this misunderstanding, Article 57(5) expressly states that "[n]o provision of this Article may be construed as authorising any attacks against the civilian population, civilians or civilian objects".

Article 58, on the precautions parties to the conflict should take against the effects of attacks on military objectives located within their territory or territory under their control, is far less elaborate. These parties "shall, to the maximum extent feasible":

(a) without prejudice to Article 49 of the Fourth Convention, endeavour to remove the civilian population, individual civilians and civilian objects under their control from the vicinity of military objectives;
(b) avoid locating military objectives within or near densely populated areas;
(c) take the other necessary precautions to protect the civilian population, individual civilians and civilian objects under their control against the dangers resulting from military operations.

Article 49 of the Fourth Geneva Convention of 1949, while generally prohibiting individual or mass forcible transfers in or from occupied territory, nonetheless permits the occupying power to "undertake total or partial evacuation of a given area if the security of the population or imperative military reasons so demand".

For the rest, it is a truism that effective separation of civilians and civilian objects from combatants and military objectives provides the best possible protection of the civilian population. It is equally obvious that in practice, this may be very difficult, if not impossible, to realise. This much is certain, however, that parties must, "to the maximum extent feasible", endeavour to bring about and maintain the above separation. That they are precluded from doing the opposite was already evident from the express terms of Article 51(7).

As mentioned before, Article 56(5) also contains a provision on precautions against the effects of attacks on military objectives. In language closely resembling that of Article 58(b), it prescribes that "[t]he Parties to the conflict shall endeavour to avoid locating any military objectives in the vicinity of the works or installations mentioned in paragraph 1" (that is, the specially protected dams, dykes and nuclear electrical generating stations). This obligation is immediately followed by a long sentence aiming to meet the evident desire to provide in the defence of these "works and installations", just in case they might be attacked in spite of the prohibition in Article 56(1). Providing that "installations erected for the sole purpose of defending the protected works or installations from attack are permissible and shall not themselves be made the object of attack", it adds the condition that the defence installations "are not used in hostilities except for defensive actions necessary to respond to attacks against the protected works or installations and that their armament is limited to weapons capable only of repelling hostile action against the protected works or installations".

If one attempts to visualise how all this could work in practice, the difficulties appear to be immense. By what means may a dam, an important dyke or a nuclear power station be defended? Would, for instance, an anti-aircraft battery be such a permissible means? After all, as became apparent in the past, an attack from the air on targets such as dams, dykes and power stations is at least as probable as any other type of attack. Does an anti-aircraft battery erected in defence of such a protected object meet the requirement that "its armament is limited to weapons capable only of repelling hostile action against the protected work or installation"? An anti-aircraft battery may be equally capable of being used against aircraft in overflight as against attacking aircraft. Then again, not much else helps against attacking aircraft except the projectile of an anti-aircraft battery.

The solution may lie in restraint on both sides, with the battery crew avoiding all possible misunderstanding as to the purpose of the defence installation by not targeting aircraft in overflight, and the crew of those aircraft tolerating the presence of the battery as being of no harm "in the circumstances ruling at the time".

4.1.5i 'New' rules and nuclear weapons

As noted in Section 4.1.4a, the drafting history of Protocol I makes it clear that any 'new' principles and rules it contains were not designed to take into account the use of nuclear weapons. Without going into the difficulties of determining what constitutes a 'new' rule, one clear example is the principle of protection of the natural environment, laid down in Article 35(3), complemented in Article 55 with the element of "prejudice to the health or survival of the population".

New are also the prohibitions on attacks by way of reprisal against the civilian population, civilians and civilian objects (on this, see Section 4.3.3b). In theory, and as far as this part of international law is concerned, a nuclear power whose cities are under nuclear attack could therefore still feel entitled to carry out a counter-attack by similar means on the grounds of reprisal – provided always that the counter-attack constitutes an ultimate means, is preceded by a due warning, does no more damage to enemy cities than is proportionate to the damage inflicted on its own cities and is terminated as soon as the enemy discontinues its unlawful attacks. The question remains, of course, what good this type of legal reasoning could do in the face of what is sometimes euphemistically referred to as a 'nuclear exchange'.

There remain the principles and rules embodied in the Protocol on 'general protection' of the civilian population, as the most likely candidates to have an impact on the use of nuclear weapons. It may be safe to say that these provisions reflect pre-existing principles of customary or treaty law. Yet their actual formulation and elaboration into minute detail at times amount to a complete renovation. Articles 57 and 58 on precautions in attack and against the effects of attacks provide striking instances of this type of development.

In this respect, it may be noted that any conceivable process of rational decision making relative to the eventual use of nuclear weapons may be expected to take place at a level of command where the factors set out in Article 57 will be taken into account as a matter of course, without the decision-makers asking themselves whether they are applying norms they are, or are not, legally bound to respect – they will, in effect, consider many other factors as well. Yet this cannot alter the conclusion that, as a matter of law, the adoption and entry into force of Protocol I has not modified the legal position as depicted in Section 3.3.5 with respect to the use of nuclear weapons. Specifically, neither the new rules nor novel formulations of existing law found in the Protocol can be deemed to bind decision-makers considering the possible use of nuclear weapons.

Here again, one may wonder what value such legal reasoning has in the face of the rather formidable characteristics of nuclear weapons. There are many more sides to the actual use, and even to the threat of use, of these weapons, and these necessitate a broader assessment of the admissibility of such use or threat. (On the 1996 Advisory Opinion of the International Court of Justice on the *Legality of the Threat or Use of Nuclear Weapons*, see Section 5.3.2a.)

4.1.5j Localities and zones under special protection

Article 59(1) repeats the rule of Article 25 of the Hague Regulations: "It is prohibited for the Parties to the conflict to attack, by any means whatsoever, non-defended localities." In the past, this ostensibly simple rule had often led to much uncertainty: when could a locality be deemed to be non-defended, and who was empowered to determine this? Paragraphs 2–9 of Article 59 provide detailed answers to these questions.

According to Article 59(2), the 'appropriate authorities' of a party to the conflict may unilaterally "declare as a non-defended locality any inhabited place near or in a zone where armed forces are in contact which is open for occupation by an adverse Party". Such a locality must meet the following four stringent conditions:

(a) all combatants, as well as mobile weapons and mobile military equipment, must have been evacuated;
(b) no hostile use shall be made of fixed military installations or establishments;
(c) no acts of hostility shall be committed by the authorities or by the population; and
(d) no activities in support of military operations shall be undertaken.

Condition (d) prohibits activities such as the transport from the locality of munitions and similar supplies to an armed force engaged in a military operation, or the transmission to that armed force of information on movements of opposing forces, etc.

To avoid that the unilateral declaration remains an empty gesture, the authorities must address it to the adverse party. Article 59(4) orders the latter party to "acknowledge its receipt". This party is then also obliged to "treat the locality as a non-defended locality unless the conditions laid down in paragraph 2 are not in fact fulfilled, in which event it shall immediately so inform the Party making the declaration". Even then, the locality continues to "enjoy the protection provided by the other provisions of this Protocol and the other rules of international law applicable in armed conflict". This much is clear, though, that a unilateral declaration will not be sufficient in all cases to bind the hands of the adverse party, especially in the not unlikely event of a difference of opinion regarding the fulfilment or interpretation of the above four conditions.

Such difficulties can be avoided when the parties to the conflict agree on the establishment of a particular non-defended locality. Paragraphs 5 and 6 deal with this possibility, especially with respect to localities that "do not fulfil the conditions laid down in paragraph 2".

Article 59(7) deals with the situation of a locality ceasing to fulfil the conditions (either those of paragraph 2 or those agreed between the parties) that underlie its status as a non-defended locality. Not surprisingly, the locality then loses its status; yet, as in paragraph 4, here too protection under the other applicable rules continues unabated.

As is apparent from its definition, while a non-defended locality may not be attacked, it is "open for occupation" by the adverse party. If the parties to the conflict also wish to exclude this latter eventuality, they must expressly agree on this. It is then no longer a question of a non-defended locality, though, but of a 'demilitarised zone' in the sense of Article 60. This article provides that the status of 'demilitarised zone' can only be conferred by agreement. Paragraph 2 specifies that this "shall be an express agreement, may be concluded verbally or in writing, either directly or through a Protecting Power or any impartial humanitarian organisation, and may consist of reciprocal and concordant declarations". Such agreements can be concluded in peacetime or, perhaps somewhat more likely in practice, after the outbreak of hostilities, when the need has made itself felt.

The protection a demilitarised zone is designed to provide follows from paragraphs 1 and 6. According to paragraph 1, "It is prohibited for the Parties to the conflict to extend their military operations" to such a zone, "if such extension is contrary to the terms of [the] agreement". Paragraph 6 specifies that "[i]f the fighting draws near to a demilitarised zone, and if the Parties to the conflict have so agreed, none of them may use the zone for purposes related to the conduct of military operations or unilaterally revoke its status".

While it is for the parties to agree on the conditions for demilitarisation of a particular zone, Article 60(3) assists them by providing a sort of model set of conditions. The list closely resembles the list of conditions laid down in Article 59(2) for a non-defended locality, with one marked difference: while the latter paragraph under (d) prohibits "activities in support of military operations", Article 60(3)(d) requires that "any activity linked to the military effort must have ceased". The term 'military effort' is narrower than the all-encompassing 'war effort' we came across in Section 4.1.5c, but it must have been meant as something wider than 'military operations'. Thus, activities such as agriculture or the import or export of raw materials or general industrial products may not fall under it, but the production of military goods like munitions, tanks or military aircraft probably does. Given the likelihood of divergent interpretations, especially in a situation of armed conflict where the immediate interests of the parties may inspire quite extreme positions, the concluding sentence of Article 60(3) admonishes the parties to the conflict to "agree upon the interpretation to be given to the condition laid down in sub-paragraph (d)".

Article 60 provides further details about the marking of a demilitarised zone, the presence in the zone of police forces and similar matters. We pass them over in silence, except for the point that a 'material breach' by one party to the conflict of the provisions of paragraphs 3 or 6 releases the other party from its obligations under the agreement establishing the demilitarised zone. The zone thereby loses its protected status. Once again, however, the normal rules for the protection of the civilian population and civilian objects continue to apply.

It should be noted that the 'localities and zones under special protection' of Articles 59 and 60 have nothing to do with the type of 'safe haven' like those established in the 1990s by the United Nations in Gorazde, Srebrenica and other places in the territory of the former Yugoslavia and which were set up as militarily defended areas.

4.1.5k   Civil defence

Organised protection of the civilian population against the dangers of hostilities, or 'civil defence', proved its importance in the course of the Second World War, in the context of the massive bombardments of cities and similar places of civilian habitation. Yet, the subject was not taken up in Part II ('General Protection of Populations against Certain Consequences of War') of the Fourth Convention of 1949, despite its obvious relationship to matters such as the position of civilian hospitals and medical convoys, which did find a place in that Part. It hence remained for the Diplomatic Conference of 1974–7 to lay down, for the first time, rules on this subject. These rules, contained in Chapter VI of Part IV, Section I, of Protocol I, clearly show their relationship to the matters just indicated.

The chapter opens with a definition of what 'civil defence' means "for the purposes of this Protocol". Article 61(a) defines this function as follows:

> the performance of some or all of the undermentioned humanitarian tasks intended to protect the civilian population against the dangers, and to help to recover it from the immediate effects, of hostilities or disasters and also to provide the conditions necessary for its survival.

It then provides a detailed list of what these tasks are:

(i) warning;
(ii) evacuation;
(iii) management of shelters;
(iv) management of blackout measures;
(v) rescue;
(vi) medical services, including first aid, and religious assistance;
(vii) fire-fighting;
(viii) detection and marking of danger areas;
(ix) decontamination and similar protective measures;
(x) provision of emergency accommodation and supplies;
(xi) emergency assistance in the restoration and maintenance of order in distressed areas;
(xii) emergency repair of indispensable public utilities;
(xiii) emergency disposal of the dead;
(xiv) assistance in the preservation of objects essential for survival;
(xv) complementary activities necessary to carry out any of the tasks mentioned above, including, but not limited to, planning and organisation.

The enumeration is meant to be exhaustive. Yet the 'task' defined under (xv) provides an opening to bring activities not mentioned in the list under the scope of the chapter, provided the activities are "necessary to carry out any of the tasks mentioned" under (i)–(xiv).

The above definition in Article 61(a) of the *function* of 'civil defence' is followed by sub-paragraphs (b)–(d) defining 'civil defence organisations', the 'personnel' and the 'materiel' of such organisations, respectively. The decisive factors are that the organisations "are organised or authorised by the competent authorities of a Party to the conflict to perform any of the tasks mentioned under sub-paragraph (a)" and that they "are assigned and devoted exclusively to such tasks".

Article 62 addresses the protection of civilian civil defence organisations. These have to perform their tasks under a variety of circumstances: in the event of attacks against targets in the hinterland, in zones of combat or in occupied territory. Paragraph 1 lays down that they "shall be respected and protected" in all circumstances, and that they "shall be entitled to perform their civil defence tasks except in case of imperative military necessity". Article 63 adds to this general principle a series of provisions specifically for the purpose of enabling the organisations to continue to perform their tasks even in the event of occupation.

An obvious question is what protection may realistically be expected for the personnel, buildings and materiel of civilian civil defence organisations. The risk of harm will be greatest in the event of attacks from the air: supposing that the chosen target is a military objective located within a built-up area and the attacks result in fires spreading beyond the target, the deployment of civil defence units to combat the fires will not prevent the enemy from continuing the attacks. Or consider the effects of exploding delayed-action bombs dropped outside the target area. In any such event, the members of the civil defence unit clearly run far greater risks than the rest of the civilian population. Yet they may not expect, for themselves and their equipment, anything better than the general protection afforded the entire civilian population. Article 62(3) expressly states so with respect to the "buildings and matériel used for civil defence purposes": these objects "are covered by Article 52". The same applies to "shelters provided for the civilian population".

In other situations, for instance when a town is conquered street by street, the above risks may be diminished by clearly marking the personnel, buildings and materiel of the civil defence organisation, as well as the shelters provided for the civilian population. On this matter of identification Article 66 contains a number of provisions relating, among other things, to the use of an "international distinctive sign of civil defence". This is described in paragraph 4 as "an equilateral blue triangle on an orange ground". To the extent that "medical and religious personnel, medical units and medical transports", which are normally identified by a red cross or red crescent, are used for civil defence purposes, paragraph 9 permits the continued use of the latter signs (see also hereafter, in Section 4.1.6).

The distinctive sign of civil defence may be used in time of peace, with the consent of the competent authorities, to identify civil defence personnel, buildings and materiel as well as civilian shelters (Art. 66(7)). Article 66(8) requires the contracting parties and, as the case may be, the parties to the conflict to "take the measures necessary to supervise the display" of the sign and "to prevent and repress any misuse thereof".

Article 67 makes provision for the event that individual members of the armed forces or entire military units are "assigned to civil defence organisations". Such members or units "shall be respected and protected", provided that they fulfil a long list of conditions, the essence of which is that they are "permanently assigned and exclusively devoted to the performance of any of the tasks mentioned in Article 61" and "are clearly distinguishable from the other members of the armed forces by prominently displaying the international distinctive sign of civil defence".

4.1.6   Wounded, sick and shipwrecked

4.1.6a   General remarks

Like Part IV on the 'Civilian Population', Part II of Protocol I, on the 'Wounded, Sick and Shipwrecked', also contains many important improvements over the pre-existing law. This despite the fact that comparatively little time had passed since its codification in the Geneva Conventions of 1949.

A first point of interest concerns the title of Part II. While in 1949 the wounded, sick and shipwrecked of the armed forces came under Conventions I and II, and wounded and sick civilians under Convention IV, Part II of Protocol I brings them all together under the general heading of 'wounded, sick and shipwrecked'. The unification is apparent from Article 8, defining, "for the purposes of this Protocol", the 'wounded and sick' and 'shipwrecked', respectively, as follows:

(a) 'wounded' and 'sick' mean persons, whether military or civilian, who, because of trauma, disease or other physical or mental disorder or disability, are in need of medical assistance or care and who refrain from any act of hostility. These terms also cover maternity cases, newborn babies and other persons who may be in need of immediate medical assistance or care, such as the infirm or expectant mothers, and who refrain from any act of hostility;

(b) 'shipwrecked' means persons, whether military or civilian, who are in peril at sea or in other waters as a result of misfortune affecting

them or the vessel or aircraft carrying them and who refrain from
any act of hostility. These persons, provided that they continue to
refrain from any act of hostility, shall continue to be considered shipwrecked during their rescue until they acquire another status under
the Conventions or this Protocol.

Note, first, the wide definition of sickness, with the "need of medical
assistance or care" as a key element. It is beyond question that not only
physical trauma but mental illness as well brings a person under the category of the 'sick' in the sense of the Protocol.

Note also that persons who are wounded, sick or shipwrecked will
enjoy protection as such only so long as they refrain from "any act of hostility". This brings to mind two rules dealt with before. One is the prohibition in Article 42(2)(c) of attacks against a person who is *hors de combat*
because he "has been rendered unconscious or is otherwise incapacitated
by wounds or sickness, and therefore is incapable of defending himself,
provided that ... he abstains from any hostile act and does not attempt to
escape". The other is the rule in Article 51(3) that civilians enjoy general
protection as such, "unless and for such time as they take a direct part in
hostilities".

The category of 'shipwrecked' persons comprises, besides the classical
'shipwrecked at sea', also persons who are in peril in 'other waters', such as
rivers or lakes. The definition makes clear that being 'shipwrecked' represents a transitory stage; it comes to an end as soon as the person in question is put ashore and, with that, acquires a different status, for instance,
that of prisoner of war, of a wounded person or of a civilian, whether in
occupied or non-occupied territory.

Emphasising the non-discriminatory character of this part and in
broadest possible terms, Article 9(1) excludes "any adverse distinction
founded on race, colour, sex, language, religion or belief, political or other
opinion, national or social origin, wealth, birth or other status, or on any
other similar criteria" in its application.

Article 9(2) reverts to a provision in Article 27 of Convention I, which
has to do with the condition of the personnel of a recognised Red Cross or
Red Crescent Society of a "neutral country" (see Section 3.4.3). Purporting
to broaden the quoted words, Article 9(2) under (a) specifies that these
shall encompass "a neutral or other State which is not a Party to the conflict"; the addition of the "other" state serves to place beyond question that
the provision also covers those states that have not formally declared their
neutrality and, perhaps, do not in all respects abide by the strict rules of

traditional neutrality law; we shall refer to all types of non-participating state as 'neutral states', a term which in our view adequately describes the "other" situation as well.

Article 10 lays down the principles of protection and care of the wounded, sick and shipwrecked. Paragraph 1 emphasises that "[a]ll the wounded, sick and shipwrecked, to whichever Party they belong, shall be respected and protected". Paragraph 2, first sentence, requires that "[i] n all circumstances they shall be treated humanely and shall receive, to the fullest extent practicable and with the least possible delay, the medical care and attention required by their condition". Elaborating this point, the second sentence specifies that medical grounds are the only ones that can justify any distinction in their treatment.

Article 11, strikingly, is not confined to the wounded, sick and ship-wrecked but generally concerns all those persons, whether healthy or sick, "who are in the power of the adverse Party or who are interned, detained or otherwise deprived of liberty" as a result of a situation amounting to an international armed conflict. Paragraph 1 prohibits to endanger their "physical or mental health" by "any unjustified act or omission", such as "any medical procedure which is not indicated by the state of health of the person concerned and which is not consistent with generally accepted medical standards which would be applied under similar medical cir-cumstances to persons who are nationals of the Party conducting the pro-cedure and who are in no way deprived of liberty".

Article 11(2) prohibits in particular "to carry out on such persons, even with their consent", procedures amounting to "physical mutilations", "medical or scientific experiments" or "removal of tissue or organs for transplantation", which cannot be justified on medical grounds. Article 11(3) permits exceptions to the last-mentioned prohibition only in the case of entirely voluntary "donations of blood for transfusion or of skin for grafting"; the donations must moreover be made "for therapeutic purposes, under conditions consistent with generally accepted medical standards and controls designed for the benefit of both the donor and the recipient".

Article 11(4), on the criminal character of certain violations of the above rules, is referred to in Section 4.3.4 on individual responsibility.

Article 11(5) lays down the right of the persons described in para-graph 1 "to refuse any surgical operation". In case of such a refusal, the medical personnel concerned shall endeavour to document it by means of "a written statement to that effect, signed or acknowledged by the patient".

Article 11(6) provides guidelines for the registration of medical procedures undertaken with respect to the persons identified in paragraph 1.

4.1.6b   Medical units, medical personnel, religious personnel

Articles 12–15 supplement the existing rules on the protection of medical units and civilian medical and religious personnel. The first point to note is how these categories are defined in the Protocol. Article 8(e) defines medical units as:

> establishments and other units, whether military or civilian, organised for medical purposes, namely the search for, collection, transportation, diagnosis or treatment – including first-aid treatment – of the wounded, sick and shipwrecked, or for the prevention of disease. The term includes, for example, hospitals and other similar units, blood transfusion centres, preventive medical centres and institutes, medical depots and the medical and pharmaceutical stores of such units. Medical units may be fixed or mobile, permanent or temporary.

Note that this definition, rather than being confined to an enumeration of activities relating to the treatment of wounded, sick and shipwrecked, also mentions the prevention of disease. This extension is directly related to the wide scope of Article 11, mentioned above. (We shall encounter this point once again in the discussion of Article 16, in Section 4.1.6e.)

Medical personnel, as defined in Article 8(c), are "those persons assigned, by a Party to the conflict, exclusively to the medical purposes enumerated under sub-paragraph (e) or to the administration of medical units or to the operation or administration of medical transports. Such assignments may be either permanent or temporary." Article 8(c) lists three categories of persons who are included under the term in any event:

(i) medical personnel of a party to the conflict, whether military or civilian, including those described in the First and Second Conventions, and those assigned to civil defence organisations;

(ii) medical personnel of national Red Cross, Red Crescent and Red Lion and Sun Societies, and other national voluntary aid societies duly recognised and authorised by a party to the conflict;

(iii) medical personnel of medical units or medical transports described in Article 9, paragraph 2.

The units or transports indicated under (iii) are those units or transports that have been "made available to a Party to the conflict for humanitarian purposes" by a neutral state or aid society of such a state or by an impartial international humanitarian organisation.

The above definition is once again wide in scope, not only on account of its reference to sub-paragraph (e), but also because it includes administrative and technical personnel. It is not, on the other hand, completely open-ended: the personnel in question must have been expressly assigned by a party to the conflict. In the eyes of the authors of the text, only somewhat sizeable organisations would normally qualify for such an assignment: the hospital with its personnel would qualify, but not the individual medical practitioner or pharmacy.

'Religious personnel', as defined in Article 8 (d), means:

> military or civilian persons, such as chaplains, who are exclusively engaged in the work of their ministry and attached:
>
> (i) to the armed forces of a party to the conflict;
> (ii) to medical units or medical transports of a party to the conflict;
> (iii) to medical units or medical transports described in Article 9, paragraph 2; or
> (iv) to civil defence organisations of a party to the conflict.

Here again, the attachment may be either permanent or temporary. While the Conventions of 1949 simply refer to "chaplains", the present text refers to them merely as one example of persons constituting "religious personnel". This leaves room for a more flexible interpretation than would previously have been possible, perhaps even to the inclusion of personnel providing spiritual assistance not, strictly speaking, of a 'religious' character in the narrow sense of being devoted to the service of, and seeking reliance in, a specific god or gods.

Article 12, on the protection of medical units, states in its first paragraph the general principle that these "shall be respected and protected at all times and shall not be the object of attack". To make this principle effective, the parties may resort to a variety of measures. As regards fixed medical units, they may notify the adverse party of their location. Paragraph 3 invites them to do this, adding that the "absence of such notification shall not exempt any of the Parties from the obligation" to abide by the principle set forth in paragraph 1. As another obvious measure for ensuring protection, paragraph 4 obliges the parties, whenever possible, to ensure that medical units, whether fixed or mobile, "are so sited that attacks against military objectives do not imperil their safety".

Over and above these and similar measures, a point of major importance is the possibility to mark a given object as a medical unit. As the need of identification applies to medical personnel and medical transports as well, it is discussed separately in Section 4.1.6d.

For a *civilian* medical unit, such as a civilian hospital or blood transfusion centre, to qualify for the protection of Article 12(2), it must either belong to a party to the conflict, be "recognised and authorised by the competent authorities" of such a party, or have been made available by a neutral state or organisation as mentioned above.

When civilian medical units "are used to commit, outside their humanitarian function, acts harmful to the enemy" they lose their protection but only, as specified in Article 13, after a due "warning has remained unheeded". The article provides a list of situations that are not "considered as acts harmful to the enemy", such as the carrying of "light individual weapons" for the defence of the personnel or the wounded and sick, and the presence of combatants in the unit "for medical reasons".

Article 14 reaffirms the obligation laid down in Article 55 of the Fourth Convention, for an occupying power "to ensure that the medical needs of the civilian population in occupied territory continue to be satisfied". Elaborating this principle, paragraph 2 puts specific limits to the power of the party concerned to "requisition civilian medical units, their equipment, their *matériel* or the services of their personnel".

Article 15 states and elaborates the principle that civilian medical and religious personnel "shall be respected and protected".

Addressing the situation "in an area where civilian medical services are disrupted by reason of combat activity", paragraph 2 requires that the personnel shall be afforded "all available help". Although the paragraph does not specify who is to afford this help, it may be safe to say that the obligation rests on every party to the conflict in a position to do so.

Article 15(3) reaffirms and reinforces the obligations of an occupying power under Article 56 *et seq.* of the Fourth Convention and requires the occupant to "afford civilian medical personnel in occupied territories every assistance to enable them to perform, to the best of their ability, their humanitarian functions". It may not, conversely, compel them to act in a manner that is "not compatible with their humanitarian mission".

Article 15(4) provides in general terms, and without reference to any particular situation of danger, disruption of services or occupation, that the personnel "shall have access to any place where their services are essential"; both in their own interest and in that of the relevant party to the conflict, this right of access is "subject to such supervisory and safety measures" as this party "may deem necessary".

Article 15(5) makes both the general rule of respect and protection, and the relevant specific "provisions concerning the protection and identification of medical personnel" applicable to civilian religious personnel as well.

4.1.6c   Medical transportation

Leaving aside for the moment Articles 16–20, we now take up the provisions relating to medical transportation in Section II of Part II. The definitions of the various key concepts concerned are once again found in Article 8.

Article 8(f) defines the function of 'medical transportation' as "the conveyance by land, water or air of the wounded, sick, shipwrecked, medical personnel, religious personnel, medical equipment or medical supplies protected by the Conventions and by this Protocol".

'Medical transports', as the means for carrying out this function, are defined in Article 8(g) as "any means of transportation, whether military or civilian, permanent or temporary, assigned exclusively to medical transportation and under the control of a competent authority of a Party to the conflict". "Control of a competent authority" is decidedly more exacting than mere prior 'recognition' or 'authorisation', and it must persist as long as the object in question is "assigned exclusively to medical transportation".

Sub-paragraphs (h)–(j) distinguish as separate categories of medical transports: 'medical vehicles', 'medical ships and craft' and 'medical aircraft', for transport by land, by water and by air, respectively.

The protection of medical vehicles (such as ambulances) requires no more than a single provision of Section II: Article 21 lays down that they "shall be respected and protected in the same way as mobile medical units under the Conventions and this Protocol".

The remainder of the section provides supplementary rules on the use and protection of hospital ships and coastal rescue craft (Art. 22) and other medical ships and craft (Art. 23), and it deals at length with the position of medical aircraft (Arts. 24–31).

As noted in Section 3.4.3, fear of possible abuse of medical aircraft had led in 1949 to the adoption of rules severely curtailing their use, to the point that this had become virtually impossible. This situation needed to be redressed. An important factor in the deliberations was the necessity, inherent in modern air warfare, of rapid decisions concerning the classification of moving objects in the air and the measures, if any, to be taken against them. Taking this and other relevant factors into account, Articles

24–31 were drafted with a view to providing medical aircraft with the maximum protection that may realistically be expected in each distinct situation.

Article 24 states the principle: "Medical aircraft shall be respected and protected, subject to the provisions of this Part."

The use of medical aircraft is subject to certain general restrictions. Article 28(1) provides that they shall not be used "to attempt to acquire any military advantage over an adverse Party" or "in an attempt to render military objectives immune from attack", and paragraph 2 prohibits their use "to collect or transmit intelligence data" or for the transport of any persons or cargo not included within the above definition of the function of 'medical transportation'. A further obvious restriction is that medical aircraft are in principle precluded from carrying any weapons; exception is made in paragraph 3 only for "small arms and ammunition taken from the wounded, sick and shipwrecked on board and not yet handed to the proper service, and such light individual weapons as may be necessary to enable the medical personnel on board to defend themselves and the wounded, sick and shipwrecked in their charge".

Articles 25–27 distinguish three specific situations: medical aircraft may be in "areas not controlled by an adverse Party"; in "contact or similar zones"; or in "areas controlled by an adverse Party". The first situation gives rise to the least problems: Article 25 confirms that in and over such areas "the respect and protection of medical aircraft of a Party to the conflict is not dependent on any agreement with an adverse Party". Yet, for greater safety, and "in particular when such aircraft are making flights bringing them within range of surface-to-air weapons systems of the adverse Party", notification of the latter party may be advisable. The areas are defined in the article as "areas physically controlled by friendly forces, or sea areas not physically controlled by an adverse Party".

Greater difficulties arise when medical aircraft are in or over "contact or similar zones". A 'contact zone', as defined in Article 26(2), is "any area on land where the forward elements of opposing forces are in contact with each other, especially where they are exposed to direct fire from the ground". Paragraph 1 deals with the situation of medical aircraft "in and over those parts of the contact zone which are physically controlled by friendly forces" as well as "in and over those areas the physical control of which is not clearly established". For a 'fully effective' protection of medical aircraft in and over such areas "prior agreement between the competent military authorities of the Parties to the conflict" is required. In the absence of such agreement, medical aircraft "operate at their own risk". Even then, though, they must be respected "after they have been recognised as such".

Most problematic is the situation of medical aircraft of a party to the conflict "flying over land or sea areas physically controlled by an adverse Party". Article 27(1) provides that medical aircraft shall be protected even in this situation, "provided that prior agreement to such flights has been obtained from the competent authority of that adverse Party". In the event of a medical aircraft flying over such an area "without, or in deviation from the terms of, an agreement provided for in paragraph 1, either through navigational error or because of an emergency affecting the safety of the flight", it is obviously at risk of being attacked; in order to minimise this risk, Article 27(2) requires it to "make every effort to identify itself and to inform the adverse Party of the circumstances". As soon as that party has recognised the medical aircraft for what it is, it "shall make all reasonable efforts to give the order to land or to alight on water … or to take other measures to safeguard its own interests"; only if all these measures have remained without effect may it attack the aircraft.

Medical aircraft flying over contact or similar zones (Art. 26) or over areas controlled by an adverse party (Art. 27) "shall not, except by prior agreement with the adverse Party, be used to search for the wounded, sick and shipwrecked"; thus Article 28(4). The text is the result of debate at the CDDH about the status of search-and-rescue helicopters: could they be marked with the emblem and then be safe from attack, or was their function another one than the function of medical transportation as defined in Article 8(f)? The outcome was a compromise: medical aircraft, including helicopters properly so marked, could be used to "search for the wounded, sick and shipwrecked", but only with the "prior permission" of the adverse party. The outcome in practice has been that the helicopters used to search for, and collect the wounded, sick or shipwrecked (or, generally, friendly personnel) in contested areas or areas under enemy control are not marked with the emblem, are fully armed and carry out their missions at their own risk.

The remaining articles of this section deal with the procedures to be followed with respect to notifications and requests for prior agreements (Art. 29), landing and inspection of medical aircraft (Art. 30), and flying over or landing in the territory of neutral states (Art. 31).

4.1.6d   Identification

Effective respect for and protection of medical units, medical and religious personnel and medical transports depends to a very great extent on recognising them as such. Traditionally, the red cross or red crescent, applied so as to ensure maximum visibility, have served this purpose. Visibility, though, depends in turn on factors such as the dimensions of the distinctive emblem, the distance between emblem and observer, and the time available for its recognition, not to mention circumstances affecting visibility such as rain, fog or darkness.

Article 18, on identification, prescribes in paragraph 1 that "[e]ach Party to the conflict shall endeavour to ensure that medical and religious personnel and medical units and transports are identifiable". More concretely, paragraph 2 requires each such party to "endeavour to adopt and to implement methods and procedures which will make it possible to recognise medical units and transports which use the distinctive emblem and distinctive signals". The use of distinctive *signals* constitutes a novelty. Paragraph 5 makes their use dependent on authorisation by the party concerned, and detailed provisions on the use of distinctive signals are contained in Chapter III of Annex I to the Protocol, as amended in 1993. Provision is made for the use of a light signal (a flashing blue light), a radio signal (the urgency signal and distinctive signal described in specified regulations of the International Telecommunication Union), and means of electronic identification using the Secondary Surveillance Radar system. Further improvements and developments in this field are continually sought. As noted before, the characteristics of modern air warfare make the timely identification of medical units and transports extremely important.

With respect to the identification of civilian medical and religious personnel, Article 18(3) prescribes that in "occupied territory and in areas where fighting is taking place or is likely to take place" they "should be recognisable by the distinctive emblem and an identity card certifying their status". Chapter I of Annex I provides indications concerning the design and format of the identity card.

4.1.6e   General protection of medical duties

Article 16, on the 'general protection of medical duties', breaks new ground. It deals with the problems that may arise in connection with 'medical activities' relating to the treatment of wounded and sick, with 'medical ethics' serving as the yardstick by which these activities are to be measured. The article does not give a definition of 'medical activities', and neither does it indicate who are thought to be carrying out these activities. Yet the link with 'medical ethics' makes clear that its drafters had in mind those who practise the medical profession, and the professional activities of these persons: indeed, of *all* such persons, irrespective of whether they belong to the category of 'medical personnel' or not.

Article 16 lays down three basic rules. The first, in paragraph 1, prohibits punishing any person "for carrying out medical activities compatible with medical ethics, regardless of the person benefiting therefrom".

The second rule, in paragraph 2, prohibits to compel "persons engaged in medical activities" to perform acts "contrary to the rules of medical ethics" or other relevant rules or, to refrain from performing acts that are "required by those rules and provisions".

The third rule, in paragraph 3, prohibits to compel any person engaged in medical activities to give "any information concerning the wounded and sick who are, or who have been, under his care, if such information would, in his opinion, prove harmful to the patients concerned or their families". The sole (and very serious) exception to this last prohibition concerns information the person is required to give to their own party in accordance with the law of that party. They are, moreover, bound to respect existing regulations for the compulsory notification of communicable diseases.

It may be clear from this brief outline that Article 16 deals with a topical yet delicate issue: the tendency is strong to regard the provision of medical aid to wounded adversaries and not informing one's authorities accordingly, as a betrayal of one's own cause.

4.1.6f   Role of the civilian population and of aid societies

Article 17 deals with the role of the civilian population and of aid societies from various angles. Paragraph 1, first sentence, addresses the not-so-humanitarian tendencies of the civilian population:

> The civilian population shall respect the wounded, sick and shipwrecked, even if they belong to the adverse Party, and shall commit no act of violence against them.

The remainder of Article 17(1) deals with the positive role the population can equally well play. Both the civilian population in general and aid societies (such as national Red Cross or Red Crescent Societies) "shall be permitted, even on their own initiative, to collect and care for the wounded, sick and shipwrecked, even in invaded or occupied areas". No one, the paragraph concludes significantly, "shall be harmed, prosecuted, convicted or punished for such humanitarian acts".

While the initiative in Article 17(1) lies with the civilian population, paragraph 2 deals with the converse situation, where the authorities ("the

Parties to the conflict") appeal to the civilian population and aid societies "to collect and care for the wounded, sick and shipwrecked, and to search for the dead and report their location". The parties are then obliged to "grant both protection and the necessary facilities to those who respond to this appeal". The paragraph even lays down that if the adverse party gains control of the area, it shall "afford the same protection and facilities for so long as they are needed".

4.1.6g   Other matters

Part II, Section I, contains two more articles on matters of a general nature. Article 19 lays down an obligation for neutral states to "apply the relevant provisions of this Protocol to persons protected by this Part who may be received or interned within their territory, and to any dead of the Parties to that conflict whom they may find".

Article 20, continuing the line set out in the Conventions of 1949, prohibits reprisals "against the persons and objects protected by this Part". On this, see Section 4.3.3b.

Section III of Part II is devoted to 'missing and dead persons'. Any armed conflict of some duration and covering a somewhat extended area entails uncertainty about the fate of vast numbers of individuals, combatants and civilians alike. Accordingly, the Conventions of 1949 already contain provisions designed to facilitate the tracing of missing and dead persons. The rules in Section III supplement these provisions. Article 32 expresses the rationale behind the rules: the primary concern lies with "the right of families to know the fate of their relatives".

Article 33 deals with missing persons, that is, "persons who have been reported missing by an adverse Party". The party to the conflict that has received such reports has the duty, "as soon as circumstances permit, and at the latest from the end of active hostilities", to search for the persons in question, inter alia, on the basis of relevant information transmitted by the adverse party (paragraph 1). In order to facilitate this collection of information, paragraph 2 requires the parties concerned to record, in the course of the armed conflict, specified data relating to persons who have been detained for some time or who died "as a result of hostilities or occupation". Paragraph 3 prescribes that information as well as requests for information shall be transmitted either directly or through the protecting power, the Central Tracing Agency of the International Committee of the Red Cross or national Red Cross or Red Crescent Societies; the parties must ensure that the information, no matter how transmitted, is always also supplied to the Central Tracing Agency.

Article 33(4) urges the parties to the conflict to "endeavour to agree on arrangements for teams to search for, identify and recover the dead from battlefield areas". An obvious form of such an arrangement is the local ceasefire. The search party may be composed of personnel of one or, as appropriate, both parties to the conflict. The paragraph specifies that "[p]ersonnel of such teams shall be respected and protected while exclusively carrying out these duties".

Article 34 provides rules on the treatment of the remains of persons who have died as a result of hostilities or occupation, and on the maintenance of and access to their grave sites.

4.1.7   Relief in favour of the civilian population

While we encountered the civilian population in Article 17 of the Protocol as a potentially active party in collecting and caring for the wounded, sick and shipwrecked, it figures as a group itself in need of relief in Section II ('Relief in Favour of the Civilian Population') of Part IV ('Civilian Population').

As far as occupied territory is concerned, Convention IV already regulates the subject in a fairly satisfactory manner (see Section 3.4.6d). Accordingly, Article 69 of the Protocol merely adds to the "food and medical supplies of the population" that Article 55 of the Convention obliges the occupying power to ensure, a catalogue of other 'basic needs' it must also meet: "clothing, bedding, means of shelter, other supplies essential to the survival of the civilian population of the occupied territory and objects necessary for religious worship". The inclusion of "other supplies essential to survival" removes the danger, inherent in any such detailed specification, that the omission of a particular item is used as an argument that it is not covered by the obligation.

In contrast with the rules for occupied territory, the provisions in Convention IV relating to relief for the civilian population in non-occupied territory were totally inadequate. Article 70 of the Protocol is designed to fill this gap, to the extent this proved acceptable to the contracting states. The main obstacle was states' inclination to regard the well-being of their own population as a domestic affair and, accordingly, to reserve to themselves the right to decide whether, and by whom, relief shall be provided. A compromise between this aspect of state sovereignty and the fundamental idea of aid according to need was the maximum that could be achieved.

The compromise is evident in Article 70(1). It opens with the ostensibly firm statement that "[i]f the civilian population [in non-occupied territory] is not adequately provided with the supplies mentioned in Article 69, relief actions which are humanitarian and impartial in character and conducted without any adverse distinction shall be undertaken", but adds that such actions shall be "subject to the agreement of the Parties concerned in such relief actions". In an attempt to forestall possible objections of the recipient state, Article 70(1) goes on to state that offers of relief "shall not be regarded as interference in the armed conflict or as unfriendly acts". In a closing sentence it lays down that in the distribution of relief consignments, priority shall be given to specially protected persons "such as children, expectant mothers, maternity cases and nursing mothers".

Strikingly, while the need of the civilian population has been phrased in objective terms ("*is* not adequately provided"), the text specifies neither who should undertake the relief actions, nor who are the "Parties concerned" in the relief actions. As regards the first question, it appears that the 'actor' may be any individual or organisation, whether governmental or non-governmental, the sole condition being that the action is "humanitarian and impartial in character and conducted without any adverse distinction".

Among the "Parties concerned", two appear to be of crucial interest: the receiving party, and an adverse party in a position to prevent the passage of relief consignments, for instance, because it has established a blockade. The article provides no further details concerning the position of the receiving party: in particular, whether it is obliged to permit necessary relief actions. Yet one feels inclined to infer the existence of such an obligation in a situation where all conditions are fulfilled, notably the condition that in any reasonable assessment the civilian population is threatened in its survival.

As regards other parties concerned, and especially the adverse party, Article 70(2) provides that they "shall allow and facilitate rapid and unimpeded passage of all relief consignments, equipment and personnel provided in accordance with this Section, even if such assistance is destined for the civilian population of the adverse Party". This language effectively precludes the practice, applied sometimes in blockades, of cutting off literally all supplies with enemy destination. In fact, this provision requires all states parties to allow and facilitate rapid and unimpeded access of all relief consignments, equipment and personnel.

The remaining paragraphs of Article 70 deal with practical aspects of relief actions, including international co-ordination. Finally, Article 71 lays down rules relating to the position of the personnel involved in relief

actions, both in occupied and non-occupied territory. In particular, it
provides that such personnel shall be respected, protected and assisted in
carrying out their relief mission.

4.1.8   Treatment of persons in the power
of a party to the conflict

The above phrase is the title of the final Section of Part IV. Opening
Chapter I ('Field of Application and Protection of Persons and Objects'),
Article 72 states that the provisions of the section are additional, not only
to "the rules concerning humanitarian protection of civilians and civilian objects in the power of a Party to the conflict contained in the Fourth
Convention", but to "other applicable rules of international law relating to
the protection of fundamental human rights during international armed
conflict" as well. These other rules include provisions of international
human rights law.

Article 73, on 'refugees and stateless persons', provides that "[p]ersons
who, before the beginning of hostilities, were considered as stateless persons or refugees" under relevant rules of international or domestic law
"shall be protected persons within the meaning of Parts I and III of the
Fourth Convention, in all circumstances and without any adverse distinction". The purpose of this provision is to ensure that, if the territory
where these persons are living is occupied by the party to the conflict
from whose territory they fled or whose nationality they were deprived
of before the outbreak of hostilities, that party will grant them the guarantees and protection to which they are entitled as 'protected persons',
regardless of the fact that they had previously fled that party's territory.

While Article 73 is not concerned with people who flee their homes
after the beginning of hostilities, Article 74 addresses at least part of
that problem, and one that often assumes staggering proportions, viz.,
the break-up of families "as a result of armed conflicts". The article provides that all parties (that is, all states parties to the Protocol, and first
and foremost the parties to the conflict) "shall facilitate in every possible
way the reunion" of such families. The parties are moreover placed under
an obligation to "encourage in particular the work of the humanitarian
organisations engaged in this task in accordance with the provisions of
the Conventions and of this Protocol and" – unavoidable safety clause –
"in conformity with their respective security regulations".

The clearest example of a human rights-type provision in Section III of
Part IV is Article 75. It provides an extensive catalogue of fundamental,

human rights-type guarantees for the protection of persons in the power of a party to the conflict, such as their right to life and personal integrity (paragraph 2) and minimum standards to be observed in the arrest and criminal procedures against them (paragraphs 3–7). Special reference should be made to paragraph 7, which places beyond doubt that the principles of fair trial apply equally to "persons accused of war crimes or crimes against humanity". Paragraph 8, finally, expressly excludes a reading of the article that would deprive a person of the protection of "any other more favourable provision granting greater protection".

It may be noted in passing that Article 75 thus reaffirms a number of the basic, equally human rights-type principles embodied in common Article 3 of the 1949 Conventions, applicable in *non*-international armed conflicts.

The 'persons in the power of a party to the conflict' who qualify for the protection of Article 75 are, first, those persons who have fallen into the hands of an adverse party and do not benefit from more favourable treatment under the Conventions or under the Protocol. An example is the guerrilla fighter who, in an unusual combat situation as defined in Article 44, has failed to meet the minimum requirement of carrying arms openly "during each military engagement, and during such time as he is visible to the adversary while he is engaged in a military deployment preceding the launching of an attack in which he is to participate" and thus has forfeited the right to be a prisoner of war. Another category is the mercenary of Article 47, who "shall not have the right to be a combatant or a prisoner of war".

An open question is whether the protection of Article 75 also extends to nationals of a party to the conflict whom that party, for reasons related to the armed conflict, deprives of their liberty or subjects to criminal procedures. The article provides no answer to this question, leaving the possibility of divergent views.

Chapter II of Section III contains 'measures in favour of women and children'. Article 76, on 'protection of women', provides in paragraph 1, first, that women must be "the object of special respect", and then, reflecting a never-ending list of tragic experiences, specifies that they "shall be protected in particular against rape, forced prostitution and any other form of indecent assault".

Article 76(2) and (3) deal with pregnant women and mothers with dependent infants. When "arrested, detained or interned for reasons related to the armed conflict", their cases must be "considered with the utmost priority" (paragraph 2). In respect of the death penalty, paragraph

3 requires the parties to the conflict to "endeavour to avoid the pronounce-ment" of this punishment on these women "for an offence related to the armed conflict", and it provides that this penalty for such offences shall "not be executed on such women".

Article 77 deals with various aspects of the protection of children. We mention, first, the restrictions paragraphs 2 and 3 place on the direct par-ticipation of children in hostilities. Children below the age of fifteen years ought not to take a direct part in hostilities; this is the idea underlying the text of paragraph 2. It should be immediately added that this rule, with its specific age limit of fifteen years, represents a more or less arbitrary compromise between those who would have preferred a far lower limit, or even no specific limit at all, and those who favoured a distinctly higher limit, of eighteen or even twenty-one years.

As it stands, Article 77(2) obliges the parties to the conflict to "take all feasible measures" to ensure that children below fifteen are kept from taking a direct part in hostilities; "in particular, they shall refrain from recruiting them into their armed forces". For the event that, despite this express rule, children below the set age limit "take a direct part in hostil-ities and fall into the power of an adverse Party", Article 77(3) provides that "they shall continue to benefit from the special protection accorded by this Article, whether or not they are prisoners of war". Elements of this special protection are: special respect, protection against indecent assault, and "the care and aid they require" (paragraph 1), and quarters in principle "separate from the quarters of adults" (paragraph 4). On child participation in hostilities, see also Section 5.2.4.

An aspect that deserves to be highlighted concerns the death penalty. Article 77(5) prohibits the execution of this penalty for offences related to the armed conflict "on persons who had not attained the age of eighteen years at the time the offence was committed". The only decisive factor here is the age of the offenders at the time they *committed* the offence: irre-spective of the age at which they are tried, and even if they are then *con-demned* to death, that penalty shall not be *executed* on them if they were below eighteen at the time they perpetrated the crime.

Article 78 is designed to prevent the arbitrary evacuation of children to a foreign country. Their evacuation is prohibited in principle; exception may only be made in their own interest: viz., "where compelling reasons of the health or medical treatment of the children or, except in occupied territory, their safety, so require". For these exceptional cases, the article provides several precise rules to be observed in preparing and carrying out their evacuation.

Chapter III of Section III consists of one single article: Article 79, on 'measures of protection for journalists'. The persons envisaged here are those journalists who, without being accredited to the armed forces as war correspondents, are "engaged in dangerous professional missions in areas of armed conflict" – a type of activity the dangerous character of which too often comes to light in fatal incidents. The conundrum is what can be done to protect journalists engaged in such missions without at the same time depriving them of their freedom of movement and of collecting and imparting information.

Two situations need to be distinguished here. Journalists whose 'dangerous professional mission' has brought them into an area where combat is actually being waged may, either, be able to move around freely in the area, or may find themselves apprehended and detained by one of the parties to the conflict. Article 79, which does not explicitly identify these situations, must be regarded as applicable to both.

With regard to the first situation, the law evidently cannot do overly much to protect our journalist against the immediate effects of combat – the bullets, the bombs, the mines. Article 79(1) confines itself to a statement of the obvious: journalists "shall be considered as civilians within the meaning of Article 50, paragraph 1". Article 79(2) adds that "[t]hey shall be protected as such under the Conventions and this Protocol, provided that they take no action adversely affecting their status as civilians". The point is, of course, that they *are* civilians, but civilians with the peculiar propensity to seek out situations of acute danger in which the rules on protection of civilians are bound to be of limited effect.

As for journalists who find themselves in the hands of a party to the conflict, their two main concerns will probably be to keep their equipment and materials intact and to regain as rapidly as possible their liberty and freedom of movement. Article 79 does not squarely address either of these issues; rather, paragraphs 1 and 2 apply in this situation too: the journalist "shall be considered as a civilian" and "shall be protected as such". One question is whether such captives will be believed in their assertions that they actually are journalists. In this respect, paragraph 3 provides that a journalist setting out on a dangerous mission "may obtain an identity card … issued by the government of the State of which [he] is a national or in whose territory he resides or in which the news medium employing him is located". Such an official identity card may contribute to convincing the detaining party that the person in question is not a spy or a saboteur but, rather, a respectable person doing a respectable job.

At the same time, to obtain the card from the government concerned may imply the acceptance of a measure of official supervision that journalists consider irreconcilable with the requirements of their profession. In view of this dilemma, paragraph 3, rather than firmly prescribing the possession of an identity card attesting to the status of its bearer as a journalist, leaves the journalist entirely free to acquire such a document, or not.

4.2   Protocol II

After the above, lengthy discussion of Protocol I, much less need be said about Protocol II. For one thing, it counts a mere 28 articles (as opposed to the 102 articles of Protocol I). For another, several of its provisions are copies of provisions in Protocol I.

As indicated by Article 1, Protocol II "develops and supplements Article 3 common to the Conventions of 1949". In a similar vein, the preamble recalls "that the humanitarian principles enshrined in Article 3 ... constitute the foundation of respect for the human person in cases of armed conflict not of an international character", adding that "international instruments relating to human rights offer a basic protection to the human person".

The preamble defines what may be regarded as the basic concern of Protocol II, as "the need to ensure a better protection for the victims" of internal armed conflicts. These 'victims' are all those persons who take no direct part in the hostilities. A particularly important 'supplement' to common Article 3 are therefore the rules of the Protocol specifically designed for their protection.

Since a complete or perfect regulation of this and other topics could not be reached at the CDDH, the preamble concludes with a simplified version of the Martens clause, stating that "in cases not covered by the law in force, the human person remains under the protection of the principles of humanity and the dictates of the public conscience".

4.2.1   Scope of application

As indicated in its title, Protocol II applies in 'non-international' armed conflicts. Article 1(1) specifies that this means situations that are not international armed conflicts as defined in Protocol I (including wars of national liberation). Article 1(2) excludes "situations of internal disturbances and tensions, such as riots, isolated and sporadic acts of violence and other acts of a similar nature, as not being armed conflicts".

The area of internal armed conflict lying between these two extremes encompasses widely different situations, ranging from a short-lived rebellion to the full-fledged civil war. Whereas Article 3 common to the 1949 Geneva Conventions covers all of these situations, Protocol II is confined to the upper segment: as specified in Article 1(1), it only applies to internal armed conflicts that "take place in the territory of [a contracting state] between its armed forces and dissident armed forces or other organised armed groups which, under responsible command, exercise such control over a part of its territory as to enable them to carry out sustained and concerted military operations and to implement this Protocol".

A first point to note is that this language excludes the case of (even major) fighting in a country between various armed groups but with no involvement of the governmental armed forces – as in the Lebanese civil war in the 1970s. Regrettable though this exclusion may be, even greater importance attaches to the catalogue of conditions the 'adverse party' is required to meet and which tend to exclude any argument that the Protocol should be deemed to apply to an internal armed conflict simply because it results in a large number of victims. Similarly, the Protocol does not appear designed to apply to a situation where the 'adverse party' is an underground guerrilla movement that can only incidentally, here and there, carry out actions of the hit-and-run type.

Another point is that the qualification of a situation as an armed conflict under the Protocol (or common Article 3, for that matter) is left first and foremost to the discretion of the state concerned. Much will therefore depend on the policy of the authorities in the state concerned and, as the case may be, on such pressure as the outside world may be able and willing to bring to bear. Obviously, and as noted earlier in Sections 3.1 and 4.1.2, international judicial bodies are empowered to make their own determination about the application of Protocol II, as of common Article 3, to given situations of internal violence.

As expressly stated in paragraph 1, Article 1 does not purport to modify the "existing conditions of application" of Article 3 common to the Conventions: that article remains applicable to those situations of internal armed conflict that are not considered to meet the requirements of Article 1(1) of the Protocol.

An armed conflict presupposes the existence of parties to the conflict. It is, therefore, a striking fact that although Article 1 speaks of at least two opposing armed forces, it does not refer to 'parties to the conflict'. The same goes for the rest of the Protocol: one may read about a situation of 'armed conflict', with 'hostilities' and 'military operations' – but without so much as a single reference to the 'parties to the conflict'. This utter silence reflects the fear of many governments that the mere reference to an adverse party might in concrete instances be interpreted as a form of recognition.

The same fear resulted in the adoption of Article 3 on 'Non-intervention'. Paragraph 1 provides that "[n]othing in this Protocol shall be invoked for the purpose of affecting the sovereignty of a State or the responsibility of the government, by all legitimate means, to maintain or re-establish law and order in the State or to defend the national unity and territorial integrity of the State". Paragraph 2 adds, for good measure, that nothing in the Protocol "shall be invoked as a justification for intervening … in the armed conflict or in the internal or external affairs of the High Contracting Party in the territory of which that conflict occurs".

The complete silence on the existence of an 'adverse party' might give rise to the question of whether the Protocol is binding on non-state parties to a conflict. While possible hesitations on this score might be strengthened by the (regrettable) absence of any procedure, comparable to that of Article 96(3) of Protocol I, by which the leadership of "other organised armed groups" might express the will to respect its obligations under the Protocol, its drafting history leaves no doubt that the negotiating parties intended both sides to a Protocol II-type conflict to be bound to implement its provisions.

4.2.2   Protected persons

In terms similar to those usually found in human rights conventions, Article 2(1) defines the 'personal field of application' of Protocol II as: "all persons affected by an armed conflict as defined in Article 1". It emphasises that the Protocol "shall be applied without any adverse distinction founded on race, colour, sex, language, religion or belief, political or other opinion, national or social origin, wealth, birth or other status, or on any other similar criteria". It may be evident that this prohibition of discrimination on any ground is in striking contrast to the practice of parties in many internal armed conflicts.

A major lacuna of Protocol II, as compared to Protocol I, is that while the latter recognises certain categories of persons as 'combatants' and makes provision for their protection against the employment of certain methods and means of warfare, the notion of 'combatant' does not figure in Protocol II, and neither does that of 'prisoner of war'. It obviously does recognise the occurrence of hostilities. Indeed, the only provision that affords protection precisely to those who take part in hostilities, is the prohibition in the closing sentence of Article 4(1) "to order that there shall be no survivors": the classical no-quarter prohibition in a human rights-oriented environment. In addition, the provisions of Protocol II are without exception designed to protect, in the words of the first sentence of the quoted paragraph, all those "who do not take a direct part in hostilities or who have ceased to take part in hostilities".

4.2.3   Humane treatment

Under the above title, Part II opens the series of substantive provisions of Protocol II. It starts out with the statement of principle that all persons who do not or who have ceased to take a part in hostilities, "whether or not their liberty has been restricted, are entitled to respect for their person, honour and convictions and religious practices"; they shall "in all circumstances be treated humanely", once again, "without any adverse distinction" (Art. 4(1)).

Article 4(2) elaborates this general principle into a long list of "acts against the persons referred to in paragraph 1" that "are and shall remain prohibited at any time and in any place whatsoever". The list repeats a number of acts prohibited already by virtue of Article 3 common to the Conventions, and adds such diverse acts as (in the order in which they figure in the text) "corporal punishment", "acts of terrorism", "outrages upon personal dignity" including "rape, enforced prostitution and any form of indecent assault", "slavery and the slave trade in all their forms", and "pillage". The list ends with "threats to commit any of the foregoing acts".

Article 4(3) concerns the specific problem of the protection of children. Here too, the paragraph opens with a general principle: "Children shall be provided with the care and aid they require." This is followed by a set of specific provisions, which in effect represents a simplified version of the comparable list in Articles 77 and 78 of Protocol I. Attention is drawn in particular to the provision that "children who have not attained the age of fifteen years shall neither be recruited in the armed forces or groups nor allowed to take part in hostilities". On this, see also Section 5.2.4.

Article 5, on "persons whose liberty has been restricted", provides striking evidence of the wide gulf separating the treaty rules of humanitarian law applicable in international and internal armed conflicts, respectively. As compared to the elaborate and detailed rules in the Geneva Conventions on the treatment of prisoners of war and civilian internees in a situation of international armed conflict, Article 5 does little more than indicate some main lines concerning the treatment of all persons deprived of, or restricted in, their liberty for reasons related to the internal armed conflict. Yet, as compared to common Article 3, Article 5 of the Protocol represents a significant development.

Article 5 does not make any distinction according to the reasons a person's liberty is restricted other than that it must be for "reasons related to the conflict". The fact should be underscored once again that there is no special prisoners-of-war regime in Protocol II: it is immaterial whether a person is taken prisoner, say, as a 'participant in hostilities' or on the suspicion that they have "incited to armed rebellion against the legitimate government", were engaged in espionage for one or the other side, or provided medical aid to a wounded victim of the conflict.

Two paragraphs of Article 5 deal in particular with persons who are interned or detained. Paragraph 1 lays down rules that "shall be respected as a minimum", regarding appropriate medical treatment, individual or collective relief, practising one's religion, and spiritual assistance. The persons in question shall also, "to the same extent as the local civilian population, be provided with food and drinking water and be afforded safeguards as regards health and hygiene and protection against the rigours of the climate and the dangers of the armed conflict".

Paragraph 2 adds a series of provisions that "those who are responsible for the internment or detention" of the persons concerned are bound to respect "within the limits of their capabilities". Allowing the internees or detainees to send and receive letters and cards falls in this category, as well as, surprisingly, a prohibition to endanger their "physical or mental health and integrity" by "any unjustified act or omission"; the paragraph specifies that it is accordingly "prohibited to subject the persons described in this Article to any medical procedure which is not indicated by the state of health of the person concerned, and which is not consistent with the generally accepted medical standards applied to free persons under similar medical circumstances". One would rather have expected to find this prohibition in paragraph 1, among the rules that have to be "respected as a minimum".

Article 5(3) provides that persons who are not interned or detained but "whose liberty has been restricted in any way whatsoever for reasons related to the armed conflict shall be treated humanely". This humane treatment must be in accordance, in particular, with certain named provisions of Articles 4 and 5 relating, among other things, to individual or collective relief, religion and spiritual assistance, and correspondence.

Article 5(4), finally, makes provision for the event that "it is decided to release persons deprived of their liberty": in that case, "necessary measures to ensure their safety shall be taken by those so deciding".

The "prosecution and punishment of criminal offences related to the armed conflict" is the subject of Article 6. The standards of 'due process' laid down in the article are based on existing human rights conventions. Thus, any sentence and the execution of any penalty require "a conviction pronounced by a court offering the essential guarantees of independence and impartiality"; an accused must be afforded "all necessary rights and means of defence"; and the act or omission must have constituted "a criminal offence, under the law, at the time when it was committed".

Article 6(4) prohibits to pronounce the death penalty on "persons who were under the age of eighteen years at the time of the offence", and to execute it on "pregnant women or mothers of young children".

Whereas the formulation of the rules in Article 6 might permit their application by a non-governmental party, in the perception of governmental authorities the matter of 'prosecution and punishment of criminal offences' is something exclusively reserved to the judicial apparatus of the state. To meet the conditions set forth in the article for fair trial and execution of punishments may moreover usually, even in a long-lasting internal armed conflict (as in Colombia), be beyond the capacities of the adverse party (in this case, the FARC).

Article 6(5), on amnesty at the end of hostilities, is discussed in Section 4.3.4.

4.2.4   Wounded, sick and shipwrecked

It may be recalled that on this subject, Article 3 common to the Conventions of 1949 merely provides that "[t]he wounded and sick shall be collected and cared for", and that they, like all other persons not taking or no longer taking active part in hostilities, must be treated humanely and without discrimination. Part III of Protocol II reaffirms and develops these basic rules: with respect to 'protection and care' in Article 7, and with respect to 'search', including for the dead, in Article 8.

According to Article 7(1), "all the wounded, sick and shipwrecked, whether or not they have taken part in the armed conflict" are entitled to protection and care. Paragraph 2 establishes the principle of medical care without discrimination:

> In all circumstances they shall be treated humanely and shall receive, to the fullest extent practicable and with the least possible delay, the medical

care and attention required by their condition. There shall be no distinction among them founded on any grounds other than medical ones.

Article 9(1) adds that "[m]edical and religious personnel shall be
respected and protected and shall be granted all available help for the
performance of their duties", and it prohibits to compel such personnel
"to carry out tasks which are not compatible with their humanitarian
mission". Paragraph 2 specifically forbids to require medical personnel,
in the performance of their duties, to "give priority to any person except
on medical grounds".

Under the heading of 'general protection of medical duties', Article 10
lays down rules similar to those found in Article 16 of Protocol I: prohibition to punish any person "for having carried out medical activities
compatible with medical ethics, regardless of the person benefiting therefrom" (para. 1); prohibition to compel persons engaged in such activities
"to perform acts or to carry out work contrary to ... the rules of medical
ethics or other rules designed for the benefit of the wounded and sick, or
this Protocol", or, conversely, to compel them to refrain from acts required
by such rules (para. 2); and protection of professional obligations, including patient confidentiality (paras. 3, 4). Needless to say, these rules are
even harder to maintain in internal armed conflict than they are in an
international one.

Article 11 provides basic protection for medical units and transports: unless "used to commit hostile acts, outside their humanitarian
function", these objects "shall be respected and protected at all times and
shall not be the object of attack". Article 12 deals in equally brief terms
with the "distinctive emblem": the red cross or red crescent, when displayed, under the "direction of the competent authority concerned",
"by medical and religious personnel and medical units" or "on medical
transports", "shall be respected in all circumstances"; on the other hand,
it "shall not be used improperly".

4.2.5   Civilian population

As mentioned before, apart from the no-quarter prohibition, Protocol II
has nothing to say about methods and means of warfare. Yet this almost
complete silence could not in common decency be maintained with
regard to one aspect of internal armed conflict that attracted at the time,
and to this day continues to attract, a great deal of attention, viz., the often
miserable fate of the civilian population in a country torn by civil strife.
Yet, as the Protocol recognises neither the existence of 'combatants' nor

(with one curious exception) of 'military objectives', the civilian population and civilian objects could not be defined with reference to these concepts either. The effect of this silence is that the provisions in Part IV on protection of the civilian population dangle in the air. They are also considerably shorter than the comparable provisions in Protocol I. In practice, fortunately, parties are inclined to seek guidance in Protocol I for their interpretation of the relevant provisions in Protocol II.

Article 13(1) lays down the principle that "[t]he civilian population and individual civilians shall enjoy general protection against the dangers arising from military operations". It is accordingly prohibited to make them the object of attack, and so are "[a]cts or threats of violence the primary purpose of which is to spread terror among the civilian population" (para. 2). Here too, the rule applies that civilians enjoy this protection "unless and for such time as they take a direct part in hostilities" (para. 3). However, given the confusion often characterising situations of internal armed conflict and the absence of definitions in Protocol II that separate combatants from civilians, application of this rule may be even more difficult here than it is in international armed conflicts.

Articles 14 to 16 prohibit acts of war directed against specified objects, namely: "objects indispensable to the survival of the civilian population" (on the basis of the principle that "[s]tarvation of civilians as a method of combat is prohibited", Art. 14); "works and installations containing dangerous forces, namely dams, dykes and nuclear electrical generating stations" (even, remarkably, if they are "military objectives": this being the single reference to that concept in the Protocol, Art. 15); and the "historic monuments, works of art or places of worship which constitute the cultural or spiritual heritage of peoples", Art. 16).

Article 17(1) prohibits ordering the displacement of the civilian population for reasons related to the conflict "unless the security of the civilians involved or imperative military reasons so demand"; and paragraph 2 forbids under any circumstances to compel civilians "to leave their own territory" for reasons related to the conflict.

Article 18 contains the few provisions applicable in internal armed conflicts on 'relief societies and relief actions'. Paragraph 1 provides, first, that relief societies "located in the territory" of the state afflicted by the conflict, such as Red Cross or Red Crescent organisations, "may offer their services for the performance of their traditional functions in relation to the victims of the armed conflict". It should be noted that, in contrast with Article 81 of Protocol I (see below, in 4.3.5a), this paragraph does not expressly refer to the ICRC and the International Federation of Red Cross and Red Crescent Societies. It does, on the other hand, provide a role for the civilian population: as stated in the second sentence, the population "may, even on its own initiative, offer to collect and care for the wounded, sick and shipwrecked". The silence in Article 18 on the role of the ICRC cannot detract from its right under common Article 3 to "offer its services to the Parties to the conflict".

Article 18(2) broaches the question of relief to the civilian population. If this "is suffering undue hardship owing to a lack of the supplies essential for its survival, such as foodstuffs and medical supplies", relief actions "shall be undertaken"; the paragraph stops at that: it does not specify who is to carry out this obligation. The paragraph does specify, on the other hand, that the actions must be "of an exclusively humanitarian and impartial nature" and be "conducted without any adverse distinction". The actions require, moreover, "the consent of the High Contracting Party concerned", that is, of the recognised government of the state, whether the relief has to be brought to the civilian population in territory under its control or under the effective control of the (formally non-recognised) adverse party. It may be noted that the absolute respect implicit in this rule for the sovereignty of the territorial state and the authority of the established government, at times proves more than can be maintained in practice.

4.3   Implementation and enforcement

Article 1(1) of Protocol I states, in terms identical to Article 1 of the Geneva Conventions of 1949, that the contracting states "undertake to respect and to ensure respect for this Protocol in all circumstances". The scope of this formula, originally conceived in the context of the law of Geneva, is herewith explicitly expanded to the law of The Hague as codified and developed in the Protocol.

A similar formula is absent from Protocol II. It should not be deduced from this silence that a state party to that Protocol does *not* undertake "to respect and to ensure respect" for it. It is simply that in their general tendency to reduce the expression of their obligations under Protocol II to the barest minimum, states this time preferred to leave this formula out.

Indeed, Protocol II is remarkably silent on all aspects of 'implementation and enforcement'. The single provision on this subject is Article 19, which reads in full: "This Protocol shall be disseminated as widely as possible". Especially in light of the total absence of provisions on other aspects of implementation and enforcement, this one, passively formulated provision gains overwhelming importance in the attempts to bring the message of Protocol II home.

The situation under Protocol I is very different. Both Parts I ('General Provisions') and V ('Execution of the Conventions and of this Protocol') provide a series of measures designed to improve the implementation and enforcement of humanitarian law.

4.3.1   Instruction and education

Opening Part V, Article 80 emphasises the duty of all contracting states, and of states parties to an international armed conflict in particular, to take "without delay ... all necessary measures for the execution of their obligations under the Conventions and this Protocol"; to issue "orders and instructions to ensure observance" of these instruments; and to "supervise their execution".

Article 83 reinforces the duty of states parties to provide for the necessary dissemination of knowledge of humanitarian law. As provided in paragraph 1, states parties undertake, "in time of peace as in time of armed conflict ... to include the study [of the Conventions and the Protocol] in their programmes of military instruction and to encourage the study thereof by the civilian population", with the aim that "those instruments may become known to the armed forces and to the civilian population". Paragraph 2 adds that "[a]ny military or civilian authorities who, in time of armed conflict, assume responsibilities in respect of the application of the Conventions and this Protocol shall be fully acquainted with the text thereof".

Article 82 introduces an interesting instrument for improved dissemination and compliance in the armed forces. It obliges, again, both the contracting states at all times and parties to the conflict in time of armed conflict, to ensure the availability of legal advisers "to advise military commanders at the appropriate level on the application of the Conventions and this Protocol and on the appropriate instruction to be given to the armed forces on this subject". This provision has already proved its usefulness in numerous situations, with commanders being more adequately informed about applicable rules and troops better acquainted with their basic obligations under humanitarian law.

The overriding importance of dissemination of humanitarian law, first but not exclusively among the armed forces, can hardly be exaggerated. The better the rules of humanitarian law are known and understood, the greater the chance that they will be respected in practice. To support states in their endeavours, Red Cross and Red Crescent Societies, under the guidance of the ICRC and the International Federation of Red Cross and Red Crescent Societies, are running programmes of dissemination, both among their members and beyond that circle, and, occasionally, even for the armed forces. Needless to say, these activities of the Red Cross and Red Crescent Movement cannot in any way absolve the authorities from their responsibilities. It may be repeated that at least the dissemination of the applicable law is a 'must' under Protocol II as well (Art. 19).

4.3.2   Protecting powers and 'other humanitarian agencies'

As related in Section 3.5.2, the Geneva Conventions of 1949 assign a function of supervision to protecting powers or, in their absence, to an impartial humanitarian organisation such as the ICRC. In the past, when diplomatic relations were severed a third state would take over the protection of the conflicting states' interests, and upon the outbreak of hostilities that state would almost automatically assume the duties of a protecting power. Since 1949 this system has hardly worked and the appointment of protecting powers has proved almost impossible to achieve. Moreover, although under Article 10 of Conventions I–III and Article 11 of Convention IV states that detained protected persons are obliged to accept an offer by the ICRC or other humanitarian organisation to assume the functions of protecting powers should it prove impossible to arrange protection by means of protecting parties, the functioning of such substitutes in practice remained dependent on the consent of the party or parties concerned.

Articles 5 and 6 of Protocol I are designed to improve this situation. They are preceded by a definition of 'protecting power', in Article 2(c):

> a neutral or other State not a Party to the conflict which has been desig-
> nated by a Party to the conflict and accepted by the adverse Party and has
> agreed to carry out the functions assigned to a Protecting Power under
> the Conventions and this Protocol.

The definition makes it clear that the appointment of a protecting power involves a triangular arrangement. For a given state to act as protecting power on behalf of one party to the conflict and in the territory of the adverse party, the consent of all three states is needed.

Article 5(1) states the principle that "[i]t is the duty of the Parties to a conflict from the beginning of that conflict to ensure the supervision and implementation of the Conventions and of this Protocol by the application of the system of Protecting Powers"; that system includes, inter alia, "the designation and acceptance of those Powers, in accordance with the following paragraphs".

Article 5(1) adds that "Protecting Powers shall have the duty of safeguarding the interests of the Parties to the conflict". This language closely resembles the formula found in the Geneva Conventions. However, in the Conventions this formula simply refers to a factual situation ("the Protecting Powers whose duty it is to safeguard the interests of the Parties to the conflict"), which reflects the old practice of states almost automatically slipping into the role of protecting powers, as a natural consequence of their earlier acceptance of the function of diplomatic representation on behalf of one of the parties to a dispute that since has evolved into an armed conflict. In Article 5(1), in contrast, it assumes the character of an obligation, laid upon a state that in the course of an armed conflict is designated and accepted, and itself accepts, to act as a protecting power. In the context of the Protocol, this obligation cannot be understood as a reference to a general duty of diplomatic representation: rather, the 'interests' the protecting power is asked to safeguard must specifically be the interests of a party to the conflict to see its nationals in enemy hands treated in accordance with applicable standards of international humanitarian law, and probably also, to a certain extent, with their own customs and culture.

Paragraphs 2 and 3 of Article 5 lay down detailed procedures designed to facilitate the 'designation and acceptance' of protecting powers. If all this remains without result, it is the turn of a 'substitute'. As defined in Article 2(d), this "means an organisation acting in place of a Protecting Power in accordance with Article 5". Article 5(4) explains how this can be brought about: the ICRC or "any other organisation which offers all guarantees of impartiality and efficacy" *may*, "after due consultations with [the parties to the conflict] and taking into account the result of these consultations", offer to the said parties to act as a substitute; if, after such thorough preparation, the organisation makes an offer, "the Parties to the conflict shall accept [it] without delay".

One difference between a protecting power and a substitute such as the ICRC is that, while the former is obliged to safeguard the interests of the party to the conflict it represents, the emphasis in respect of the substitute is on its impartiality. For an organisation like the ICRC, it is evident that its focus is primarily on the interests of the victims of the conflict.

A practical problem attending the possible activities of protecting powers is that, in order to carry out their supervisory functions, they need to have at their disposal sufficient qualified personnel. Article 6 aims to ensure that the parties to the Protocol will already do whatever is necessary to train such personnel in peacetime.

The above attempt to revive the institution of protecting powers with the aid of a series of new provisions has thus far remained without success. However, the system is available and may be resorted to in a future armed conflict. What then may be expected of the supervision by protecting powers or their substitute? On the one hand, they may be expected to effectively supervise conditions in places where wounded and sick, prisoners of war or other detainees or internees are kept or put to work, or to oversee the health situation and provision with essential foodstuffs of a civilian population in occupied territory. On the other hand, any supervisory activities with respect to combat activities proper and the relevant rules applying between combatants may be expected to be accidental and indirect at best. The functions of protecting powers do not normally include investigation into whether attacks were carried out according to the rules. An exception to this general statement should perhaps be made in respect of the use of chemical weapons; as past experience shows, the traces of such use may sometimes be found in the target area, and this investigation can be carried out equally well by delegates of a protecting power or a substitute as by anyone else.

It may be noted, finally, that Protocol II makes no mention of anything similar to the protecting powers system. An interesting question is whether such a mechanism or something comparable to it could be applied in an internal armed conflict. It should be noted that the ICRC frequently conducts visits to persons deprived of their liberty in connection with internal armed conflicts falling within the scope of Protocol II (or common Article 3, and even in situations of political conflict).

4.3.3 Collective responsibility

As mentioned in Section 3.5.3, the state party to an international or internal armed conflict is the first to be held responsible for violations of international humanitarian law committed in that conflict.

In this regard, mention should be made of the combined effect of Articles 1(4) and 96(3) of Protocol I. As noted in Section 4.1.2, Article 1(4) recognises certain 'wars of national liberation' as international armed conflicts, and Article 96(3) creates the possibility for the authority representing the people fighting such a war to address to the Depositary a declaration by which it undertakes to apply the Conventions and the

Protocol. This brings the Conventions and the Protocol into force for that party to the conflict "with immediate effect", and renders these instruments "equally binding upon all Parties to the conflict". In consequence, from the moment this situation was effectuated (which, as noted earlier, has not happened in practice) the leadership of the people fighting a liberation war would become fully accountable for any violations of the body of international humanitarian law.

Regrettably, a similar possibility has not been provided in Protocol II. Although, as argued in Section 3.5.3, non-state armed groups involved in an internal armed conflict must of necessity be held responsible for violations committed by their members – a responsibility that in an armed conflict of the Protocol II type comprises all the provisions of that Protocol – a provision along the lines of Article 96(3) of Protocol I would have been helpful.

4.3.3a   Reciprocity

As noted in Section 3.5.3a, a state party to the 1949 Conventions cannot invoke negative reciprocity ("I am no longer bound to respect the law because you have not respected it") as a ground to withdraw from its obligations under the Conventions. The matter was not so entirely clear with respect to the law of The Hague, though. The question arises how matters stand with Protocol I, which, as we have seen, combines elements of Geneva and Hague law.

Article 1(1) expresses the undertaking of the states parties "to respect and to ensure respect for this Protocol in all circumstances". This clause is identical to the text of Article 1 common to the Geneva Conventions. The conclusion must be that negative reciprocity is excluded with respect to the entire terrain covered by the Protocol, including the rules on methods and means of warfare and on the protection of the civilian population against the effects of hostilities.

Positive reciprocity ("I am bound to respect the law because you undertake to do so too") has equally found a place in Protocol I, notably in relation to the wars of national liberation of Article 1(4). As mentioned, a declaration made pursuant to Article 96(3) would not only have the effect of bringing the Conventions and this Protocol into force for the people fighting the war "with immediate effect", but would render these instruments "equally binding upon all Parties to the conflict".

Protocol II contains no comparable provisions on 'negative' or 'positive' reciprocity. Yet its very application requires that not only the armed forces of the state but the "other organised armed groups as well … exercise such control over a part of its territory as to enable them ... to implement this Protocol". Once this condition is satisfied and the Protocol therefore in force in the conflict, a strong case can be made that its rules for the protection of victims of the conflict are so essentially humanitarian in nature that they cannot be set aside on the sole ground that the other side is violating them.

As for positive reciprocity, too much should perhaps not be expected in an internal armed conflict of the force of a good example. Yet respect by one side may be used as an argument in the hands of third parties trying to promote respect of international humanitarian law by all sides.

4.3.3b   Reprisals

Rules prohibiting recourse to reprisals are found both in Part II ('Wounded, sick and shipwrecked') and Part IV ('Civilian population') of Protocol I.

Article 20, supplementing the prohibitions already enshrined in the Conventions of 1949, prohibits reprisals against all persons and objects protected by Part II. This prohibition was adopted without any difficulty.

Part III, on 'Methods and means of warfare, combatant and prisoner-of-war status', does not contain a prohibition on reprisals. However, reprisals in respect of some provisions of this part are excluded because they are prohibited elsewhere. Thus, the rule forbidding "to make improper use of the distinctive emblem of the red cross [or] red crescent" (Art. 38) is 'reprisal-proof' by virtue of the prohibition in Article 20. Failing such a specific prohibition elsewhere the question remains whether other rules of Part III can still be set aside by way of reprisals.

It seems an entirely defensible position that reprisals are no longer justifiable in derogation of rules unmistakably designed to protect named categories of persons, such as the prohibition of perfidy in Article 37, or the rules on quarter and protection of an enemy *hors de combat* in Articles 40 and 41. At the same time, the restrictions in Protocol I on the use of weapons or enemy uniforms (Arts. 35, 39) arguably remain subject to reprisals.

As reported in Section 3.5.3b, in 1970 the UN General Assembly included in Resolution 2675 (XXV) a clause to the effect that "civilian populations, or individual members thereof, should not be the object of reprisals". At the CDDH, this extension of the prohibition of reprisals proved a hard nut to crack. In contrast with the almost automatic reaffirmation of the ban on reprisals in the framework of the protection of the wounded, sick and shipwrecked, the debate on reprisals in the context of the protection of the civilian population was long and difficult.

Two main currents opposed each other: those who advocated a categorical ban in this area too, and those who wished to maintain a possibility of recourse to reprisals against the civilian population.

Both sides had strong arguments. Representatives of the 'ban' group argued that just like reprisals against prisoners of war, measures of reprisal against the civilian population are bound to hit persons not responsible for the violation. Moreover, the chance that a particular measure of reprisal would result in the adverse party giving up its unlawful behaviour was deemed slight at best.

Members of the opposite group argued, in contrast, that civilian populations may not always be entirely innocent of what the political and military leadership are doing; that reprisals against the civilian population may not be ineffective in all cases, and, last but not least, that parties to the conflict simply have no other immediate means at their disposal to bring about a change in the attitude of a non-complying adversary. Representatives of this group also felt that, if the prohibition of attacks in reprisal against the civilian *population* could not be avoided, then at least the possibility of reprisals against civilian *objects* needed to be maintained.

Proponents of the latter position also introduced proposals for a strict regulation of permissible recourse to reprisals. These proposals contained elements such as: express warning in advance; no execution of the reprisal unless it is apparent that the warning has gone unheeded; infliction of no greater amount of suffering to the enemy civilian population than the adversary has caused to one's own population; and termination of the reprisal measure as soon as the adverse party has discontinued its unlawful attacks.

After prolonged debate and negotiations the 'ban' current won a total victory, resulting in prohibitions on attacks by way of reprisal against the civilian population or individual civilians (Art. 51(6)), civilian objects (Art. 52(1)), cultural objects and places of worship (Art. 53(c)), objects indispensable for the survival of the civilian population (Art. 54(4)), the natural environment (Art. 55(2)), and works and installations containing dangerous forces (Art. 56(4)) – a situation of overkill, so to speak.

These categorical prohibitions now doubtless form part of the law. Equally doubtless, in practice they will remain vulnerable to considerations of 'negative reciprocity'. It should be kept in mind, moreover, that a number of the provisions relating to the protection of the civilian population are complicated and phrased in terms that in practice may easily give rise to differences of opinion as to whether they are being respected or violated. To the extent that this may be a matter of fact-finding, mention may be made here of the possibility, created in Article 90 of the Protocol, for parties to a conflict to engage the services of the International Humanitarian Fact-Finding Commission. Early recourse to this Commission in appropriate cases could contribute to curbing the tendency to take recourse to reprisals. (See further Section 4.3.5 below.)

In 1986, in ratifying Protocol I, Italy declared that it "will react to serious and systematic violations by an enemy of the obligations imposed by … Articles 51 and 52 with all means admissible under international law in order to prevent any further violation". While this text does not specify what "means" Italy regards as "admissible under international law", the phrase in all likelihood was meant to reflect the traditional requirements for a lawful reprisal.

The declaration made by the United Kingdom upon ratification, in 1998, is explicit on this point. It reads, in relevant part:

> If an adverse Party makes serious and deliberate attacks, in violation of Article 51 or Article 52 against the civilian population or civilians or against civilian objects, or, in violation of Articles 53, 54 and 55, on objects or items protected by those articles, the UK will regard itself as entitled to take measures otherwise prohibited by the articles in question to the extent that it considers such measures necessary for the sole purpose of compelling the adverse Party to cease committing violations under those articles, but only after formal warning to the adverse Party requiring cessation of the violations has been disregarded and then only after a decision taken at the highest level of government. Any measures thus taken by the UK will not be disproportionate to the violations giving rise thereto and will not involve any action prohibited by the Geneva Conventions of 1949 nor will such measures be continued after the violations have ceased. The UK will notify the Protecting Powers of any such formal warning given to an adverse Party, and if that warning has been disregarded, of any measures taken as a result.

This is an accurate formulation of the traditional requirements for recourse to belligerent reprisals. The declaration (which has not been the subject of complaint by other contracting states) may be understood to imply that the United Kingdom, while accepting the prohibition of 'reprisals' in the sense of plain retaliation, retains the right of recourse to duly considered, open, official, formal and strictly circumscribed acts of reprisal. One consequence is that potential adversaries of the United Kingdom will have the same right, again under the same strict conditions.

It may be noted that the United Kingdom (like Italy before it) has also recognised the competence of the International Humanitarian

Fact-Finding Commission. Again, one would hope that in actual practice, recourse to that Commission would replace recourse to reprisals.

A last point to note is that since the adoption of the Protocol there appear to have been no instances of attacks on an enemy civilian population or civilian objects announced as reprisals and meeting the conditions therefor. On the other hand, parties to armed conflicts on numerous occasions have viciously retaliated against enemy civilian populations. The international community, far from condoning these practices, has more than once strongly reacted to such behaviour. Even so, it seems unlikely, also in light of the Italian and UK declarations, that the prohibitions of reprisals against the civilian population in Articles 51 *et seq.* have become rules of customary law.

None of the above is reflected in Protocol II. Discussion at the CDDH on the issue of reprisals in internal armed conflict led to the negative conclusion that nothing would be said about it in the Protocol. One argument was that reprisals do not have a place in the law relating to internal armed conflict. In a strict sense, the argument is correct: the rules on justifiable belligerent reprisals as developed in inter-state practice (warning, ultimate means, proportionality, limitation in time) have no counterpart in the history of internal armed conflicts. From another point of view, the argument is a bit of a nonsense; the prohibitions of reprisals in the Conventions and Protocol I serve first and foremost to outlaw the almost blind gut reaction to intolerable violations: "he killed my people, now I'll kill his". This type of reaction is probably even more common in situations of internal armed conflict than it is in international ones. The real point at the Conference was that states, although probably not in favour of such acts of blind retaliation in internal armed conflict as well, did not wish to bind their hands by including a ban on reprisals in Protocol II.

4.3.3c   Compensation

State responsibility in the classical sense is expressly dealt with in Article 91 of Protocol I:

> A Party to the conflict which violates the provisions of the Conventions or of this Protocol shall, if the case demands, be liable to pay compensation. It shall be responsible for all acts committed by persons forming part of its armed forces.

The article amounts to an adaptation of Article 3 of the 1907 Hague Convention on Land Warfare (where liability was strictly speaking confined to violations of the Regulations) to the new situation of 'confluence',

or intermingling of Hague and Geneva law in the Protocol. The implication is that the rule on responsibility, including the liability to pay
compensation, has acquired a much broader scope. Although formally
written for the Conventions and the Protocol as treaties, it is not too dar-
ing to regard it as applicable to the whole of international humanitarian
law, whether or not written.

Another consequence of the language adopted in 1977 flows from the
reference to "a Party to the conflict" and "its armed forces". A state party's
responsibility covers, by virtue of Article 43(1), "all organised armed
forces, groups and units which are under a command responsible to [it]
for the conduct of its subordinates". If a 'people' fights a war of national
liberation under the terms of Article 1(4) in conjunction with Article
96(3), that 'party to the conflict' will be equally responsible for all that is
done by its 'armed forces' as defined in Article 43(1).

For a discussion of the possibilities and difficulties in attempts to apply
the rule of Article 3 of 1907, see Section 3.5.3c. The same considerations
apply to application of Article 91 of the Protocol.

The second sentence of Article 91 may be read in an entirely different light as well, as an indication that a party to the conflict may be held
responsible, not only by the party suffering the damage, but by all other
states party to the Protocol, or by public opinion. This aspect of the matter
is discussed further in Section 4.3.5.

4.3.4   Individual responsibility

4.3.4a   Individual criminal liability

Article 85(1) makes the system for the repression of 'grave breaches' and
other violations of the Conventions applicable to similar encroachments
of Protocol I. At the same time, this Protocol significantly adds to and
improves the system.

The system could easily be made applicable to those provisions of the
Protocol designed, just as with the Conventions, to protect clearly specified categories of persons and objects that are either in the power of
the adverse party or can be recognised as being under special protection
by virtue of a distinctive sign (such as a red cross). Thus, Article 85(2)
counts among the provisions the violation of which constitutes a "grave
breach" those relating to participants in hostilities who fall into enemy
hands without being entitled to prisoner-of war status. Similarly, in Part
II ('Wounded, Sick and Shipwrecked') Article 11(4) turns into a grave
breach any "wilful act or omission" violating one of the rules laid down in

the article and that "seriously endangers the physical or mental health or integrity of any person who is in the power of a Party other than the one on which he depends".

More circumspection was needed when it came to applying the system to the provisions in Parts III and IV of Protocol I on protection of the civilian population against the effects of hostilities. For one thing, these parts are not, generally speaking, designed to protect well-defined, sufficiently restricted categories of 'protected persons'. Also, it is often very difficult to establish the true facts about hostilities and their effects. Parties to an armed conflict are generally inclined to present a propagandistically coloured version of the facts. How then could they be expected to give a fair trial to an adversary accused, say, of having bombed a residential district?

These considerations are reflected in Article 85(3). Take, by way of example, a violation of the prohibition on indiscriminate attacks (Art. 51(4)): for such an attack to amount to a grave breach it not only must be "committed *wilfully*, in violation of the relevant provisions of this Protocol, and causing death or serious injury to body or health", but it must be launched "in the *knowledge* that such attack will cause excessive loss of life, injury to civilians or damage to civilian objects, as defined in Article 57, paragraph 2(a)(iii)". The italicised requirements of intent and knowledge serve to prevent overly hasty, primarily propagandistic criminal charges.

The attack on an adversary *hors de combat* provides another example. Article 41(1) prohibits an attack on an adversary "who is recognised, or who, in the circumstances, *should be recognised* to be *hors de combat*". Here too, the attack will only constitute a grave breach if the act was done wilfully and in the knowledge that the victim was *hors de combat* – in other words, if the victim was actually so recognised and was attacked nonetheless (Art. 85(3)).

Not every provision of Parts III and IV has been brought under the operation of the system of grave breaches. Left out were, for instance: the basic rules prohibiting the use of weapons of a nature to cause superfluous injury or unnecessary suffering, and of methods or means of warfare that are intended, or may be expected, to cause widespread, long-term and severe damage to the environment (Art. 35(2) and (3)); use of enemy uniforms (Art. 39(2)); and attacks against objects indispensable to the survival of the civilian population, such as foodstuffs, crops and livestock (Art. 54).

On the other hand, Article 85(4) introduces an entirely novel set of grave breaches, including "unjustifiable delay in the repatriation of prisoners of war or civilians" and "practices of *apartheid* and other inhuman and degrading practices involving outrages upon personal dignity, based on racial discrimination", in either case "when committed wilfully and in violation of the Conventions or the Protocol". These 'grave breaches' reflect specific concerns of the 1970s (Pakistan v. India, South Africa). Here too, the text has been drafted with an eye to preventing all too facile application.

Article 85(5) states that grave breaches of the Conventions and of the Protocol "shall be regarded as war crimes". This phrase, which may look like a statement of the obvious, is mainly of historical interest: states of the then Soviet bloc had thus far, for reasons connected with the war crimes trials conducted after the Second World War, refused to recognise that grave breaches of the Conventions fell under the general notion of war crimes.

Article 88 reinforces and improves the rules in the Geneva Conventions on "assistance in connection with criminal proceedings brought in respect of grave breaches of the Conventions or of this Protocol". Provision has been made in particular for improved cooperation in the matter of extradition.

4.3.4b   Superior responsibility

The Geneva Conventions of 1949 do not state in so many words that 'a failure to act when under a duty to do so' may by itself constitute a breach. Article 86(1) mends this defect. The second paragraph adds to this ostensibly simple rule a provision on the most important problem arising in connection with 'failure to act': that is, the responsibility of superiors for the behaviour of their subordinates. It reads as follows:

> The fact that a breach of the Conventions or of this Protocol was committed by a subordinate does not absolve his superiors from penal or disciplinary responsibility, as the case may be, if they knew, or had information which should have enabled them to conclude in the circumstances at the time, that he was committing or was going to commit such a breach and if they did not take all feasible measures within their power to prevent or repress the breach.

Elaborating this principle in particular with a view to the obligations of military commanders, Article 87(1) adds that states parties and parties to a conflict shall place them under a duty, "with respect to members of the armed forces under their command and other persons under their control, to prevent and, where necessary, to suppress and to report to competent authorities breaches of the Conventions and of this Protocol".

Given these duties, military commanders need to be able to know with a sufficient degree of certainty what conduct will be regarded as amounting to a 'breach' of these instruments. Given the complex structure of the Geneva Conventions and the Protocols, commanders will often need expert advice on the interpretation of these instruments. As mentioned in Section 4.3.1, Article 82 obliges the parties to "ensure that legal advisers are available, when necessary, to advise military commanders *at the appropriate level* on the application of the Conventions and this Protocol and on the appropriate instruction to be given to the armed forces on this subject". The implication is not that platoon leaders always need a legal adviser at their side. However, determination of the "appropriate level" will depend in each case on the factual situation.

While the Protocol deals with the responsibility of superiors for acts of their subordinates, it is silent on the reverse question of the liability to punishment of a subordinate who has either acted pursuant to an order of the government or a superior and thereby has committed a war crime, or who has refused to obey such an order precisely because it would constitute such a crime. In the CDDH the issue was debated at length and on the basis of numerous written proposals. In the end, none of these proposals carried a sufficient majority. With that, the question was left to the domestic legislation of states and to further development on the international plane.

4.3.4c   Protocol II

In the absence of comparable provisions in Protocol II, punishment for violation of its rules is a matter within the discretion of the parties to the conflict. As noted in Section 4.2.3, governments do not much favour the idea of non-state organised armed groups setting up a judiciary of their own. Punishment (or, indeed, detention) on the governmental side is often for the hostile acts themselves, that is, for the direct participation in the hostilities, which may for instance be considered as treason, rather than for violations of international humanitarian law.

Making up for this absence of provisions on punishment of violations, Article 6(5) addresses the converse and particularly delicate problem that frequently arises at the end of an internal armed conflict. The termination of hostilities should mean that the one-time adversaries will resume their normal lives next to, and with, each other, as more or less peaceful citizens of the state that until recently was the scene of their violent activities. It will then be important to create circumstances conducive, as far as possible, to such peaceful co-existence. As one means to this end, the paragraph calls upon "the authorities in power" to "grant the broadest possible amnesty to persons who have participated in the armed conflict, or those deprived of their liberty for reasons related to the armed conflict, whether they are interned or detained".

This provision, although broadly worded, should not lead to a situation where even the worst offences against humanitarian law (as against human rights) go unpunished, as this may in turn entail deep dissatisfaction with the manner by which the conflict has been brought to an end. To avoid this long-term effect requires a careful balance between the requirements of justice and peace. Past history as well as current experience show that this balance usually is difficult to find.

4.3.5   Other measures of implementation and enforcement

This heading covers diverse matters that figure in different places in the 1977 Protocols and that are all more or less loosely connected with implementation and enforcement, without fitting under earlier headings of this section.

4.3.5a   Activities of the Red Cross and Red Crescent and other humanitarian organisations

Article 81 of Protocol I deals with those activities of the ICRC, the national Red Cross and Red Crescent organisations and the International Federation of Red Cross and Red Crescent Societies that relate directly to a particular armed conflict (and not, therefore, to their other tasks of humanitarian assistance).

With respect to the ICRC, Article 81(1) provides that parties to an armed conflict are bound to grant it "all facilities within their power so as to enable it to carry out the humanitarian functions assigned to it by the Conventions and this Protocol in order to ensure protection and assistance to the victims of conflicts". It adds that the ICRC "may also carry out any other humanitarian activities in favour of these victims, subject to the consent of the Parties to the conflict concerned".

The Red Cross and Red Crescent organisations of the parties to the conflict must also be granted facilities, notably those "necessary for carrying out their humanitarian activities in favour of the victims of the conflict, in accordance with the provisions of the Conventions and this Protocol and the fundamental principles of the Red Cross as formulated by the International Conferences of the Red Cross" (Art. 81(2)).

The term 'organisations' in Article 81(2) was chosen to include bodies that have not yet been, or cannot be, recognised as a Red Cross or Red

Crescent Society in the proper sense of the term: recently established organisations not yet meeting all requirements for international recognition. At the time, this included the Palestine Red Crescent Society: this could not be recognised since Palestine was not an internationally recognised state. At the same time, the Israeli Magen David Adom Society could not be recognised on account of its emblem, the Red Shield of David. As mentioned earlier, a solution of these delicate problems was found in 2005, with the creation of an additional emblem, the 'red crystal'. (See further Section 5.2.5, and on the Red Cross and Red Crescent Movement in general, Section 5.3.9.)

Article 81(3) adds an obligation, both for states parties and the parties to the conflict, to "facilitate in every possible way the assistance" that Red Cross or Red Crescent organisations and the International Federation "extend to the victims of conflicts" – provided always that this assistance is in accordance with the Conventions, the Protocol and the aforesaid fundamental principles.

Article 81(4), finally, requires states parties and the parties to the conflict, as far as possible, to "make facilities similar to those mentioned in paragraphs 2 and 3 available" to other humanitarian organisations that are duly authorised by the parties to the conflict and that "perform their humanitarian activities in accordance with the provisions of the Conventions and this Protocol".

Reference was made in Section 4.2.5 to Article 18 of Protocol II, which treats the position of "relief societies located in the territory" of the state in conflict, such as Red Cross and Red Crescent organisations. Rather than being granted any specific entitlements, they are simply permitted to "offer their services for the performance of their traditional functions in relation to the victims of the armed conflict".

Although Article 18 does not mention the ICRC, it often performs its traditional functions in countries involved in internal armed conflict, not least among which is the dissemination of international humanitarian law throughout the country, wherever it can get access and often in close cooperation with the Red Cross or Red Crescent Society "located in the territory".

4.3.5b International activities for the promotion of international humanitarian law

Attempts to strengthen the role of the international community in the promotion of respect for international humanitarian law have resulted in the introduction into Protocol I of two provisions, one located in

Part I ('General Provisions') and the other in Part V ('Execution of the Conventions and of this Protocol').

Article 7 in Part I provides that the Depositary of the Protocol (that is, Switzerland) shall convene a meeting of the states parties, "at the request of one or more of the said Parties and upon the approval of the majority of the said Parties, to consider general problems concerning the application of the Conventions and of the Protocol". The reference to "general problems" indicates that the purpose of such a meeting is not to examine and expose specific alleged violations of the Conventions and the Protocol. Yet delegates at such meetings may wish to illustrate "general problems concerning the application" with specific examples, and in practice it might prove difficult to distinguish such specific examples from direct accusations.

The other provision is Article 89, in Part V. Under the heading "co-operation" the article provides that in "situations of serious violations of the Conventions or of this Protocol" the states parties "undertake to act, jointly or individually, in co-operation with the United Nations and in conformity with the United Nations Charter". This is a rather bland statement, leaving all questions about its real significance and practical utility wide open. It might arguably be used equally for a UN-concerted severance of diplomatic relations as for outright armed intervention, again under the aegis of the United Nations.

It may be noted that the Security Council often passes resolutions calling upon parties to an armed conflict to respect their obligations under relevant instruments of humanitarian law, both in relation to international armed conflicts and, more frequently today, to internal armed conflicts (see further Section 5.3.1a).

UN organs as well as other international bodies have eagerly adopted the term 'serious violation' of rules of international humanitarian law. The term makes its first appearance in Article 89 and is equally utilised in the next article to be dealt with, Article 90.

4.3.5c   International Humanitarian Fact-Finding Commission

The responsibility of a party to the conflict for violations of the Conventions or of the Protocol presupposes that the violations have actually occurred; that, in other words, the facts have been duly established. It was noted earlier that with respect to many rules of the Protocol, this often will be a difficult task. Take the case of an alleged attack on a hospital: was the attack directed against the hospital, or against a military objective in its immediate vicinity (which should not have been there in the first place)? How much damage was really done to the hospital? Was this caused by bombs dropped from the air, or by other factors? An objective observer is rarely present at such occasions, and experience shows that more often than not the parties to the conflict will give diametrically opposed versions of the facts. Whom then to believe?

In this quandary, Article 90 makes provision for the establishment of an "International Fact-Finding Commission". The Commission, composed of "fifteen members of high moral standing and acknowledged impartiality", was established in 1991 when twenty contracting states had "agreed to accept the competence of the Commission", by means of a unilateral declaration "that they recognise[d] *ipso facto* and without special agreement, in relation to any other High Contracting Party accepting the same obligation, the competence of the Commission to enquire into allegations by such other Party, as authorised by this Article".

The Commission, which added "Humanitarian" to its name to avoid confusion with other fact-finding bodies, is competent to examine the facts concerning alleged serious violations of the Conventions or of the Protocol, and to "facilitate, through its good offices, the restoration of an attitude of respect for the Conventions and this Protocol" – a phrase that reflects similar descriptions of competence in human rights instruments. The Commission is mandated to exercise its functions on the basis of the concordant unilateral declarations of states involved in an international armed conflict, or, in the absence of such declarations, with the ad hoc consent of the parties concerned, where necessary in the shape of an agreement between the parties involved.

The activities provided for in Article 90 are designed to contribute to the speedy and fair settlement of disputes arising from allegations of serious violations of the Conventions or the Protocol, and to help reduce tensions attending such allegations and, with that, the possibility of recourse to 'reprisals' or its even uglier relative, plain retaliation.

While at the time of writing seventy-one states have made the declaration of Article 90, no situation has yet occurred where the services of the Commission were actually invoked. It is realised that it has to compete with other fact-finding procedures: both those operating in the human rights sphere and the ad hoc teams the UN, and notably the Security Council, occasionally establish for such purposes. A case in point was the establishment by the Secretary-General, in 1992, of a commission of experts to collect and sort out evidence concerning allegations of serious violations of international humanitarian law in the territory of the former

Yugoslavia. Two members of that commission were actually members of the Fact-Finding Commission – which was not asked whether it was prepared to carry out this task.

Although Protocol II is silent on the matter, the Commission has repeatedly confirmed that it is willing and able to entertain requests for investigation into alleged violations in situations of internal armed conflict as well. This will again require the consent of the parties: the state, and the organised armed group or groups concerned. Even more than in an international armed conflict, this requirement has proved to be the major stumbling block for the Commission actually to become engaged in any such activity.

The Commission has also frequently made it known to UN organs, in particular the Security Council, that it holds itself available to act on their request. In effect, the Security Council on 11 November 2009 adopted Resolution S/Res/1894 on the protection of civilians in armed conflict which, underlining the importance of "timely, objective, accurate and reliable" information on alleged violations of the applicable law, recognises "the possibility, to this end, of using the International Humanitarian Fact-Finding Commission".

On 16 December 2009, the UN General Assembly by its Resolution 64/121 granted the Commission observer status.

5

Post-1977 developments

5.1 Developments in the law on weapons

5.1.1 *Prohibitions or restrictions on use of conventional weapons*

As noted in Section 2.4, the CDDH (1974-7) had not been able to conclude the lawmaking process relating to the use of conventional weapons at the same time as the work on the two Additional Protocols. The Conference did, however, adopt a resolution at its last meeting, recommending that another conference should be convened "not later than 1979" to finish the work on conventional weapons. The new conference should attempt to reach agreement, not only on "prohibitions or restrictions" on the use of specific conventional weapons, but on a review mechanism as well.

Duly convened in 1979, the 'United Nations Convention on Prohibitions or Restrictions on the Use of Certain Conventional Weapons Which May be Deemed to be Excessively Injurious or to Have Indiscriminate Effects' concluded its work in 1980 with the adoption of the Convention with the same long title – a title that had caused difficulties at the Conference because it could be read as suggesting that choosing a weapon for discussion already implied its illegality. The weapons in question could certainly be regarded as 'dubious weapons' (a term coined in the 1960s by the distinguished Dutch international lawyer, Professor Bert Röling): dubious, because the weapons themselves or the manner they were used might be at variance with principles of humanitarian law. For brevity's sake we shall simply refer to the Convention as 'Conventional Weapons Convention' or 'CCW'.

If reaching agreement on the text of the Additional Protocols of 1977 had been no mean task, the negotiations preceding the adoption of the Conventional Weapons Convention with its annexed Protocols involved even greater difficulties. The task in hand was to find agreement on restrictions on the use of specific weapons, many of which had long formed part of the arsenals of armed forces and, indeed, were in common use in many theatres of war. Accordingly, the positions of delegations at the Conference varied widely. To give just one example: while one group favoured a total ban on use of incendiary weapons, another group saw no reason to protect combatants from the impact of incendiary weapons, nor were they convinced of the need to supplement the rules in Protocol I of 1977 on protection of the civilian population with rules protecting civilians against the use of such weapons in particular. With the points of departure so far apart, the texts that emerged from the negotiations on this and similar questions cannot but bear all the marks of compromise.

The Conventional Weapons Convention (an 'umbrella convention') does not itself contain substantive provisions on use of certain conventional weapons but, rather, deals with matters such as the scope of application, entry into force and revision of the Convention and its Protocols. The substantive rules adopted in 1980 are found in the original three Protocols: Protocol I on 'Non-Detectable Fragments', Protocol II on 'Prohibitions or Restrictions on the Use of Mines, Booby Traps and Other Devices', and Protocol III on 'Prohibitions or Restrictions on the Use of Incendiary Weapons'. To this were subsequently added: Protocol IV on 'Blinding Laser Weapons' (1995), Amended Protocol II on 'Prohibitions or Restrictions on the Use of Mines, Booby Traps and Other Devices' (1996) and Protocol V on 'Explosive Remnants of War' (2003). The Protocols are presented here in their chronological order. The discussion of conventional weapons concludes with brief references to two related Conventions: the Ottawa Convention on Anti-Personnel Mines and the Convention on Cluster Munitions.

5.1.1a   The Convention on Conventional Weapons

As mentioned at the end of Chapter 2, the CCW was concluded under the auspices of the United Nations. This sets it somewhat apart from the other treaties on the humanitarian law of armed conflict, including the Additional Protocols of 1977. Yet its subject matter is closely connected with that of the other treaties. The connection is obvious in the preamble, where the states parties recall "the general principle of the protection of the civilian population against the effects of hostilities" as well as the principles of unnecessary suffering and protection of the environment: these principles derive directly from Protocol I of 1977.

In a similar vein, the states parties once again repeat the Martens clause, in confirming their determination:

> that in cases not covered by this Convention and its annexed Protocols or by other international agreements, the civilian population and the combatants shall at all times remain under the protection and authority of the principles of international law derived from established custom, from the principles of humanity and from the dictates of public conscience.

Here, as in 1899, the clause was introduced for a specific purpose. The negotiations left no doubt that several proposals would not be accepted nor, hence, be reflected in specific rules. For such cases the clause preserves the admittedly vague and ill-defined, yet non-negligible protection of the applicable 'principles of international law'.

The preamble brings out yet another, perhaps less obvious relationship: the link between the subject matter of the Convention with its annexed Protocols and the question of disarmament. On this point, the preamble expresses the desire of the states parties "to contribute to international détente, the ending of the arms race and the building of confidence among states, and hence to the realisation of the aspiration of all peoples to live in peace", adding that positive results achieved in the area of prohibition or restriction of use of certain conventional weapons "may facilitate the main talks on disarmament with a view to putting an end to the production, stockpiling and proliferation of such weapons".

Article 1, as originally adopted, contained one single paragraph that defined the scope of application of the CCW and its annexed Protocols by referring to Article 2 common to the Geneva Conventions of 1949 and Article 1(4) of Protocol I of 1977. This limited the scope of the Convention to international armed conflicts, including wars of national liberation and, by implication, excluded application in internal armed conflicts.

As amended in 2001 (and in force since 18 November 2003 for states that have accepted the amendment), the original text of Article 1 now constitutes its first paragraph. Paragraph 2 expands the scope of the CCW and the annexed Protocols to "situations referred to in Article 3 common to the Geneva Conventions of 12 August 1949" – the broadest possible definition of internal armed conflict; this with the same bottom line as applies for common Article 3 and Protocol II: excluded are "situations of internal disturbances and tensions, such as riots, isolated and sporadic acts of violence, and other acts of a similar nature, as not being armed conflicts". Paragraph 3 states that in a case of internal armed conflict, "each Party to the conflict shall be bound to apply the prohibitions and restrictions of this Convention and its annexed Protocols". This oft-repeated clause is succeeded, in turn, by three equally usual clauses serving to safeguard the political and territorial sovereignty of the state.

Article 2 excludes any interpretation of the Convention or its Protocols that would detract from "other obligations imposed on the High Contracting Parties by international humanitarian law applicable in armed conflict". This implicitly refers to the Geneva Conventions and the Additional Protocols.

Another implicit reference to, or reliance on, the Geneva Conventions and Protocols may be seen in Article 6, which obliges states parties "in time of peace as in time of armed conflict, to disseminate this Convention and those of its annexed Protocols by which they are bound as widely as possible in their respective countries and, in particular, to include the study thereof in their programmes of military instruction, so that those instruments may become known to their armed forces". No matter how welcome, this reaffirmation of the need to disseminate the law is the only duty the Convention imposes on the parties in the sphere of implementation. Compliance with and enforcement of the Convention and the annexed Protocols may on the other hand be expected – or at least hoped – to go hand in hand with the efforts to promote the Geneva Conventions of 1949 and the Additional Protocols of 1977.

In other respects, the Conventional Weapons Convention stands apart from the earlier treaties. While the 1977 Protocols are open only to states parties to the 1949 Conventions, all states may become party to the CCW (Arts. 3, 4). Yet this does not imply any great difference, given that today all states are party to the Geneva Conventions. (Although negotiated under the aegis of the United Nations, the Convention is not open to accession by that or any other international organisation.)

The fact that the Convention is itself devoid of substantive rules on use of weapons reflects the uncertainty at the time whether states would eventually "consent to be bound" by all the prohibitions and restrictions the participants at the Conference might be able to agree on. The solution was to group the rules together according to categories of weapon and distribute them over separate Protocols, which states would be free in principle to accept or not.

This set-up entailed the possibility that some states would be bound by one particular Protocol, and others by a different one. To cope with what might become a confusing situation, Article 4 provides that to become party to the Convention, a state must accept at least two of the (then) three Protocols. At any time thereafter it may "consent to be bound by any annexed Protocol by which it is not already bound"; all of this through notification to the Depositary: in this case, as provided by Article 10, the UN Secretary-General.

This cleverly devised system, complemented by rules on relations between states party to the Convention but to different sets of Protocols (Art. 7), had little practical significance since, rare exceptions apart, states that became party to the Convention accepted all three original Protocols. The system has come into play with the adoption of Protocols IV and V and Amended Protocol II: states accepted one or other of the new Protocols at widely different dates.

For completeness' sake, reference is made to Article 7(4), which makes provision for all the variations and permutations that may arise in the event of the Convention and one or more of its Protocols being applied in a war of national liberation waged under the conditions of Article 1(4) in conjunction with Article 96(3) of Additional Protocol I of 1977.

Another matter that required a complex set of rules concerns review and amendment. The Conference was leaving a number of appeals for prohibitions or restrictions on the use of specific (categories of) weapons unfulfilled. Delegations that saw their proposals rejected were keen to include, in the Convention, rules that would facilitate the subsequent revision of accepted texts and the addition of new rules or even entirely new protocols. Their opponents were more inclined to restrict the possibilities for review and amendment.

Article 8, reflecting this controversy, contains a number of hard-won compromises. It distinguishes between amendments to the CCW and the annexed Protocols (paragraph 1) and the addition of new protocols (paragraph 2). Both paragraphs provide that at any time after the entry into force of the Convention any state party may table relevant proposals. The Depositary notifies such a proposal to all states parties and "shall seek their views on whether a conference should be convened to consider the proposal". The conference is only convened if a majority and at least eighteen – of the states parties so agree, and it then has power to consider and decide upon the proposals. If the purpose is to amend the Convention or a Protocol, only parties to those instruments may adopt the proposals. New protocols, on the other hand, may be adopted by a conference on which all states may be represented, whether they are parties to the Convention or not.

While these provisions still left the chance that unwilling states would block the convening of further conferences, paragraph 3 closed the gap by providing that if ten years after the entry into force of the CCW no conference had been held, any state party could ask the Depositary to convene a conference "to review the scope and operation of this Convention and the Protocols annexed thereto and to consider any proposal for amendments"; this time, with no majority required and, again, with states non-parties present, as observers.

With the entry into force of the Convention and the three annexed Protocols in December 1983, the procedure of paragraph 3 could be set in motion, resulting in the first Review Conference, which, in two sessions (late 1995 and early 1996), adopted Protocol IV and Amended Protocol II. The second Review Conference was held in 2001, and the third, in 2006.

5.1.1b   Protocol I on Non-Detectable Fragments

Protocol I consists of one single provision, prohibiting "to use any weapon the primary effect of which is to injure by fragments which in the human body escape detection by X-rays".

The provision is a direct application of the principle prohibiting the use of weapons "of a nature to cause superfluous injury or unnecessary suffering" (in the terms of Article 35(2) of Protocol I of 1977). It is therefore primarily designed to protect combatants – a rare exception in the whole of the CCW and Protocols. It is, however, of limited practical significance: at the time of the Conference, weapons meeting the above description were only rumoured to exist, and even today, they do not belong to the standard arsenals of the vast majority of states. It was, in effect, the rather limited significance of the prohibition in Protocol I that led to the requirement in Article 4(3) of the Convention that in order to become a party a state must accept to be bound by at least two of the annexed Protocols: acceptance of nothing but the Protocol on Non-Detectable Fragments would have been devoid of significance.

The limited significance of the Protocol cannot be illustrated better than by pointing out that its single line is the sole remnant of attempts to ban whole categories of actually used explosive munitions such as projectiles with a pre-fragmented casing (designed to explode according to a set pattern into fragments of predetermined dimensions) or filled with very small round 'pellets' or nail-like 'fléchettes'. All these attempts had foundered on the argument that compared with other existing and commonly used types of munitions, such as the high-explosive bomb or artillery shell, the 'fragmentation' types of explosive ammunition could not be said to be of a nature to cause superfluous injury or unnecessary suffering.

5.1.1c Protocol II on Mines, Booby Traps and Other Devices

While the Non-Detectable Fragments Protocol in 1980 was the almost imperceptible result of efforts that had aimed much higher, the Mines Protocol was its opposite in this as in most other respects. A great deal of energy had gone into the elaboration of detailed rules for the use of various types of mine-like munitions, in an attempt, to quote the classic formula, to "protect the civilian population as much as possible" against the often horrendous and long-lasting effects of this class of weapon. After its adoption and entry into force, the need for stronger rules was soon perceived, and this came about in 1996 with the adoption of the Amended Protocol. Since this does not replace the 1980 Protocol and not all states which are party to the 1980 Protocol have also accepted the Amended Protocol of 1996 (and vice versa), it remains necessary to expound the 1980 Protocol first.

According to Article 1, the Protocol applies on land, including "beaches, waterway crossings or river crossings", but not to "the use of anti-ship mines at sea or in inland waterways". It encompasses a wide category of weapons that, in contrast with what their name might suggest, need not all be explosive. A 'mine' is explosive: as defined in Article 2(1), it is "any munition placed under, on or near the ground or other surface area and designed to be detonated or exploded by the presence, proximity or contact of a person or vehicle". In contrast, the 'booby trap' is not necessarily explosive: Article 2(2) defines it as "any device or material which is designed, constructed or adapted to kill or injure and which functions unexpectedly when a person disturbs or approaches an apparently harmless object or performs an apparently safe act". The 'other devices' may also be explosive or otherwise: Article 2(3) defines them as "manually emplaced munitions and devices designed to kill, injure or damage and which are actuated by remote control or automatically after a lapse of time".

The goal of protection of the civilian population is pursued, first, by subjecting the use of all of these munitions to general restrictions, inspired by the provisions on the same subject in Additional Protocol I of 1977. As provided in Article 3, they are threefold: a prohibition on the use of the munitions "either in offence, defence or by way of reprisals, against the civilian population as such or against individual civilians"; a prohibition on indiscriminate use; and an injunction to take all feasible precautions to protect civilians from the effects of use of the munitions. Article 3 defines "indiscriminate use" in terms identical to those used in Protocol I of 1977; the same applies to the definitions of "military objective" and "civilian object" in Article 2(4) and (5).

The "general restrictions" of Article 3 are by no means redundant: not all states party to the Weapons Convention are also party to Protocol I of 1977. Apart from that, Article 3 places beyond doubt that the use of mines, booby traps and 'other devices' falls under the concept of 'attack' as defined in Article 49 of Protocol I of 1977.

Articles 4 and 5 make provision for the protection of the civilian population. Article 4 restricts the use of all the weapons (except for remotely delivered mines) in "any city, town, village or other area containing a similar concentration of civilians" if no actual fighting between ground forces is going on or is imminent. Use of the weapons in these circumstances is prohibited unless "they are placed on or in the close vicinity of a military objective belonging to or under the control of an adverse Party" (in an act of sabotage, for instance); or when they are placed as part of defensive measures, on the condition that "measures are taken to protect civilians from their effects, such as the posting of warning signs, the posting of sentries, the issue of warnings or the provision of fences".

Article 5 deals with the use of "remotely delivered mines" (that is, according to Article 2(1), mines "delivered by artillery, rocket, mortar or similar means or dropped from an aircraft"). Such remote delivery is only permitted "within an area which is itself a military objective or which contains military objectives", and under the further condition that, either, "their location can be accurately recorded", or "an effective neutralising mechanism is used on each such mine" for the event that the mine no longer serves the purpose for which it was placed in position. Also required is effective advance warning "of any delivery or dropping of remotely delivered mines which may affect the civilian population, unless circumstances do not permit".

The rules in Article 6, prohibiting "the use of certain booby traps", are designed to protect combatants as much as civilians. Recalling "the rules of international law applicable in armed conflict relating to treachery and perfidy", paragraph 1 goes on to prohibit, "in all circumstances", the use, first, of "any booby trap in the form of an apparently harmless portable object which is specifically designed and constructed to contain explosive material and to detonate when it is disturbed or approached", and, second, of a long list of booby traps "attached to or associated with" such items as (to give just a few examples) the red cross emblem, a sick, wounded or dead person, medical items or children's toys.

Article 6(2) prohibits, equally "in all circumstances", the use of "any booby trap which is designed to cause superfluous injury or unnecessary suffering". This prohibition, again a direct application of the well-known principle of 1899, was included in particular with a view to a practice of which the memory was still fresh, of constructing carefully hidden holes with sharp bamboo spears erected on the bottom: the person who fell into such a trap was likely to suffer grievous injuries and die a slow and painful death.

While the above provisions deal with the use of mines (etc.) in the course of hostilities, Article 7 addresses the dangers that minefields, scattered mines and booby traps continue to pose to the civilian population long after the cessation of active hostilities. The provisions of Article 7 amount to an obligation to record whenever possible the location of all minefields, mines and booby traps, and to use those records after the cessation of hostilities in taking "all necessary and appropriate measures" for the protection of civilians, either by the party that had recorded the data or through an exchange of information. A technical annex to the Mines Protocol provides detailed 'guidelines on recording'.

Article 7 does not refer to enemy occupation in so many words; this despite the fact that in such a situation any minefields laid beforehand for the defence of the territory may pose as much of a threat to the civilian population as in any other case of 'cessation of active hostilities'. This ostensible silence finds its explanation in the opposition, in particular, of Yugoslavia (as it then was), whose constitution expressly excluded the acceptance of a situation of enemy occupation. Its delegation was therefore not in a position to accept any rule expressly referring to occupation. In the light of this bit of drafting history, 'cessation of active hostilities' must be interpreted as covering the case of enemy occupation.

Article 8 makes provision for the event that a UN force or mission is performing "functions of peacekeeping, observation or similar functions" in a given area (where the presence of mines or booby traps may severely hamper its movements). Paragraph 1 obliges each party to the conflict, if so requested and to the extent of its abilities, to "remove or render harmless all mines or booby traps in that area"; to take all other necessary measures for the protection of the force or mission, and to make all relevant information in its possession available to the head of the force or mission. For the specific case of a UN fact-finding mission (which may roam over a wider and more unpredictable stretch of territory than other missions), paragraph 2 repeats the duties of protection and information, leaving out the obligation to remove the danger of mines (etc.) from the area of the mission's activities.

Article 9, finally, urges the parties to cooperate, after the cessation of hostilities, "both among themselves and, where appropriate, with other states and with international organisations", in the removal or neutralisation of minefields, mines and booby traps placed in position during the conflict.

Even in retrospect, the Mines Protocol remains a carefully balanced instrument that provides significant protection to civilian populations on just one condition: that its rules be scrupulously observed by a professional armed force conducting war with the restraint that is implied in the military principle of economy of force, and in a theatre that lends itself to that type of warfare. Practice, however, has proved very different, with whole countries being literally strewn with all types of land-mines and booby traps of the most perfidious kinds. This massive, unrestricted use in theatres such as Afghanistan and Angola led to an outcry from the international community, and this, in turn, to endeavours to further restrict the use of these munitions. While these endeavours have led to positive results, with the adoption of the 1995 Amended Protocol followed by the 1996 Ottawa Convention, the original Protocol II is still in force and hence, whenever applicable, requires compliance and enforcement.

5.1.1d   Protocol III on Incendiary Weapons

Protocol III, on 'Prohibitions or Restrictions on the Use of Incendiary Weapons', comprises just two articles, each the result of a hard battle at the Conference. Article 1 defines what, for the purpose of the Protocol, are "incendiary weapons" and what munitions are not included in its scope; it also defines some other notions, such as "military objective" and "civilian object". Article 2 contains rules on the "protection of civilians and civilian objects".

An "incendiary weapon" is defined in Article 1(1) as "any weapon or munition which is primarily designed to set fire to objects or to cause burn injury to persons through the action of flame, heat, or a combination thereof, produced by a chemical reaction of a substance delivered on the target". All sorts of munitions meet this description; the paragraph gives some examples: "flame throwers, fougasses, shells, rockets, grenades, mines, bombs and other containers of incendiary substances". This list of examples is not, however, of material significance in the Protocol, since none of the listed devices has been made the subject of separate regulation, whether prohibition or restriction. The same applies to napalm, which, in spite of the strong objections to its use voiced at the time of the Convention, was not even mentioned in the list. (It appears to have been phased out of most military arsenals.)

Of greater practical significance is the enumeration, in the same paragraph, of munitions that the Protocol does *not* regard as incendiary weapons. They are, first, munitions "which may have incidental incendiary effects, such as illuminants, tracers, smoke or signalling systems". A tracer is a projectile primarily designed to show the trajectory followed by a stream of projectiles, say, from a machine gun; it does this by radiating light caused by a chemical reaction of a substance it carries to that purpose. When the tracer hits the target which the other projectiles are also aimed at, the same chemical reaction may cause fire or burn injury: this will then be an incidental rather than a primary effect.

Munitions "designed to combine penetration, blast or fragmentation effects with an additional incendiary effect" are also excluded. In this category fall, for instance, anti-tank munitions whose armour-piercing effect is based on the development of an extremely high temperature. Munitions of this type, in which "the incendiary effect is not specifically designed to cause burn injury to persons", are also commonly used against other, so-called 'hard' targets.

As noted above, the other article of the Protocol, Article 2, provides protection for "civilians and civilian objects". It does not, in other words, protect combatants at all against the effects of incendiary weapons, whether included or excluded in the definition, nor, indeed, against the effects of fire by any other cause.

Article 2(1) reaffirms the main rule of protection of the civilian population: "It is prohibited in all circumstances to make the civilian population as such, individual civilians or civilian objects the object of attack by incendiary weapons." Of course, this prohibition applies to any other weapon as well.

Paragraphs 2 and 3 are both designed to protect "concentrations of civilians" – a notion already known from Additional Protocol I of 1977. Article 1(2) defines it anew, adding further examples; it "means any concentration of civilians, be it permanent or temporary, such as in inhabited parts of cities, or inhabited towns or villages, or as in camps or columns of refugees or evacuees, or groups of nomads". Civilians in such situations are extremely vulnerable to fire spreading from attacks with incendiary weapons on military objectives located in their midst. Accordingly, Article 2(2) categorically prohibits to make any military objective so located "the object of attack by air-delivered incendiary weapons".

As for attacks by other than air-delivered incendiary weapons, paragraph 3 permits these solely under the twofold condition that, first, the military objective "is clearly separated from the concentration of civilians" and, second, that "all feasible precautions are taken with a view to limiting the incendiary effects to the military objective and to avoiding, and in any event to minimising, incidental loss of civilian life, injury to civilians and damage to civilian objects". It should be emphasised that the protection provided by these prohibitions covers only the fire caused by incendiary weapons as defined, and not fire as an incidental effect of use of a munition that does not fall under the definition.

Paragraph 4, finally, contains a provision of protection of the environment: "forests or other kinds of plant cover" must not be made "the object of attack by incendiary weapons except when such natural elements are used to cover, conceal or camouflage combatants or other military objectives, or are themselves military objectives". The built-in series of exceptions, covering all conceivable motives a belligerent party might have to attack a forest by incendiary weapons (or any other weapons, for that matter) deprives the paragraph of practical significance.

5.1.1e   Protocol IV on Blinding Laser Weapons

As widespread and common as is the use of mines, booby traps and incendiary weapons, so infrequent and novel appeared to be the use of blinding laser weapons, the topic of Protocol IV. The adoption of this Protocol in 1995 represents a rare instance of limits being set to the use of a specific weapon before it has become entrenched in states' arsenals to the point where its removal becomes almost impossible to achieve.

Over a comparatively short period of time, laser systems have become indispensable in a wide range of military operations, for functions such as target marking or projectile guidance. When the 'target' is a manned weapon system, the laser beam may hit a human eye, and this can have a temporary or permanent blinding effect. It is also possible purposely to train a laser beam on the eyes of enemy personnel, in an attempt to temporarily blind them. While the first case is accidental and the second, as long as it causes no more than a brief loss of eyesight, might be a permissible method of disabling the adversary, the assessment was different as regards permanent blinding: this was deemed unacceptable suffering for the victim as well as to the community they belong to; hence, Protocol IV.

Article 1 prohibits "to employ laser weapons specifically designed, as their sole combat function or as one of their combat functions, to cause permanent blindness to unenhanced vision" (that is, with or without glasses or lenses). "Permanent blindness" is defined in Article 4 as "irreversible and uncorrectable loss of vision which is seriously disabling with no prospect of recovery". "Serious disability" is in turn defined in terms that will enable an optician to establish with precision whether a person's loss of eyesight meets the definition.

Article 2 prescribes that in the employment of laser systems, contracting states must "take all feasible precautions to avoid the incidence of permanent blindness to unenhanced vision", inter alia, by appropriate "training of their armed forces and other practical measures". Article 3 adds that blinding "as an incidental or collateral effect of the legitimate military employment" of such systems, including those "used against optical equipment, is not covered by the prohibition of this Protocol".

Article 1 contains an interesting second sentence. It provides that contracting states "shall not transfer [weapons as defined in the quoted first sentence] to any State or non-State entity". This is a disarmament-type provision and therefore an unusual sight in a humanitarian law text. It is also conspicuous for its reference to non-state entities. This includes terrorist or other opposition groups, regardless of whether they are involved in armed conflict. Again, this is a considerable step beyond the general scope of application of the CCW.

5.1.1f   Amended Protocol II on Mines, Booby Traps and Similar Devices

The process of amending the Mines Protocol has resulted in an instrument that is different in many respects from the other Protocols. Whereas the latter Protocols clearly fit under the umbrella of the Convention, the Amended Protocol II has its own chapter (called Article 1) on scope of application, its own section (called Article 8) on transfers, and its own part (Arts. 11–14) on implementation, enforcement, international consultation and cooperation. It is also a highly complicated instrument, of which only some highlights are mentioned here.

The first point to highlight is its scope of application. Article 1(2) provides that it also applies in internal armed conflicts. Paragraphs 2–6 then reiterate the same list of clauses, including those safeguarding the sovereignty of states, found in Additional Protocol II of 1977 (and now in Article 1 of the CCW as well). The provision in paragraph 3 that in such an internal armed conflict, "each Party to the conflict shall be bound to apply the prohibitions and restrictions of this Protocol", poses no mean task on those who venture to instruct especially the non-state parties (and perhaps not only those) about their obligations under the Protocol.

From the long list of definitions (Art. 2) one is selected here: an "antipersonnel mine" is "a mine primarily designed to be exploded by the presence, proximity or contact of a person and that will incapacitate, injure or kill one or more persons" (Art. 2(3)). The definition is important because, in contrast with its predecessor, the Amended Protocol places restrictions specifically on that type of mine.

Article 3 places a series of general restrictions on the use of mines (etc.). Some of these restrictions correspond to the relevant provisions in the 1980 Protocol, while others reaffirm principles and rules for the protection of combatants (against unnecessary suffering) and civilians (against the effects of hostilities, including the prohibition of reprisals) as found in the Additional Protocols of 1977.

In this mass of provisions, Article 3(2) stands on its own, declaring that each contracting state and other party to the conflict is "responsible for all mines, booby traps and other devices employed by it". The sentence does not stop there; it continues: "and undertakes to clear, remove, destroy or maintain them as specified". Yet the question may be asked what is the extent of this responsibility: does it cover only the removal of the devices in question, or also all the harm their illegitimate use may cause, including the financial consequences thereof? In view of the gigantic amounts of money potentially involved in the latter interpretation, this may not be what the drafters had in mind. Even so, it does not appear legally unsound and deserves its day in court.

The use of anti-personnel mines in particular is regulated in (parts of) Articles 4–6. Article 4 prohibits the use of such mines "which are not detectable" (as specified in a technical annex to the Protocol). Article 5 places technical and other restrictions on the use of non-remotely delivered anti-personnel mines, and Article 6 on remotely delivered mines, including anti-personnel mines. The restrictions are designed to prevent harm to persons other than enemy combatants.

Article 7, on the use of booby traps and other devices, reaffirms most of the comparable provisions in the 1980 Protocol. It does not repeat the prohibition to use booby traps "designed to cause superfluous injury or unnecessary suffering" (which would have only been repetitive). It adds restrictions on the use of booby traps in areas containing a "concentration of civilians in which combat between ground forces is not taking place or does not appear to be imminent". A similar provision in the 1980 Protocol covered mines as well.

The part of the Protocol on implementation contains rules on transfers (Art. 8); recording and use of information about mines (etc.) (Art. 9); removal of same, and international cooperation (Art. 10); technological cooperation and assistance (Art. 11); protection of a variety of missions, including those of the ICRC (Art. 12); consultations among contracting states, including an annual conference (Art. 13); and, last but not least, compliance (Art. 14).

Article 14(1) urges a contracting party to "take all appropriate steps, including legislative and other measures, to prevent and suppress violations of this Protocol by persons or on territory under its jurisdiction or control". The references to "persons or territory" and "jurisdiction or control" imply a wide territorial scope for these measures, covering invaded or occupied parts of enemy territory – as well as, and this should not be forgotten, a state's own territory in the event of an internal armed conflict.

Article 14(2) provides that the measures of paragraph 1 "include appropriate measures to ensure the imposition of penal sanctions against persons who, in relation to an armed conflict and contrary to the provisions of this Protocol, wilfully kill or cause serious injury to civilians and to bring such persons to justice". While stopping short of explicitly creating a 'grave breach' as in the 1949 Geneva Conventions and Protocol I of 1977, this provision doubtless defines a 'serious violation of international humanitarian law'.

All of these innovative steps are most welcome and may contribute to giving the Protocol enhanced effect. More traditional are the obligations in Article 14(3), requiring contracting parties to ensure that their armed forces receive the right instructions and training, and paragraph 4, on the possibility of bilateral or multilateral consultation among the parties.

A final comment concerns, once again, the ostensibly independent character of the Amended Protocol II. True, it has a number of features that set it apart from the other Protocols annexed to the Weapons Convention. Yet technically, it is just another annexed Protocol; specifically, it has no provisions of its own on ratification, entry into force, treaty relations and so on. In this regard it is interesting to note that one (mini-)state, Monaco, in becoming party to the Convention in 1997, chose to be bound only by Protocol I on Non-Detectable Fragments and Amended Protocol II on Mines – the least and the most exacting respectively of the five, but including the one that gives it access to the annual Review Conference.

5.1.1g   Protocol V on Explosive Remnants of War

While in the 1970s the use of 'fragmentation bombs' had already become the object of heated discussion, further development of this weapon led to the introduction of so-called 'cluster munitions', which upon explosion disperse a quantity of small explosive devices over a wide area. If only combatants are assembled in the area, that is all right. As experience shows, this often is not the case, with numbers of casualties among the civilian population as a consequence. Moreover, not all of the bomblets explode upon hitting persons, objects or the ground in the target are, thus exposing anyone entering the area after the fighting is over to the risk of becoming gravely wounded. Other unexploded ordnance poses the same risk.

In September 2000, the ICRC proposed to an expert meeting convened in Switzerland that a protocol on these explosive remnants of war ("ERW") be negotiated. In 2001, at the second CCW Review Conference, this idea gained wide support and a group of government experts was set up to draft a text. Their work resulted in a text that, on 28 November 2003, was adopted at a meeting of states parties to the Convention. Having received the requisite twenty ratifications, Protocol V on Explosive Remnants of War entered into force on 12 November 2006.

The Protocol is applicable in any armed conflict, whether international or internal (Art. 1(3)). It defines explosive remnants of war as "unexploded" or "abandoned" explosive ordnance. The term "explosive ordnance" is defined as "conventional munitions containing explosives" with the exception of the "mines, booby traps and other devices" of the Amended Mines Protocol. "Unexploded" ordnance (or "UXO") has actually been used in an armed conflict and "should have exploded but failed to do so". "Abandoned" ordnance ("AXO") has not been used and "has been left behind or dumped by a Party to an armed conflict", and "is no longer under control" of that party (all of this in Art. 2).

While ERW pose a risk from their very inception, the risk increases exponentially when the territory where they are located ceases to be an area of active hostilities and the inhabitants resume their normal outdoor activities. Measures for their protection against these dangers become that much more urgent, and more practicable as well. The Protocol accordingly distinguishes general responsibilities of parties to the conflict (which apply even with active hostilities in progress) and specific responsibilities of the parties that arise after the cessation of active hostilities.

A general task for parties responsible for the delivery or abandonment of explosive ordnance is to record the relevant information. Article 4(1) provides that this must be done "to the maximum extent possible and as far as practicable": a reminder that at a time of active hostilities other concerns may stand in the way of proper bookkeeping.

Equally carefully circumscribed is the task of parties to the conflict in control of a territory where ordnance has become ERW: Article 5 provides that they must take "all feasible precautions" to protect "the civilian population, civilians and civilian objects" from the "risks and effects" of these devices; and "feasible" means "practicable or practicably possible, taking into account all circumstances ruling at the time, including humanitarian and military considerations" – a well-known safeguarding clause, but one that is understandable in the "circumstances ruling at the time". On the practical side, the article suggests "risk education", warnings, and the "marking, fencing and monitoring of territory affected by" ERW.

After the cessation of active hostilities, the obligations on both sides become more stringent. Article 4(2) now requires the party that "used or abandoned explosive ordnance which may have become" ERW to make the information it recorded about such use or abandonment available to the party in control of the "affected area", and this "without delay" but still "as far as practicable, subject to [its] legitimate security interests". The article suggests routes for the transfer of the information via the United Nations or "other relevant organisations", inter alia, if direct delivery to the party in control of the territory appears to be impracticable.

This leaves the party with ERW in territory under its control: it now must "mark and clear, remove or destroy" the ERW "as soon as possible", and giving priority to areas assessed to pose a "serious humanitarian risk" (Art. 3(2)). Paragraph 3 sets forth the steps required to "survey and assess the threat"; to "assess and prioritise needs and practicability" of measures to remove the risk; to actually take these measures; and to "mobilise resources to carry out these activities".

In all of this, the party concerned must "take into account international standards, including the International Mine Action Standards" (Art. 3(4)). These standards, or IMAS, are developed and maintained by the United Nations Inter-Agency Policy: Mine Action and Effective Coordination (UNMAS) with the assistance of the Geneva International Centre for Humanitarian Demining. Originally written for the combat against landmines, these standards have been adapted, where necessary, to cover ERW as well.

Further articles of Protocol V deal with the "protection of humanitarian missions and organisations from the effects of" ERW, by, among other things, providing them with information on the location of ERW in territory where they are, or are going to, operate (Art. 6); the right to ask, and the duty to provide, assistance from other states or international entities (Art. 7); and "cooperation and assistance" in the fields of marking etc. of ERW, risk education, and care, rehabilitation and reintegration of victims of ERW (Art. 8). Article 9 encourages states parties "to take generic preventive measures aimed at minimising the occurrence of" ERW – meaning that they should improve the technical features of explosive ordnance, so that the weapons will not become ERW.

Article 10 makes provision for consultations among the states parties "on all issues related to the operation of this Protocol", notably through the same system of review conferences as has been created for the CCW. With a first conference in November 2007, these review conferences are being held on a yearly basis. The work of the conferences includes "review of the status and operation" of the Protocol and a look at its implementation on the national level. On this, Article 11 obliges states parties to see to it that their armed forces "issue appropriate instructions and operating procedures" and that the training of the personnel is "consistent with the relevant provisions of this Protocol".

Altogether, Protocol V may contribute considerably to reducing the misery caused by ERW. It remains to note that many interested parties (states as well as organisations including the ICRC) remained dissatisfied with the fact that cluster munitions had not been prohibited outright from use as well as production, development and so on. Their efforts resulted in the adoption of the Convention on Cluster Munitions (see below, Section 5.1.2b).

5.1.1h   Note on reciprocity and reprisals in the CCW Protocols

Article 3(2) of the 1980 Mines Protocol and Article 3(7) of the 1996 Amended Mines Protocol prohibit "*in all circumstances* to direct weapons to which this Article applies, either in offence, defence *or by way of reprisals*, against the civilian population as such or against individual civilians". Article 6(2) of the 1980 Protocol, which prohibits the use of "any booby trap which is designed to cause superfluous injury or unnecessary suffering", and Article 3(3) of the 1996 Protocol which does the same in relation to "any mine, booby trap or other device" which is so designed, are equally reinforced with the phrase 'in all circumstances', and so is the prohibition in Article 2 of the Incendiary Weapons Protocol "to make the civilian population as such, individual civilians or civilian objects the object of attack by incendiary weapons". These latter provisions do not add the reference to reprisals.

The phrase 'in all circumstances' in these provisions implies that use of the weapons in question on grounds of (negative) reciprocity will be unlawful. This is precisely, however, where the notion of 'reprisal' comes in: a reprisal is by definition an unlawful act but one which is legitimised by its purpose (to compel the adverse party to mend its ways) and by the strict conditions under which it can be resorted to.

As regards reprisal attacks against the civilian population or individual civilians, the Mines Protocols explicitly prohibit such recourse while the Incendiary Weapons Protocol has no comparable clause. The difference does not imply any significant conclusions, however. The reference in the Mines Protocols to "reprisals", as a sort of logical follow-up to "offence or defence", merely reiterates the general prohibition of reprisal attacks against the civilian population or civilians embodied in Article 51(6) of Additional Protocol I. The absence of the comparable phrase in the Incendiary Weapons Protocol is simply the consequence of a slightly different construction of the article in question, and the *a contrario* argument that use by way of reprisal of incendiary weapons against the civilian population remains permissible is obviously fallacious.

There remain the "superfluous injury or unnecessary suffering" provisions in the Mines Protocols. These are primarily, if not exclusively, designed to protect combatants, a category of persons protected from reprisals only if they are wounded or sick or are in enemy hands as prisoners of war. Given the lack of specific language on this point in the Mines Protocols, and for want of unambiguous practice one way or the other, the only conclusion one may draw is that the legitimacy of use in reprisal of mines, booby traps and other devices, as of other prohibited weapons, against the armed forces of the adverse party remains a debatable point.

5.1.2   Prohibitions on use, production, etc. of weapons

5.1.2a   The Ottawa Convention on Anti-Personnel Mines

The Convention, officially entitled 'Convention on the Prohibition of the Use, Stockpiling, Production and Transfer of Anti-Personnel Mines and on Their Destruction', is not only a humanitarian treaty but an interstate disarmament instrument as well: as its title indicates, apart from use, it focuses on all aspects of the very existence of these mines. It is therefore mentioned here only briefly. Although adopted at Oslo, on 18 September 1997, it is usually referred to as the Ottawa Convention after the place where it was opened for signature, on 3 and 4 December 1997. The Convention is the result of a forceful, well-organised and persistent campaign of civil society (the International Campaign to Ban Landmines, launched in 1992) that, convinced that the restrictions of Protocol II to the CCW did not go far enough, strove (and succeeded) to achieve a categorical ban on all use of anti-personnel mines.

Giving clear expression to the motives underlying the Convention, the first paragraph of the preamble declares that the states parties are:

> Determined to put an end to the suffering and casualties caused by anti-personnel mines, that kill or maim hundreds of people every week, mostly innocent and defenceless civilians and especially children, obstruct economic development and reconstruction, inhibit the repatriation of refugees and internally displaced persons, and have other severe consequences for years after emplacement.

Another paragraph of the preamble stresses the role of public conscience and recognises the efforts of "the International Red Cross and Red Crescent Movement, the International Campaign to Ban Landmines, and numerous other non-governmental organisations around the world". The closing paragraph recalls the fundamental principles of humanitarian law: the absence of an unlimited right to choose methods or means of warfare; the prohibition on use of weapons of a nature to cause unnecessary suffering; and the principle of distinction between civilians and combatants.

Turning to substance, Article 1(1) sets forth the undertaking of each state party "never under any circumstances ... to use anti-personnel mines". This is followed by equally absolute prohibitions on the development, production, acquisition, stockpiling or transfer of these weapons, and on assisting, encouraging or inducing "anyone to engage in any activity prohibited to a State Party under this Convention". Paragraph 2 adds the undertaking "to destroy or ensure the destruction of all anti-personnel mines in accordance with the provisions of this Convention". It should be noted that while the article categorically prohibits the use of anti-personnel mines in any armed conflict, its disarmament-type prohibitions on development and so on bind only states.

Article 2 defines some key notions. Paragraph 1, defining "anti-personnel mine", adopts the definition in the 1996 Protocol but leaves out the word "primarily" as an element qualifying the design of the mine. The next sentence excludes anti-vehicle mines equipped with an "anti-handling device" that, as explained in paragraph 3, protects the mines from attempts to "tamper with or otherwise intentionally disturb" them. Such a device, and the mine with it, may be caused to explode by the person doing the tampering. Neither the mine nor the "anti-handling device" are designed or emplaced in an anti-personnel mode; hence the exclusion.

The remainder of the Convention deals with organisational matters: destruction of mines on stock or in mined areas, cooperation and assistance, regular or special 'Meeting of the States Parties', fact-finding missions, etc. Mention is made in particular of Article 9, which obliges states parties to "take all appropriate legal, administrative and other measures, including the imposition of penal sanctions, to prevent and suppress any activity prohibited to a State Party under this Convention undertaken by persons or on territory under [their] jurisdiction or control".

A concluding remark may be that after the century-old prohibition on the use of dum-dum bullets and the recent but rather limited prohibition of use of weapons "the primary effect of which is to injure by fragments which in the human body escape detection by X-ray", the present categorical ban on use of anti-personnel mines is the third, this time highly significant, specific ban in force on what may be classified as a conventional weapon. All other specific rules in this area are confined to placing restrictions, rather than prohibitions, on use.

5.1.2b The Convention on Cluster Munitions

Adopted on 30 May 2008 at a diplomatic conference in Dublin, the Convention on Cluster Munitions is the result of a process that ran parallel with the making of Protocol V and that involved a large number of states, organisations such as the ICRC and the United Nations, and civil society (the Cluster Munition Coalition). It has been signed by many states and, having received the required thirty ratifications, it entered into force on 1 August 2010.

Whereas Protocol V attempts to forestall, reduce or help overcome the damage done by unexploded or abandoned munitions without removing the munitions from the arsenals of states, the 2008 Convention singles out cluster munitions as the object of an outright prohibition on use, production, possession and so on (Art. 1). The munitions in question are defined in Article 2, which, interestingly, begins with a very wide definition of the victims: it includes not only anyone who has been killed, injured or suffered other named types of loss caused by the use of cluster munitions, but their "affected families and communities" as well (paragraph 1).

Article 2 defines the cluster munition as "a conventional munition that is designed to disperse or release explosive submunitions each weighing less than 20 kilograms, and includes those explosive submunitions"; and the explosive submunition as "a conventional munition that in order to perform its task is dispersed or released by a cluster munition and is designed to function by detonating an explosive charge prior to, on or after impact" (paragraphs 2, 3). The article goes on to list a number of (sub)munitions that are excluded from this definition: first, those which serve for specific functions (dispense flares, smoke, pyrotechnics or chaff, produce electrical or electronic effects, or act in an air-defence role). But also excluded are munitions developed precisely "to avoid indiscriminate area effects and the risks posed by unexploded submunitions"; these must meet the following requirements: per munition no more than nine explosive submunitions; and each submunition heavier than four kilograms, designed to detect and engage a single target, and equipped with an electronic self-destruction mechanism and self-deactivating feature (all of this in paragraph 2). It may be obvious that few states take an active interest in developing munitions meeting these requirements.

The Convention lays down procedures for the destruction of existing stocks (Art. 3), clearance and destruction of cluster munition remnants in areas under the jurisdiction or control of a state party (Art. 4), and assistance to cluster munition victims in areas under the jurisdiction and control of such a state (Art. 5). Article 6 makes provision for international cooperation and assistance in pursuing these goals.

Implementation begins at the national level (Art. 9). To enhance this effort, provision is made for transparency in reporting (Art. 7) and cooperation to facilitate compliance (Art. 8). Should a dispute arise among states parties on the interpretation or application of the Convention, they must "consult together with a view to the expeditious settlement of the dispute by negotiation or by other peaceful means of their choice, including recourse to the Meeting of States Parties and referral to the International Court of Justice in conformity with the Statute of the Court" (Art. 10). The Meeting of States Parties is established in Article 11, and Review Conferences in Article 12.

The remainder of the Convention contains the usual technical treaty clauses. By way of final note, reference is made here to a clause in the preamble whereby it is "resolved" that non-state armed groups "shall not, under any circumstances, be permitted to engage in any activity prohibited to a State Party to this Convention". Instruments to enforce this prohibition are not provided in the Convention.

5.1.2c Biological and chemical weapons

With respect to nuclear weapons, it suffices to note here that given the impasse in the lawmaking field, the UN General Assembly in 1994 decided to request the ICJ for its opinion on the question whether the threat or use of nuclear weapons would ever be permissible under international law. The Court's Advisory Opinion of 1996 is dealt with in Section 5.3.2a.

As noted in earlier chapters, the use of chemical and bacteriological weapons was prohibited by the Geneva Protocol of 1925, but their production, possession and so on was not. Nor was it altogether clear whether they could be used in reprisal against earlier enemy use, either, of the identical means of warfare, or of one belonging to the same category of 'weapons of mass destruction'. The fact that for several decades now, the prohibition on use of these weapons is regarded as a rule of customary law, does not resolve this point: conceivably, a customary prohibition on use of a given weapon may be accompanied by an equally customary recognition of the right to resort to reprisal in the event of violation of the prohibitory rule.

Attempts to mend this situation ultimately resulted in the adoption of conventions banning bacteriological weapons (1972) and chemical weapons (1993). As primarily disarmament treaties, these conventions are discussed here only so far as relevant to our purposes.

The 1972 Convention on the Prohibition of Development, Production and Stockpiling of Bacteriological (Biological) and Toxin Weapons and on Their Destruction, while in its title still maintaining the term 'bacteriological' as used in the 1925 Protocol, in effect covers much more ground than the instrument that preceded it.

Article I states the fundamental obligation of the states parties:

> Each State Party to this Convention undertakes never in any circumstances to develop, produce, stockpile or otherwise acquire or retain:
>
> 1. microbial or other biological agents, or toxins whatever their origin or method of production, of types and in quantities that have no justification for prophylactic, protective or other peaceful purposes;
> 2. weapons, equipment or means of delivery designed to use such agents or toxins for hostile purposes or in armed conflict.

The broader scope of the Convention is evident from the description of the agents and toxins that fall under the prohibition. These are, interestingly, defined in a negative fashion, as having "no justification for ... peaceful purposes". The undertaking of the states parties does not repeat the prohibition on use, already laid down in the 1925 Protocol. It does, on the other hand, cover the development (etc.) "in any circumstances" – even the most adverse, it may be concluded: even, therefore, in the event of use of such weapons by the adverse party. Recourse to reprisals thus appears to be excluded.

Indeed, any violation of the Convention – and, a fortiori, any wartime use of a biological weapon or toxin – *may* lead to a complaint before the UN Security Council, which then, again, *may* initiate an investigation, the results of which it *shall* communicate to the states parties (Art. VI). What measures, if any, the Security Council decides upon depends on its appreciation of the situation in the light of the relevant Charter provisions.

Article VII of the Convention makes provision for the event that the Council "decides that [a] Party has been exposed to danger as a result of violation of the Convention"; this party may then request assistance, and "each State Party to this Convention undertakes to provide or support [such] assistance, in accordance with the United Nations Charter". Not a particularly effective enforcement system, and one that would certainly be insufficient in relation to any militarily more significant weapons – such as chemical weapons.

It took another twenty years for the international community to agree on the text of the 1993 Convention on the Prohibition of the Development, Production, Stockpiling and Use of Chemical Weapons and on Their Destruction. Accordingly, it is as complex and sophisticated as the Bacteriological Weapons Convention is simple and basic. Whereas the latter has no supervisory machinery, the Chemical Weapons Convention boasts a complete Organisation for the Prohibition of Chemical Weapons, established pursuant to Article VIII of the Convention and with head-quarters at The Hague.

As the title indicates, the Convention does not stop at prohibiting the development (etc.) of chemical weapons, but reaffirms and reinforces the prohibition on their use as well. The sixth paragraph of the preamble emphasises this:

> Determined for the sake of all mankind, to exclude completely the possi-bility of the use of chemical weapons, through the implementation of the provisions of this Convention, thereby complementing the obligations assumed under the Geneva Protocol of 1925.

Largely copying the opening article of the Bacteriological Weapons Convention, Article I(1) again reaffirms the undertaking of each state party "never under any circumstances" to develop (etc.) chemical weapons. Two differences should be noted. The article does not describe or define "chemical weapons", and paragraph 1 lists under (b) the prohib-ition "to use chemical weapons".

The matter of definition was a hot issue at the negotiating table. The result occupies the larger part of the long Article II. Yet in some respects the art-icle follows the scheme of the Bacteriological Weapons Convention: iden-tification of certain "toxic chemicals and their precursors, except where intended for *purposes not prohibited under this Convention*, as long as the types and quantities are consistent with such purposes" (sub-paragraph 1(a)), and of certain "munitions and devices, specifically designed to cause death or other harm through the toxic properties of those toxic chemicals specified in sub-paragraph (a), which would be released as a result of the employment of such munitions and devices" (sub-paragraph 1(b)). These are chemical weapons, "together or separately": a toxic chemical not intended for non-prohibited purposes constitutes by itself a chemical weapon.

More definitions follow: "toxic chemical" ("Any chemical which through its chemical action on life processes can cause death, temporary incapacitation or permanent harm to humans or animals"); "precursor" ("Any chemical reactant which takes part at any stage in the production by whatever method of a toxic chemical"); "key component of binary or multicomponent chemical systems" ("The precursor which plays the most important role in determining the toxic properties of the final product and reacts rapidly with other chemicals in the binary or multicomponent system"); and so on.

A crucial concept in the system is that of "purposes not prohibited under this Convention". As defined in Article II(9), such purposes mean:

(a) industrial, agricultural, research, medical, pharmaceutical or other peaceful purposes;
(b) protective purposes, namely those purposes directly related to protection against toxic chemicals and to protection against chemical weapons;
(c) military purposes not connected with the use of chemical weapons and not dependent on the use of the toxic properties of chemicals as a method of warfare;
(d) law enforcement including domestic riot control purposes.

It may be noted that apart from "peaceful purposes", this definition recognises the continuing need to prepare for protection, not only against toxic chemicals, but also against (the use of) chemical weapons; a poignant element of realism.

Equally realistic is the inclusion of "domestic riot control purposes" among the non-prohibited purposes. Tear gas and similar chemicals are in use as 'riot control agents' in many countries. Article II(7) defines riot control agents as "Any chemical not listed in a Schedule, which can produce rapidly in humans sensory irritation or disabling physical effects which disappear within a short time following termination of exposure." The notion of 'schedule' is clarified in notes to the sub-paragraphs defining "toxic chemicals" and "precursors": they are "contained in the Annex on Chemicals" and list those chemicals that "have been identified for the application of verification measures".

The existence of riot control agents implies the possibility of their use in situations of armed conflict. As set forth in Section 3.3.2, this is undesirable and ought to be prevented. Article I(5) accordingly contains the separate undertaking "not to use riot control agents as a method of warfare". Although not expressed in terms as categorical as the general prohibition on chemical weapons ("never under any circumstances"), this undertaking, together with all other provisions of the Convention, "shall not be subject to reservations" (Art. XXII). It may be recalled that in 1975 the United States reserved the right of "first use of riot control agents … in defensive military modes to save lives", giving as an example such use against rioting inmates of a prisoner-of-war camp. This reservation did not need to be made anew, since such use does not qualify as use "as a method of warfare". (The same goes for its reservation on first use of herbicides, which equally concerns protective, non-warfare purposes.)

The rather vague reference to use "as a method of warfare" leaves open the question of whether this covers all armed conflicts, or only international ones. The 1925 Geneva Protocol doubtless applies to 'war', that is, international armed conflict only. Arguably, the customary prohibition on use of chemical weapons had come to cover internal armed conflict as well. The tolerance of riot control agents in the Chemical Weapons Convention gives rise to the problem, however, that in a country which is the theatre of an internal armed conflict, tear gas may be used on one corner of the street in a 'riot control' mode to quell a local disturbance, and on another corner "as a method of warfare" to facilitate the capturing of members of a non-state armed group. It remains to be seen whether such warlike use in internal armed conflict can be – and should be – effectively precluded.

5.2   Other substantive developments

5.2.1   The San Remo Manual on Warfare at Sea

Like the law of war on land, law relating to warfare at sea has been in existence for centuries. However, apart from the rules for the protection of the wounded, sick and shipwrecked at sea in the Second Geneva Convention of 1949, its codification stopped almost completely after the Second Hague Peace Conference of 1907 which, as mentioned in Section 2.1, had done a great deal of work on it. The Diplomatic Conference of 1974–7, which had been given no mandate to take up the law of naval warfare, confined itself to stating in Article 49 of Protocol I that the rules on general protection of civilian populations against the effects of hostilities "apply to any land, air or sea warfare which may affect the civilian population, individual civilians or civilian objects" as well as "to all attacks from the sea or from the air against objectives on land". Again, the successive conferences that in the second half of the twentieth century codified and developed the general law of the sea, although well aware of the problem, had no such power either.

Many factors have contributed to this state of affairs. To mention just a few: matters are much more complicated now than they were in the pre-UN era; the sea is split up into more areas, the existence and activities of the United Nations have affected the relevance of neutrality, and the techniques of warfare on, beneath and over the sea waters have radically changed. In addition, relatively few states are actively involved in warfare at sea, and some of these are not keen to see the law relating thereto codified at a broadly composed international conference where all kinds of interests other than their own may determine the outcome.

In this situation (and as mentioned in Section 2.4), the San Remo International Institute of Humanitarian Law undertook to prepare and publish a document that would provide a reliable restatement of the law. The document was elaborated by a group of legal and naval experts from, or close to, governments but who participated in the work in their personal capacity, and representatives from the ICRC. It was published in 1994 as the San Remo Manual on International Law Applicable to Armed Conflicts at Sea.

The Manual covers a wide range of issues, several of them beyond the scope of this section (for instance, the relations between armed conflict and the law of self-defence; belligerent conduct and the position of neutrals in various regions of operations; interception, visit and search, diversion and capture of vessels and goods). Of interest for our purposes are Parts III (Basic rules and target discrimination) and IV (Methods and means of warfare at sea).

Section I (Basic rules) of Part III restates well-known principles: the absence of an unlimited right to choose methods or means of warfare; the principle of distinction between civilians and combatants and between civilian objects and military objectives; the definition of "military objective" as in Protocol I and the requirement that attacks be limited to military objectives – specifying that "[m]erchant vessels and civil aircraft are civilian objects unless they are military objectives in accordance with the principles and rules set forth in this document"; the prohibition of methods or means of warfare which "are of a nature to cause superfluous injury or unnecessary suffering" or are indiscriminate; the prohibition of conduct of hostilities on the basis of "no survivors"; the requirement that due regard be given to the natural environment; and, last but not least (in the light of history), the reminder that "[s]urface ships, submarines and aircraft are bound by the same principles and rules".

Section II (Precautions in attack) repeats the rules on that subject in Protocol I. Section VI adds specific precautions regarding civilian aircraft.

Section III lists classes of enemy vessels and aircraft that are exempt from attack, and the conditions for, and loss of such exemption. Exempted are, for instance: hospital ships and medical aircraft; vessels carrying supplies indispensable to the survival of the civilian population or engaged in relief actions; passenger vessels (when engaged only in carrying civilian passengers) and civilian aircraft. For vessels to be exempted they must: "(a) be innocently employed in their normal role; (b) submit to identification and inspection whenever required; and (c) not intentionally hamper the movement of combatants, and obey orders to stop and move out of the way when required" (rule 48). Non-compliance with these conditions results in loss of exemption and, with that, exposure to attack; in the case of the hospital ship, attacks are permitted only as a last resort and after other measures to mend the situation have remained without success (rules 49–51).

Both for hospital ships and other vessels that have lost exemption, attack may only follow if (rules 51, 52):

(a) diversion or capture is not feasible;
(b) no other method is available for exercising military control;
(c) the circumstances of non-compliance are sufficiently grave that the vessel has become, or may be reasonably assumed to be, a military objective; and
(d) the collateral casualties or damage will not be disproportionate to the military advantage gained or expected.

Similar rules apply to the loss of exemption of enemy aircraft and the consequences of such loss (rule 57).

For a vessel or aircraft to be, or "be reasonably assumed to be", a military objective it must make "an effective contribution to military action". In this regard, rule 58 prescribes that "[i]n case of doubt whether a vessel or aircraft exempt from attack is being used to make an effective contribution to military action, it shall be presumed not to be so used".

All other enemy merchant vessels may be attacked only if they meet the definition of a military objective. Section IV enumerates the activities that may render such vessels military objectives, for instance: carrying troops; being incorporated into the enemy intelligence-gathering system; sailing under convoy; or "otherwise making an effective contribution to military action, e.g., carrying military materials". The section provides similar rules for enemy civilian aircraft.

Section V sets forth comparable rules determining the conditions under which neutral merchant vessels and civilian aircraft may be attacked, including the reasonable belief that a vessel is carrying contraband or breaching a blockade, or a civilian aircraft is carrying contraband.

Section I of Part IV deals with means of warfare: missiles and other projectiles, torpedoes and mines. According to rule 78, "missiles and other projectiles, including those with over-the-horizon capabilities, shall be used in conformity with the principles of target discrimination as set out" in the basic rules and those on "precautions in attack". Torpedoes must "sink or otherwise become harmless when they have completed their run" (rule 79). Much more elaborate are the rules on use of mines (80–92). They permit "the denial of sea areas to the enemy" but add that this "shall not have the practical effect of preventing passage between neutral waters and international waters", and due regard must be paid to "the legitimate uses of the high seas by, *inter alia*, providing safe alternative routes for shipping of neutral States". Other rules lay down technical requirements for various types of mines, and provide for measures parties to the conflict are required to take after the cessation of active hostilities in order to "remove or render harmless the mines they have laid, each party removing its own mines".

Section II, on 'Methods of warfare', is in two parts. One, on blockade, begins by restating the traditional rules on that topic (including the wondrously simple rule 95 that "[a] blockade must be effective. The question whether a blockade is effective is a question of fact"). It then incorporates rules taken from other areas of humanitarian law: the prohibition of using blockades as a means of starving the civilian population, or in circumstances where a blockade may be expected to cause excessive damage to the civilian population "in relation to the concrete and direct military advantage anticipated from the blockade" (rule 102); the obligation to provide for free passage of foodstuffs and other essential supplies for the civilian population in the blockaded territory, subject to the right to prescribe technical arrangements and to the condition that the supplies are distributed "under the local supervision of a Protecting Power or a humanitarian organisation which offers guarantees of impartiality, such as the International Committee of the Red Cross" (rule 103); and the

obligation to "allow the passage of medical supplies for the civilian population or for the wounded and sick members of armed forces", again subject to a right to prescribe technical arrangements (rule 104).

The other part deals with the practice of naval powers to declare (sometimes huge) sea areas closed to all shipping that does not have express
permission to sail through such 'exclusion zones'. Tolerating the establishment of such a zone, at most, "as an exceptional measure", the Manual
emphasises that a belligerent cannot thereby be "absolved of its duties
under international humanitarian law", and specifies a series of rules the
belligerent must respect to minimise the adverse effects of the establishment of the zone.

Section III provides rules on deception, ruses of war and perfidy. One
(rule 109) relates to military and auxiliary aircraft in particular: these "are
prohibited at all times from feigning exempt, civilian or neutral status".

Rule 110 states that "ruses of war are permitted". Rather than providing
examples of permissible ruses, the rule goes on to provide a catalogue of
acts that are prohibited: "launching an attack whilst flying a false flag",
and "actively simulating the status", for instance, of hospital ships or
other vessels entitled to be identified by the emblem of the red cross or red
crescent or on humanitarian missions, or of passenger vessels carrying
civilians.

According to rule 111 "perfidy is prohibited". This provision then
repeats the definition of acts constituting perfidy in Article 37(1) of
Additional Protocol I of 1977. Instead of the list of perfidious acts in that
article, rule 111 provides its own set of examples: "Perfidious acts include
the launching of an attack while feigning: (a) exempt, civilian, neutral or
protected United Nations status; (b) surrender or distress by, e.g., sending
a distress signal or by the crew taking to life rafts."

The San Remo Manual covers much more ground than could be
reflected here. Even the above summary of Parts III and IV may be enough
to show that the authors of the document achieved the impressive feat of
merging the traditional law of sea warfare with principles and rules taken
from other areas of humanitarian law, working the whole into a set of
realistic rules that should be acceptable to naval powers – and in effect
have been adopted by several of these powers.

5.2.2   The HPCR Manual on Air and Missile Warfare

In contrast to warfare at sea, air warfare can claim no more than a century of existence. Yet, even at a time when aircraft were still a dream and

balloons the only man-made objects able to travel through the air, the potential power of flying devices as means of warfare was realised, witness Declarations III and XIV adopted, respectively, by the Hague Peace Conferences of 1899 and 1907, which temporarily prohibited "the discharge of projectiles and explosives from balloons *or by other new methods of a similar nature*".

The rapid increase, in and after the First World War, of air warfare capabilities, both in close air support and independent operations led, first, to the work of the six-member Commission of Jurists, which in 1923 produced the Hague Rules of Aerial Warfare; and in 1938, to the adoption by the Assembly of the League of Nations of a resolution that condemned the intentional bombing of civilian populations and formulated ground rules for air attacks on military objectives (see also Sections 2.1.2 and 3.3.4).

None of this had binding force, and also, after the Second World War, none of the lawmaking conferences of the period took up the task of codifying air warfare. Yet it should be noted that at the 1974–7 Diplomatic Conference, in contrast to naval warfare, the topic was not banned either; indeed, as noted before, in drafting the rules on protection of the civilian population the Conference was very much aware of, and duly took into account, the effects of attacks from the air.

Recent developments in the capabilities of air forces, both operating alone and in combination with ground forces, inspired the idea that a restatement of the law of air warfare was urgently needed. Taking up the gauntlet, the Harvard-based 'Program on Humanitarian Policy and Conflict Research' (or HPCR) in 2004 started a series of expert meetings including experienced air force officers as well as representatives of the ICRC, all of whom took part in a personal capacity, with intermittent consultations with interested outside parties. On 15 May 2009, the experts adopted the resultant 'Manual on International Humanitarian Law in Air and Missile Warfare', composed of 175 black-letter rules. The adoption was by consensus: although participants might not agree on every single rule, this did not keep them from accepting the final set of rules, at times on the understanding that their position would be reflected in the Commentary on the Manual, to be written by a core group. This was in fact done, for instance, with respect to ICRC minority positions on aspects of the notions of 'military objective' (see below in this section). Finally, on 4 March 2010, the Manual, together with the 323-page Commentary, was officially published.

The objective of the HPCR Manual being the restatement of "existing law applicable to air or missile operations in international armed conflicts" (thus, Rule 2(a) opening Section B, General Framework), the experts couched each rule in wording regarded as reflecting customary law. This might, but did not need to be (almost) identical to the text of provisions, for instance, in Protocol I of 1977. Experts were less certain about the state of customary law in non-international armed conflicts, hence the limitation to "operations in international armed conflicts". Even so, Rule 2(a) leaves open that "some of the Rules in this Manual [may apply] to noninternational armed conflicts"; the numerous instances of such application (and, with that, recognition of a rule's force as customary law in internal armed conflict) are not expressed in the text of the rule but in the Commentary.

Another matter settled in Section B concerns the position of UN forces. These may be present in the field (and in the air) in very different capacities, from observer to full-fledged fighter. Rule 3(a) states that, subject to binding Chapter VII decisions of the Security Council, the rules "also apply to all air or missile operations conducted by United Nations forces when in situations of armed conflict they are engaged therein as combatants, to the extent and for the duration of their engagement". Rule 3(b) adds that the rules "also apply to armed conflicts involving any other international governmental organization, global or regional" – think of NATO currently operating in Afghanistan. (See also Section 5.3.1b on the UN Secretary-General's Bulletin on observance by UN forces of international humanitarian law.)

As with the San Remo Manual on Sea Warfare, the HPCR Manual covers more ground than can be reflected here. No attention will be given, in particular, to the subjects of contraband, aerial blockade and neutrality. The remainder will be dealt with in succinct fashion, with focus on 'air or missile combat operations': a central notion defined in Rule 1 (composing Section A, on Definitions) as "air or missile operations designed to injure, kill, destroy, damage, capture or neutralize targets, the support of such operations, or active defence against them". (Since a missile operation is an 'air operation' as well, we use here the shorter phrase 'air operations', except in quotations.)

Rule 1 defines a weapon as "a means of warfare used in combat operations, including a gun, missile, bomb or other munitions, that is capable of causing either (i) injury to, or death of, persons; or (ii) damage to, or destruction of, objects" – in short, a weapon of war. Separately listed are: missiles ("self-propelled unmanned weapons – launched from aircraft, warships or land-based launchers – that are either guided or ballistic"), and precision-guided weapons ("weapons that can be directed against a target using either external guidance or a guidance system of their own").

Opening Section C (on Weapons), Rule 5 requires "weapons used in air and missile warfare" to comply with the principle of distinction and to respect the prohibition of unnecessary suffering. Rule 6 lists the types of (conventional, biological or chemical) weapon, the use of which is prohibited in any warfare (and that have been dealt with in earlier chapters of this book). Rule 9, rephrasing Article 36 of Protocol I, obligates states to "assess the legality of weapons before fielding them in order to determine whether their employment would, in some or all circumstances, be prohibited": a rule that has become accepted practice in more than one country.

Because of its topicality, Rule 8 deserves special attention. It asserts that a belligerent party that possesses precision-guided weapons is under "no specific obligation" to employ these. But neither does this leave the party entirely free whether to bring such weapons into play, or not: as the rule explains, there may be "situations in which the prohibition of indiscriminate attacks, or the obligation to avoid or – in any event – to minimize collateral damage, cannot be fulfilled without using precision guided weapons". In such situations, the choice is between using the available non-precision guided weapons regardless (which may imply the commission of a war crime) or desisting from the attack (and, as required, looking for an alternative, for instance, an operation by ground forces).

Section D, on attacks, like several of the sections that follow, is split into a part on general rules and one on specifics of air operations. The general part repeats well-established rules relating to attacks (Rules 10–15) and, for the party victim of the attack, to their consequences (search for and collect the wounded and sick, search for the dead; Rule 16). Of interest is the definition in Rule 10 of "lawful target", a term not found in relevant existing treaties. Listed are: combatants, military objectives and civilians directly participating in hostilities. The implication is that to the majority of the experts participating in the drafting process, the rules in the Manual relating to attacks on 'lawful targets' apply without distinction to attacks on combatants and on civilians directly participating in hostilities.

Rule 17, in the part on specifics, reserves the function of carrying out attacks to "military aircraft, including UCAVs". The acronym stands for "unmanned combat aerial vehicle", and this in turn "means an unmanned military aircraft of any size which carries and launches a weapon, or which can use onboard technology to direct such a weapon to a target": a weapon carrier that plays an important (and at times controversial) role in present-day warfare. It is noted in passing that neither the Manual nor the Commentary so much as mention the subject of 'targeted killing'.

Rule 18 repeats the rule that acts or threats of violence "cannot be pursued for the sole or primary purpose of spreading terror among the civilian population". In contrast, non-violent air operations with the same purpose are permissible. In effect, Rule 21 confines the application of the rules which prohibit "attacks directed against civilians or civilian objects, as well as indiscriminate attacks" to "air or missile attacks that entail violent effects, namely, acts resulting in death, injury, damage, or destruction".

Rule 19 requires belligerent parties "conducting, or subject to" air operations to take measures aimed at reducing the suffering caused by the operations. Most of these tasks will fall to the attacked party: it is, again, obliged to search for, collect and care for the wounded, sick and shipwrecked (a), and it should accept and facilitate the work of impartial humanitarian organisations (c). Both sides will be involved in doing what is required in (b): "whenever circumstances permit, arrange cease-fires, if necessary through a neutral intermediary, to facilitate the activities described in paragraph (a)".

Military objectives, the objects listed in Rule 10 under the 'lawful targets', are defined in Rule 1 with the exact words of Protocol I, Article 52(2). The various elements of the definition, in particular the qualifying factors 'nature', 'location', 'purpose' and 'use', are elaborated in Section E, in general (Rules 22–4) and for air operations in particular (Rules 25, 26). While much of this is self-evident, some elements deserve to be mentioned here.

Rule 22, opening Section E on military objectives, under (a) states that the 'nature' of an object "symbolizes its fundamental character", and adds a list of examples of objects that qualify as military objective in all circumstances. Under (b) ('location') it repeats and elaborates the statement made by numerous states upon ratifying Protocol I, that application of this criterion "can result in specific areas of land such as a mountain pass, a bridgehead or jungle trail becoming military objectives". Clarified is also (c) that 'purpose' refers to the "intended future use" of an object and (d) 'use' to its "present function".

Rule 23 provides a non-exhaustive list of objects which, by force of the criteria of Rules 1(y) and 22(a), may qualify as military objectives by nature: "factories, lines and means of communications (such as airfields, railway lines, roads, bridges and tunnels); energy producing facilities; oil storage depots; transmission facilities and equipment". The Commentary on Rule 23 explains that for the majority, such objects will "become military objectives by nature only in light of the circumstances ruling at the time". The minority, and the ICRC in particular, rejected the notion of a 'temporary nature' and felt that the listed objects could become military objectives only by use, purpose or location. Not surprisingly, objects meeting these descriptions figure regularly in news items questioning whether they could properly be attacked. A proper answer to such questions requires full information about the circumstances ruling at the time of the attack, including insight into what the attacking party knew or could reasonably have known.

Rule 25, opening the section on specifics, states the obvious: an aircraft may only be attacked if it is a military objective. Rule 26 adds that "[a]ll enemy military aircraft constitute military objectives, unless protected" (for instance, as a medical aircraft). And Rule 27, under the heading "activities that may render any other enemy aircraft a military objective", lists: hostile actions in support of the enemy (e.g. echoing '9/11': "being used as a means of attack"); "facilitating the military actions of the enemy's armed forces"; "assisting the enemy's intelligence gathering system"; and "refusing to comply with the orders of military authorities". Each of these categories is supplied with examples. Closing any possible gaps, the list ends with "otherwise making an effective contribution to military action".

Section F deals with the civilian taking a direct part in hostilities. Rule 28, rephrasing Article 51(3) of Protocol I, renders the law in a single line: "Civilians lose their protection from attack if and for such time as they take a direct part in hostilities." The Commentary on the rule discusses three issues that gave rise to controversy in the group of experts: the exact moments when direct participation begins and ends, the position of individuals who are members in non-state organised armed groups, and the 'revolving door' phenomenon (the 'farmer by day, fighter by night').

Rule 29 illustrates the rule with several concrete examples of activities that, "subject to the circumstances ruling at the time", may constitute such direct participation: defending military objectives against enemy attacks; engaging in electronic warfare; participation in target acquisition; operating weapon systems in air combat operations; training aircrews for specific requirements of a particular air combat operation, etc. Essential in this open-ended list is the reference to "the circumstances ruling at the time": determinant will be the details of each separate situation as these are, or may reasonably be deemed to be, known to the belligerent party facing the decision whether or not to attack particular civilians.

The Commentary on Rule 29 summarises three cumulative requirements identified in the Interpretive Guidance for an act to amount to direct participation in hostilities: the harm objectively likely to result from the act must reach a certain level and must be brought about in one causal step, and the act "must also be specifically designed to [inflict harm] in support of a Belligerent Party and to the detriment of the other" (the latter element indicated as "belligerent nexus"). The text notes that the requirements were not unanimously accepted: a number of experts maintained that "these criteria are not part of existing law and impose inappropriate constraints on the scope of direct participation in hostilities". Practice will have to show whether the criticism is justified.

The next topic in the HPCR Manual concerns precautions required of the attacking party (Section G) and of the party subject to attack (Section H). The generality of attacks on aircraft belongs in Section G; the protection of civilian aircraft in general follows in Section I; and the specific protection of civilian airliners, aircraft granted safe conduct and medical aircraft, in Sections J and L. Much (though not all) of this has to do with combat in the air, typically an area of warfare that largely remained untouched at the CDDH and therefore was most in need of expert structuring.

Rule 30, opening the general part (I) of Section G on precautions in attack, reminds the reader that "[c]onstant care must be taken to spare the civilian population, civilians and civilian objects". Rule 32 elaborates this broad principle into three specific precautions (each accompanied with an 'everything feasible' type clause): verify that a target is a lawful target and is not under special protection; choose a means or method of warfare with a view to avoiding, or at least minimising, collateral damage; and determine whether collateral damage would be excessive "in relation to the concrete and direct military advantage anticipated" (quoting the proportionality element in the definition of military objectives). Collateral damage is defined in Rule 1(l) as: "incidental loss of civilian life, injury to civilians and damage to civilian objects or other protected objects or a combination thereof, caused by an attack on a lawful target". Note that if the attack is itself unlawful, the question of whether incidental loss of life, injury or damage would qualify as collateral damage does not arise.

Part II of Section G, on specifics of air or missile operations, lists the diverse obligations upon the attacker, including the obligation to cancel or suspend an attack, that follow from the principles set forth in Part I. Worthy of note is the statement in Rule 39 that "[t]he obligation to take feasible precautions in attack applies equally to UAV/UCAV operations". A UAV, or unmanned aerial vehicle, is "an unmanned aircraft of any size which does not carry a weapon and which cannot control a weapon" but can operate, for instance, as an observer; and the UCAV, as noted before, is its armed counterpart.

Rule 40, in Part III on the specifics of attacks directed at aircraft in the air, specifies that while prior to such an attack, "all feasible precautions must be taken to verify that it constitutes a military objective", verification with "the best means available under the prevailing circumstances" should be done with due regard to "the immediacy of any potential threat" to the attacker. The rule suggests a number of relevant indicia, including pre-flight or in-flight air traffic control (ATC) information. Rule 41 adds that both belligerent and neutral states which provide such ATC service take steps to ensure that military commanders, including commanders of military aircraft, are continually informed of "designated routes assigned to, and flight plans filed by, civilian aircraft in the area of hostilities (including information on communication channels, identification modes and codes, destination, passengers and cargo)".

Rules 42–6, constituting Section H, summarise the rules in Protocol I on the precautions to be taken by the party under attack and need not be repeated here. Worthy of note is Rule 45, which, dealing with aspects of the 'human shield' problem, admonishes belligerent parties which are "actually or potentially subject to air or missile operations" not to use or profit by "the presence or movements of the civilian population or individual civilians", in order "to render certain points or areas immune from air or missile operations" or to shield or favour their own military operations, nor to themselves direct "the movement of the civilian population or individual civilians" for such purposes.

Section I deals with the specific aspects of protection of civilian aircraft. Part of the section concerns neutral aircraft; we pass this over in silence. As for enemy civilian aircraft, Rule 48(b) reaffirms that they are open to attack only if they are military objectives, and Rule 50, that this will be the case if they are "engaged in any of the activities set forth in Rule 27" referred to earlier.

Rules 53–7 deal with the "safety in flight" of civilian aircraft. These must, first, file their flight plans with the relevant ATC service. Other suggested measures include: not to deviate from designated routes (unless in unforeseen conditions, which then require immediate notification); avoid "areas of potentially hazardous military operations"; and, in the vicinity of hostilities, "comply with instructions from the military forces regarding their heading and altitude". In this respect, belligerent parties are reminded that whenever feasible, they should issue a Notice to Airmen, or NOTAM, with information about such hazardous military operations, including on "the activation of temporary airspace restrictions" (a feature, elaborated in Section P, of exclusion zones in international airspace and no-fly zones established by a belligerent party in its own or in enemy airspace).

Civilian airliners, given their role in international connections, qualify for the highest grade of feasible protection (or, as Rule 58 has it, for "particular care in terms of precautions"). Their fate – and, we note in passing, that of aircraft granted safe conduct – is the subject of Section J.

Civilian airliners are aircraft that are "identifiable as such and engaged in carrying civilian passengers in scheduled or non-scheduled service" (Rule 1(i)). The definition is wide enough to cover both the aircraft of regular airlines, those of charter companies (whose aircraft may or may not be flying on regular schedules) and business jets. It does not include civilian cargo aircraft whether "in scheduled or non-scheduled service", leaving them to the lesser general protection of Section I.

Rule 59 provides that "[i]n case of doubt, civilian airliners – either in flight or on the ground in a civilian airport – are presumed not to be making an effective contribution to military action". As for the airliner on the ground, the rule covers only the situation where it is actually "engaged in carrying civilian passengers", whether at the gate or taxiing to or from the runway. In these situations, communication with the aircraft or the control tower of the airport might be possible as well, enabling verification of the situation.

Once in flight, civilian airliners "ought to avoid entering a no-fly or an 'exclusion zone', or the immediate vicinity of hostilities". Rule 60 adds that mere entrance of such areas does not make them lose their protection.

Rule 63 discusses circumstances that "may render a civilian airliner a military objective". The first example, being on the ground in an enemy military airfield, is not of itself enough: required are also "circumstances which make that aircraft a military objective". The other examples follow the lines of Rule 27, closing with the same safety phrase as well: "otherwise making an effective contribution to military action".

Once a civilian airliner has been found to be a military objective, it may be attacked only if a series of further conditions are met. These are listed in Rule 68: diversion of the aircraft "for landing, inspection, and possible capture" is not feasible, and "military control" cannot be exercised in any other way. Then, the "circumstances leading to the loss of protection" must be "sufficiently grave to justify an attack", and "the expected collateral damage will not be excessive in relation to the military advantage anticipated and all feasible precautions have been taken". The example that again comes to mind is warding off a '9/11' type attack.

In accordance with this elevated status of protection and the difficult assessments involved, Rule 69 suggests that the actual decision to attack a civilian airliner "ought to be taken by an appropriate level of command". If the airliner is in flight, Rule 70 requires that it be warned "before any action is taken against it". In the rare cases where this situation may be expected to arise, the 'appropriate' level of command probably will have to be a fairly high military or even political one – unless instant action is required.

Under the heading 'specific protection', successive sections cover a variety of topics: medical and religious personnel, medical units and transports (K), medical aircraft (L), the environment (M) and "other persons and objects" (N) – a section that again serves as a receptacle for disparate items: civil defence, cultural property, objects indispensable to the survival of the civilian population, and UN personnel. Since many of the rules in these sections merely rephrase Protocol I language and are of limited interest from the perspective of air warfare, those rules shall not be discussed here.

Exception is made for Section L on medical aircraft, defined in Article 1(u) as "any aircraft permanently or temporarily assigned – by the competent authorities of a Belligerent Party – exclusively to aerial transportation or treatment of wounded, sick, or shipwrecked persons, and/or the transport of medical personnel and medical equipment or supplies". Such an aircraft "must be clearly marked with [the red cross, red crescent or red crystal] together with its national colours, on its lower, upper and lateral surfaces" (Rule 76(a)). A temporary medical aircraft that for one reason or another cannot be so marked, should use "the most effective means of identification available" (c), and generally, "additional means of identification" are advised (b). Rule 76(d) adds that means of identification "are intended only to facilitate identification and do not, of themselves, confer protected status". The opposite is equally true: the absence of an emblem or the lack of effective use of other means of identification do not deprive a medical aircraft of its protected status – yet expose it to greatly enhanced risk.

Rules 77 and 78 reflect the provisions in Protocol I concerning activities of medical aircraft in various areas: friendly, contested and enemy. In the latter two areas, express prior consent of the enemy is a prerequisite for effective activity. Rule 79 adds that any conditions the enemy attaches to such consent "must be adhered to strictly". Rule 86 notes that medical aircraft engaging in the search and collection of the wounded, sick or shipwrecked (a function not included in the terms of Rule 1(u)) without the requisite consent will act at their own risk. This rule also notes that "search-and-rescue aircraft used to recover military personnel, even if they are not military aircraft, are not entitled to protection".

Section O on humanitarian aid, after summarising the general rules on the topic (Rules 100–2), goes on to specify that "whenever circumstances permit", belligerent parties conducting air operations "ought to suspend air or missile attacks in order to permit the distribution of humanitarian assistance" (Rule 103). Concluding the section, Rule 104 provides examples of the "technical arrangements" that may have to be brought about in "allowing and facilitating" the "rapid and unimpeded passage of relief consignments, equipment and personnel" referred to in Rule 101. Listed are: the "establishment of air corridors or air routes"; the "organization of air drops"; "agreement on flight details (i.e. timing, route, landing)"; and "search of relief supplies".

Section P, on exclusion zones and no-fly zones, restates some important principles: establishing such zones does not absolve a belligerent party of "its obligations under the law of international armed conflict", and the zones may not be "designated for unrestricted air or missile attacks" (Rule 105). On the other hand, nothing in Section P deprives a belligerent of its rights "to control civil aviation in the immediate vicinity of hostilities" or to take defensive measures such as establishing a "war zone" (Rule 106).

Exclusion zones may be established in international airspace, and no-fly zones, in a party's own or enemy national airspace. Within an exclusion zone, no other "rules of the law of international armed conflict" apply than are applicable outside the zone, and its "extent, location and duration … and the measures imposed must not exceed what is reasonably required by military necessity" (Rule 107). No-fly zones may not only be established but be enforced as well: in particular, aircraft are warned that "entering a no-fly zone without specific permission" renders them "liable to be attacked" (Rules 108, 110).

Section Q, on 'deception, ruses of war and perfidy', follows the generally accepted lines on these topics as developed in Protocol I (Rules 111–13). Under the heading of 'Specifics of Air or Missile Operations', it lists as examples of perfidy, the feigning of diverse types of protected status as well as the feigning of surrender (Rule 114), and it specifically lists as "prohibited at all times": "Improper use by aircraft of distress codes, signals or frequencies" and "Use of any aircraft other than a military aircraft as a means of attacks" (Rule 115).

Rule 116 in turn lists several examples of ruses of war. Mentioned here is only the use of "False military codes and false electronic, optical or acoustic means to deceive the enemy (provided that they do not consist of distress signals, do not include protected codes, and do not convey the wrong impression of surrender)." Rule 117 reminds "[a]ircrews conducting military combat operations on land or on water – outside their aircraft – [that they] must distinguish themselves from the civilian population, as required by the law of international armed conflict".

Opening Section R, on 'espionage', Rule 118 defines espionage as the clandestine gathering by a spy of "information of military value in territory controlled by the enemy, with the intention of communicating it to the opposing Party". Rule 119 notes that this type of activity is "not prohibited under the law of international armed conflict". Military aircraft on information-gathering missions "are not to be regarded as carrying out acts of espionage" (Rule 123). Enemy military aircraft, whether or not so engaged, are obviously open to attack as military objectives (Rules 26, 27). Rule 124 provides that if a civilian aircraft of a belligerent party is "flying outside the airspace of or controlled by the enemy … in order to gather, intercept or otherwise gain information", that activity "is not to be regarded as espionage, although the aircraft may be attacked at such time as it is carrying out its information-gathering mission" (again, as per Rule 27, and with due regard to the precautions in attack as set forth in Sections D, I and J).

Sections S and T deal, respectively, with 'surrender' and 'parachutists from an aircraft in distress'. The sections are taken together here for the purpose of lifting out just one issue: the difficulty for a military aircrew in flight to indicate an intention to surrender. Rule 125 states the principle: "Enemy personnel may offer to surrender themselves (and the military equipment under their control) to a Belligerent Party." Coming to specifics, Rule 128 states the obvious: "Aircrews of a military aircraft wishing to surrender ought to do everything feasible to express clearly their intention to do so." As long as their aircraft is not in distress, and provided their opponents are aware that they might wish to surrender, the latter will continue to regard the aircraft as a dangerous object, though one which they may not shoot down regardless: Rule 126 recalls the prohibition "to deny quarter to those manifesting the intent to surrender". They may, on the other hand, "insist on the surrender ... being effected in a prescribed mode, reasonable in the circumstances" (Rule 129 adding that failure to obey "may render the aircraft and the aircrew liable to attack").

In the end, this 'reasonable mode' may consist of "parachuting from the aircraft", as the only credible way for the aircrew to "communicate their intentions"; thus, Rule 130. The moment they jump, the aircraft is in distress and will fall down somewhere. The crew members, on the other hand, are parachuting from an aircraft that at the moment of the jump was not in distress. This leaves them unprotected by the rule that "[n]o person descending by parachute from an aircraft in distress may be made the object of attack during his descent" (Rule 132, copying Article 42(1) of Protocol I). Even so, Rule 131 states that the crew members may not be attacked during their descent nor after touching ground, and are actually "entitled to prisoner of war status". The risk remains that they might be attacked, whether during or after their descent, by persons on the ground who are unaware of their intention to surrender. It will be for the party ordering the parachuting to communicate this circumstance to the people on the ground.

Section W, on combined operations, is the last section to be discussed here. Rule 160 defines a combined operation as "an operation in which two or more States participate on the same side of an international armed conflict, either as members of a permanent alliance or an *ad hoc* coalition" (i.e. respectively, NATO and a 'coalition of the willing'). The remaining rules deal with variations on the theme of what are the consequences, in practical terms, for a state party to Protocol I to join forces, say, with the United States which, as noted before, is not a party to the Protocol and does not regard all of its provisions as reflecting customary law. The variations boil down to statements that the legal obligations and responsibilities of the state party remain unchanged (Rules 161–3) and, interestingly, that a state "may participate in combined operations with States that do not share its obligations under the law of international armed conflict although those other States might engage in activities prohibited for the first State". In particular with respect to the last-mentioned situation, the 'first state' may wish to steer clear of those prohibited activities, if only to avoid the possibility of being held co-responsible for the acts.

5.2.3 *The Second Protocol to the 1954 Hague Convention for the Protection of Cultural Property in the Event of Armed Conflict*

The 1999 Second Protocol to the Hague Convention of 1954 for the Protection of Cultural Property in the Event of Armed Conflict, in force since 9 March 2004, "supplements the Convention in relations between the Parties" (Art. 2) and is open to states parties to the Convention (Arts. 41 and 42 in conjunction with Art. 1(d)). Retaining the definition of 'cultural property' given in Article 1 of the Convention (Art. 1(b)), it brings important changes to the rules on general protection (Chapter II), and it introduces an entirely new system of 'enhanced protection' (Chapter III), which for all practical purposes replaces the system of 'special protection' in the Convention. It has its own rule on 'scope of application' (Art. 3) and adds chapters on 'criminal responsibility and jurisdiction' (Chapter IV) and 'institutional issues' (Chapter VI).

The Protocol applies not only in international armed conflicts but also, unlike the Convention, without restriction in internal armed conflicts (Art. 3(1) in conjunction with Art. 22(1)). Article 3(2) contains the usual formula that if "one of the parties to an armed conflict is not bound by this Protocol, the Parties to this Protocol shall remain bound by it in their mutual relations", and such relations will also extend to "a State party to the conflict which is not bound by it, if the latter accepts the provisions of this Protocol and so long as it applies them". However, parties with lower case 'p', that is, non-state parties to a conflict, cannot become parties to the Protocol and thus cannot 'accept its provisions' either.

Paragraphs 2–6 of Article 22 (constituting Chapter V on 'The Protection of Cultural Property in Armed Conflicts not of an International Character') deal with the consequences of the Protocol's extended scope of application: it "does not apply to internal disturbances and tensions" (etc.), does not affect "the sovereignty of a State" (etc.), does not "prejudice the primary jurisdiction" of the state over violations of the Protocol, provides no justification for intervention, and "shall not affect the legal status of the parties to the conflict". Paragraph 7 adds that "UNESCO may offer its services to the parties" to an internal armed conflict.

Chapter II, on 'General Provisions regarding Protection', largely rewrites the rules of 1954 in the language of the 1977 Protocols. 'Imperative military necessity', the term used in the Convention to indicate when 'respect' may be waived, is no longer the sole determinant for this step and has been supplemented with a set of conditions that are derived from Additional

Protocol I. Central is the condition that a waiver on that basis "may only be invoked to direct an act of hostility against cultural property when and for as long as: (i) that cultural property has, *by its function*, been made into a military objective" (Art. 6(a)). A "military objective" is defined in Article 1(f) in terms identical to Article 52(2) of Protocol I, requiring both that the object "by its nature, location, purpose or use makes an effective contribution to military action" and that its "total or partial destruction, capture or neutralisation, in the circumstances ruling at the time, offers a definite military advantage". The term 'function' in Article 6(a) serves to emphasise that cultural property will rarely be a military objective by its nature or purpose (a nineteenth-century artillery piece may be a monument but is no longer a military objective).

Invocation of the waiver should be a high-level decision. Article 6(c) prescribes that it "shall only be taken by an officer commanding a force the equivalent of a battalion in size or larger, or a force smaller in size where circumstances do not permit otherwise". The concluding part of the sentence betrays the same sense of realism that may be perceived in the next sub-paragraph, where "an effective advance warning" is required "whenever circumstances permit". General protection, in one word, is bound to remain contingent on circumstances.

Articles 7 and 8 introduce the notions of 'precautions in attack' and 'precautions against the effects of hostilities', in terms borrowed from Articles 57 and 58 of Protocol I. Article 9 aims to reinforce the rules in the Convention for the protection of cultural property in occupied territory. It may be noted in passing that since the Protocol is supplementary to the 1954 Convention, there was no need to repeat the prohibitions, embodied in Article 4(1) and (4) of that instrument, against directing any act of hostility, and in particular any act by way of reprisals, against cultural property.

Cultural property can only be placed under 'enhanced protection' if it is: (a) "cultural heritage of the greatest importance to humanity"; (b) "protected by adequate domestic legal and administrative measures recognising its exceptional cultural and historic value and ensuring the highest level of protection"; (c) "not used for military purposes or to shield military sites"; and "the Party which has control" over the property must have made "a declaration ... that it will not be so used" (Chapter III, Art. 10).

The phrase "greatest importance to humanity" in Article 10(a) needed to be distinguished from the notion of "outstanding universal value", which is the determinant factor in the 1972 Convention Concerning the Protection of the World Cultural and Natural Heritage for recognition of objects as belonging to the 'cultural heritage'. This task of interpretation fell to the Committee for the Protection of Cultural Property in the Event of Armed Conflict, the executive organ of the Protocol that is composed of twelve states parties elected by the Meeting of the Parties (and who should "choose as their representatives persons qualified in the fields of cultural heritage, defence or international law" (Arts. 23, 24)).

The formula the Committee has drafted is that "while considering whether cultural property is of greatest importance for humanity [it] will evaluate, case by case, its exceptional cultural significance, and/or its uniqueness, and/or if its destruction would lead to irretrievable loss for humanity" (paragraph 32 of the 'Guidelines for the Implementation of the 1999 Second Protocol' (etc.), endorsed by the Third Meeting of the Parties on 24 November 2009).

Article 11 provides that a state "which has jurisdiction or control over the cultural property" may request that it be included in the List of Cultural Property under Enhanced Protection, established and maintained for that purpose by the Committee (Art. 27(1)(b)). It continues with the Committee sending the request to all states parties (which may object, by a 'representation'); as the case may be, consultation of governmental or non-governmental organisations and individual experts; and decision by the Committee, in the event of a 'representation', by a four-fifth majority. Article 11 also provides for an emergency procedure in the event of an outbreak of hostilities, which may lead to a provisional enhanced protection, pending the outcome of the regular procedure.

"Enhanced protection shall be granted to cultural property by the Committee from the moment of its entry in the List" (Art. 11(10)). This makes the Committee the grantor for the duration of the enhanced protection. The Parties (with capital P) to a conflict are the ones who must "ensure the immunity" of cultural property so protected, "by refraining from making [it] the object of attack or from any use of the property or its immediate surroundings in support of military action" (Art. 12).

Cultural property under enhanced protection loses this protection, first, "if such protection is suspended or cancelled in accordance with Article 14", and, secondly, "if, and for as long as, the property has, by its use, become a military objective" (Art. 13(1)). In the latter case, the property may be "the object of attack", but only under the stringent conditions listed in paragraph 2: (a) that the use cannot be terminated in any other feasible way; (b) that all feasible precautions are taken to avoid, or in any event minimise, damage to the property; and (c) that the order is given "at the highest operational level of command", the "opposing forces" have been effectively warned and required to terminate the forbidden use, and have been left reasonable time to "redress the situation" (the conditions under (c), except for the case of "immediate self-defence", in Art. 13(2)). Note that 'military necessity', whether imperative or other, is no longer mentioned, and the contingency factor has been reduced to the barest minimum.

While Article 13(2) deals with the military reaction to forbidden use of cultural property under enhanced protection, Article 14(2) focuses on the consequences for its legal status: when it is used "in support of military action, the Committee may suspend its enhanced protection status". When the forbidden use is continuous, "the Committee may exceptionally cancel the enhanced protection status by removing the cultural property from the List". Apart from this case of forbidden use, the Committee may suspend or cancel the status of enhanced protection whenever "cultural property no longer meets any one of the criteria" set forth in Article 10; in case of cancellation, again, the property is removed from the List (Art. 14(1)).

It may be noted that each of the above provisions, wherever necessary, is commented upon in the above Guidelines, drafted by the Committee and adopted by the Meeting of the Parties as a 'concise and practical tool' aiming to embody the 'best practices' in the implementation of the Protocol.

Opening Chapter IV, Article 15 deals with 'serious violations' of the Protocol. These are acts committed "intentionally and in violation of the Convention or this Protocol" and listed in paragraph 1. Three are especially serious: (a) "making cultural property under enhanced protection the object of attack"; (b) "using such property or its immediate surroundings in support of military action"; and (c) "extensive destruction or appropriation" of cultural property under general protection, whether under the Convention or the Protocol. The remaining two are simply 'serious': (d) making the latter class of cultural property "the object of attack", and (e) "theft, pillage or misappropriation of, or acts of vandalism against, cultural property protected under the Convention".

Each party to the Protocol must ensure that the above acts are "criminal offences" under their domestic law and are "punishable by appropriate penalties". In doing so, they must "comply with general principles of law and international law, including the rules extending individual criminal responsibility to persons other than those who directly commit the act" (Art. 15). And Article 16(1) requires each party to make sure that it has jurisdiction over the offences of Article 15:

- in respect of all those offences, when the offence is committed in its territory or by one of its nationals (the territoriality and nationality principles of jurisdiction);

- in respect of the especially serious offences listed under (a)–(c), also "when the alleged offender is present in its territory" – an application of the universality principle.

Article 16(2), while not precluding the existence of jurisdiction on other grounds, specifies that the provisions of the Protocol on criminal responsibility and jurisdiction do not apply to the members of the armed forces of a non-party state, party to the conflict, that accepts and applies the provisions of the Protocol.

Articles 17 to 20 provide rules concerning prosecution, extradition and mutual legal assistance, and grounds for refusal of extradition or mutual legal assistance. Article 21, closing Chapter IV, obliges Parties to adopt the requisite measures "to suppress the following acts when committed intentionally":

(a) any use of cultural property in violation of the Convention or the Protocol; and
(b) any "illicit export, other removal or transfer of ownership of cultural property from occupied territory", once again, in violation of the Convention or the Protocol.

Chapter VI, on institutional issues, provides for the establishment of three organs: the Meeting of the Parties and the Committee for the Protection of Cultural Property in the Event of Armed Conflict, both mentioned above, and a Fund for the Protection of Cultural Property in the Event of Armed Conflict, designed to provide financial or other assistance in peacetime in support of certain preparatory measures and, during or after armed conflict, in relation to emergency or other measures for the protection or recovery of cultural property (Art. 29).

Chapter VII contains provisions on: dissemination and instruction (specifying that "[a]ny military or civilian authorities who, in time of armed conflict, assume responsibilities with respect to the application of this Protocol, shall be fully acquainted with the text thereof" (Art. 30(3)); international cooperation in situations or serious violations (Art. 31, copying Art. 89 of Additional Protocol I but with UNESCO mentioned besides the UN); 'international assistance' by the Committee in particular in respect of cultural property under enhanced protection (Art. 32); and 'technical assistance' by UNESCO (Art. 33).

Chapter VIII, on execution of this Protocol, provides that it "shall be applied with the co-operation of the Protecting Powers responsible for safeguarding the interests of the Parties to the conflict" (Art. 34). Article 35 defines a 'good offices' function protecting powers may fulfil "where they may deem it useful in the interests of cultural property". For the (likely) event that no protecting powers are appointed, Article 36 attributes a conciliatory role to the Director-General of UNESCO as well as to the Chairman of the Committee.

5.2.4   Optional Protocol to the Convention on the Rights of the Child on the Involvement of Children in Armed Conflict

Article 38 of the Convention on the Rights of the Child (1989, in force since 1990) urges states to "ensure that persons who have not attained the age of fifteen years do not take a direct part in hostilities" and not to recruit such young persons into their armed forces; and in recruiting among children between fifteen and eighteen years of age, they must "endeavour to give priority to those who are oldest" (paras. 2, 3). The text copies Article 77(2) of Protocol I of 1977, demonstrating the close links between the Red Cross and human rights communities in their combat against child participation in hostilities.

Always on the same track, the 26th International Conference of the Red Cross and Red Crescent in 1995 included in Resolution 2 on protection of the civilian population in a period of armed conflict, a strong condemnation of "recruitment and conscription of children under the age of 15 years in the armed forces or armed groups", as well as a recommendation that "parties to conflict refrain from arming children under the age of 18 years and take every feasible step to ensure that children under the age of 18 years do not take part in hostilities". The Conference also expressed its support for the work being done by the UN Commission on Human Rights on "an optional Protocol to the 1989 Convention on the Rights of the Child, the purpose of which is to increase the protection of children involved in armed conflicts". The efforts of this Commission ultimately resulted in the adoption by the UN General Assembly, on 25 May 2000, of the Protocol with the above title (in force since 12 February 2002).

Article 1 requires states to "take all feasible measures to ensure that members of their armed forces who have not attained the age of 18 years do not take a direct part in hostilities"; and Article 2 draws the logical consequence: states must ensure that children below eighteen "are not compulsorily recruited into their armed forces".

Voluntary recruitment is the topic of Article 3. A state that permits such recruitment below the age of eighteen must (1) establish a minimum age somewhere above the bottom line of fifteen years (except for "schools operated by or under the control of the armed forces"); (2) "deposit a binding declaration" that sets forth this chosen minimum age, as well as "a description of the safeguards it has adopted to ensure that such recruitment is not forced or coerced". And it must (3) ensure that recruitment is voluntary and the recruit is informed of the duties involved in military service, has the requisite parental or legal consent, and has provided "reliable proof of age".

Article 4 tackles the delicate topic of recruitment into non-state armed groups. The formula used in the article, "armed groups that are distinct from the armed forces of a State", covers situations of both international and internal armed conflict. These groups are admonished "not, under any circumstances, [to] recruit or use in hostilities persons under the age of 18 years" (para. 1). States must do everything feasible to prevent such recruitment and use, including through "the adoption of legal measures necessary to prohibit and criminalize such practices" (para. 2). And, of course, "the application of the present article shall not affect the legal status of any party to an armed conflict".

The remaining nine articles as well as the eighteen preambular paragraphs of this Protocol may be left undiscussed here. For present purposes, it may suffice to note that the above substantive provisions signify a marked improvement over the earlier texts, both of Article 38 of the Convention on the Rights of the Child and of the 1977 Protocols. Implementation of the new rules may pose no problems in many countries where child recruitment has been abandoned for quite some time. In other countries, the detailed rules on implementation, reporting and supervision may contribute to overcoming the practical obstacles that stand in the way of age restrictions on recruitment into the armed forces.

A point of major interest is the separate provision Article 4 makes for the non-state armed groups. Especially though not exclusively in many situations of internal armed conflict, the practice of involving young children in the hostilities – or into the bestialities that went under that name – has been all too visible on the daily news. The appeal, extended to these groups, to desist from involving children in their warlike activities will need a lot of persuasion. Here, the humanitarian-law character of the rule may come to light in that often, the ICRC through its presence in the field may be better placed than are human rights bodies to bring pressure to bear on leaders and communities not to permit children to bear the brunt of the fighting. The "legal measures necessary to prohibit and criminalize" child recruitment in internal armed conflict may also help, afterwards. In this respect, it is of interest to note that the ICC is presently dealing in one of its cases with the recruitment and conscription of children under fifteen years of age and the deployment of these children as active participants in hostilities (see Section 5.3.4e).

5.2.5 Protocol III Additional to the Geneva Conventions of 1949: the 'Red Crystal'

As mentioned several times in the foregoing, from its creation in 1948 Israel has refused to use either the red cross or the red crescent as an emblem for its medical services, and instead adopted Magen David Adom, or the Red Shield of David, an emblem that had already been in use with the Jewish settlers in the area since the 1930s. On 8 December 1949, upon signing the Geneva Conventions, it made the reservation that "while respecting the inviolability of the distinctive signs and emblems of the Convention, Israel will use the Red Shield of David as the emblem and distinctive sign of the medical services of her armed forces".

Having the same emblem in its name, instead of the red cross or red crescent as required under the Statutes of the International Red Cross and Red Crescent Movement, Israel's national society could not be recognised as its official 'red cross type' organisation and thus remained excluded from membership of the movement. The Palestine Red Crescent Society could not be admitted either, because Palestine was (and is) not a recognised state (this being yet another condition of admission to the movement). Both societies were not, however, completely isolated from the outside world: they were admitted as observers to the international conferences and similar occasions – but this left the problem unresolved.

Its resolution has taken more than half a century and in the end required a series of steps. First, on 28 November 2005, a Memorandum of Understanding and an Agreement on Operational Arrangements were concluded between the Magen David Adom Society and the Palestine Red Crescent Society, about mutual respect and cooperation. This paved the way for the adoption, on 8 December 2005, by a diplomatic conference of states parties to the Geneva Conventions of 1949 convened for that purpose, of Protocol III Additional to the Geneva Conventions of 1949, creating yet another distinctive emblem. The Protocol officially styles it the 'third Protocol emblem' and defines it as "a red frame in the shape of a square on edge on a white ground" (Art. 2(2)).

The next steps came in rapid succession: on 21 June 2006, the 29th International Conference of the Red Cross and Red Crescent resolved, first, to amend the Statutes of the Movement – not by adding the Red Shield of David but – by replacing the list of emblems with the words "the distinctive emblems recognized by the Geneva Conventions and their Additional Protocols", thus enabling admission of the Magen David Adom Society. Second, the Conference decided that the new emblem would "henceforth be designated as the 'red crystal'". And third, the ICRC having announced its decision to recognise both this society and the Palestine Red Crescent Society (as required under the Statutes of the Movement), the Conference requested the Federation of Red Cross and Red Crescent Societies to admit both societies as members. The state delegations to the Conference then left the room while the delegations of the national societies, the ICRC and the International Federation of Red Cross and Red Crescent Societies constituted themselves into the General Assembly of the Federation and in that capacity welcomed the two societies with applause, thus bringing to a close a bitter dispute that long had been held insoluble.

Protocol III, a full-fledged treaty with a page-long preamble and seventeen articles, in Article 2 creates the new emblem as a distinctive and protective emblem on the same footing as the existing emblems.

Article 3 regulates the indicative use of the red crystal by national societies of those states parties which decide to use the emblem. Such a national society may "incorporate within it, for indicative purposes", emblems recognised by the Geneva Conventions (meaning the red cross and the red crescent) or "another emblem which has been in effective use by a High Contracting Party and was the subject of a communication to the other High Contracting Parties and the International Committee of the Red Cross through the depositary prior to the adoption of this Protocol" – a formula that for all practical purposes may be abbreviated to the Red Shield of David. This society may then also use the name of this other emblem (in effect, its own name), and may display it without the red crystal frame on its national territory.

Article 4 permits the ICRC and the International Federation of Red Cross and Red Crescent Societies to "use, in exceptional circumstances and to facilitate their work", the red crystal; and Article 5 opens the possibility for "medical services and religious personnel participating in operations under the auspices of the United Nations" to use, "with the agreement of participating States", any one of the distinctive emblems mentioned in Articles 1 and 2. In either case, the reason for these organisations and persons to prefer one emblem over another may be that, unfortunately, the latter emblem is being targeted rather than respected.

Protocol III entered into force on 14 January 2007, and on 22 November 2007 Israel ratified the instrument.

5.2.6   The notion of armed conflict: variations on a theme

As noted in Section 1.2, the last quarter of the twentieth century and the opening years of the twenty-first were characterised by a high incidence of at times exceedingly violent and cruel armed conflict, with many of the long-established principles and rules of international humanitarian law being openly flouted: hostage taking, express targeting of protected persons and objects (civilians, Red Cross and Red Crescent personnel, ambulances), etc. Few of these armed conflicts were international, in the proper sense of armed conflict between states. A number were internal (e.g. Sudan, Sri Lanka, Colombia) or mixed (the break-up of Yugoslavia). The remaining situations, while unmistakably armed conflicts, did not fit very well under either heading: e.g. Israel vs Hezbollah in Lebanon and vs Hamas in the Gaza Strip, the United States and allies against Al Qaeda and the Taliban in Afghanistan.

In reaction to these events, ever greater chunks of the law of armed conflict originally written for international armed conflict were made, or declared to be, applicable in situations of non-international armed conflict as well. This development is dealt with in Section 5.2.7. Another reaction has been the debate about the law that should be held applicable to conflicts of the latter type: this matter is briefly discussed here.

In immediate reaction to the attacks of 11 September 2001 on the World Trade Center in New York and the Pentagon in Washington, the President of the United States declared war on Al Qaeda, terming it a 'war on terror'. This 'war' soon assumed diverse shapes. Operation Enduring Freedom, the US-led military operations against Al Qaeda forces and the Taliban in Afghanistan, showed all the characteristics of an armed conflict. This was not the case with the stealthy operations carried out worldwide by the CIA in attempts to eliminate or capture and detain individual persons suspected of terrorist activities or inclinations: carried out outside the context of an armed conflict between territorially definable parties, these operations could more properly be styled law (or rather policy) enforcement measures, governed by the relevant rules of constitutional law, criminal substantive and procedural law, and human rights law.

Operation Enduring Freedom in its initial phase was conducted, alongside an internationally recognised but virtually absent 'government', against Al Qaeda, a non-territorially bound, evasive grouping, and the Taliban, an armed group located in the Afghan territory and exercising de facto governmental power. Once the Taliban had been ousted from government, armed activities continued in Afghanistan, with Al Qaeda even less tangible than before, the Taliban in the role of a non-state organised armed group, and an internationally recognised government no longer absent. In either situation, the operations amounted to an armed conflict. (At the same time, the UN-mandated NATO International Security Assistance Force, or ISAF, has since 2004 operated alongside the Afghan government, in what variously amounts to protecting the population, improving its living conditions, training Afghan security forces and fighting against the Taliban.)

More precisely, the first phase of Operation Enduring Freedom was an inter-state armed conflict, governed by the law of international armed conflict. In the second phase, the war between the central government and the Taliban was (and, as of this writing, is) an internal armed conflict, governed by Article 3 common to the 1949 Conventions and such further principles and customary rules as may be deemed applicable in this situation. As for the activities of the United States, given the level of its involvement and the means and methods of warfare deployed, its military operations could best be held against the yardstick of the law of international armed conflict.

In general terms, armed conflicts involving one state and a non-state armed group located in another state's territory may assume many different shades and colours. When it comes to determining what law to apply to the extraterritorial operations of a state engaging in armed conflict with a non-state armed group on another state's territory, one situation is beyond question: when the first state directs its military operations against the territorial state as well, the situation indubitably constitutes an international armed conflict. For all other situations, the main consideration should be one of law of war policy: any significant fighting on another state's territory requires the most complete, most solidly established set of principles and rules, that is, the law of international armed conflict. The sole exception might be a case of small-scale military operations joining in the efforts of the local government in an ongoing internal armed conflict – a situation that might involve respect for the locally applicable human rights norms as well.

5.2.7 Making the law of war applicable in internal armed conflict

As recorded in earlier chapters, the body of law of war applicable in internal armed conflicts has grown from its modest beginnings (Article 3 common to the four Geneva Conventions of 1949) to include ever more principles and rules. Protocol II of 1977 was written for internal armed conflict, and the 1954 Cultural Property Convention with its 1999 Second Protocol and the 1980 Conventional Weapons Convention with its Protocols became ever more completely applicable to such conflicts. Beyond treaty law, developments could be noted in the areas of principles and customary law as well. An early example was Resolution 2444 (XXIII) by which the UN General Assembly in 1968 recognised some basic principles of protection of the civilian population as applicable in all armed conflicts. Then, the ICRC in 2005 published its long-expected study on Customary International Humanitarian Law, which posits that the majority of the 161 rules it identifies have force of law in internal armed conflict as well.

A similar claim was made in 2006, with the publication by the San Remo International Institute of Humanitarian Law of a Manual on the Law of Non-International Armed Conflict, with Commentary. Like the San Remo Manual on International Law Applicable to Armed Conflicts at Sea and the HPCR Manual on International Law Applicable in Air and Missile Warfare, the Manual on the Law of Non-International Armed Conflict is presented as an authoritative restatement of the law governing internal armed conflicts, meaning that it reflects customary law without itself being a source of law. And like the ICRC study, it covers the entire range of rules of armed conflict.

This impressive mass of treaty and customary law, stated to be applicable in internal armed conflict and to be binding on non-state parties as well, stands in stark contrast to the actual practice in the field. One factor is the impossibility for non-state parties to become party to the treaties laying down the rules they are expected to respect. Nor do the treaties create the possibility for them to declare their acceptance of the rules (as extended in Protocol I of 1977 to the authorities representing peoples seeking self-determination, see Section 4.1.2).

In this respect, it may be noted that the 27th International Conference of the Red Cross and Red Crescent (1999) in its 'Plan of Action for the years 2000–2003' included a clause urging "organised armed groups in non-international armed conflict … to respect international humanitarian law. They are called upon to declare their intention to respect that law and teach it to their forces." The appeal correctly combined the mere verbally declared intention with the requirement of actual instruction of the group's armed forces, as an indispensable step towards implementation. Unfortunately, the appeal appears to have drawn no reactions, nor did subsequent International Red Cross and Red Crescent Conferences (2003, 2007) return to the point.

Another, more narrowly focused and result-oriented approach has been followed since 2000 by Geneva Call, a Geneva-based non-governmental organisation. Focusing also on non-state armed groups, it attempts gradually to convince them of the need and utility of committing themselves to the total ban of anti-personnel landmines (defined as "those devices which effectively explode by the presence, proximity or contact of a person, including other victim-activated explosive devices and anti-vehicle mines with the same effect whether with or without anti-handling devices"). A group that accepts this commitment signs a document confirming the fact (the 'Deed of Commitment under Geneva Call for Adherence to a Total Ban on Anti-Personnel Mines and for Cooperation in Mine Action'). Signature implies acceptance of monitoring and verification by Geneva Call, which may publish its findings. On the other hand, Geneva Call supports the group in its efforts at implementation through training activities, facilitating technical support for the destruction of stockpiles, etc.

Over the years and to this day, Geneva Call has succeeded in inspiring a significant number of non-state armed groups to sign and live up to the Deed of Commitment. It is presently exploring the possibility of applying the same format (of a narrowly defined commitment completed with acceptance of monitoring and verification) to two other areas, viz., the protection of children and of women.

The ICRC, for its part, applying its long-established method of work, combines advocacy with supervision in today's internal armed conflicts as well. Depending on the situation, it may broadly address all parties on the entire area of humanitarian law or, rather, focus on a specific armed group and attempt to convince it of the need (and utility) of respecting some particular rule, for instance, to keep prisoners alive; and, once this works, expand the range of accepted rules. In contrast with Geneva Call, the ICRC does not normally publish its results except in general terms.

5.3 International and domestic actors

5.3.1 The United Nations

5.3.1a The Security Council

As noted in Section 2.3, interest at the United Nations in the law of armed conflict and its development long remained rhetoric, with the General Assembly passing resolutions about items on its agenda under the heading 'human rights in armed conflicts'. Changes in the political climate, culminating in the fall of the Berlin Wall, led to a more action-oriented stance in matters of armed conflict and, with that, away from the General Assembly and onto the Security Council. Acting under its Charter mandate and with 'concern' shifting to 'condemnation', this body began to speak out against situations of "gross violations of human rights and humanitarian law". Interestingly, its resolutions and presidential statements (a means of expression below the level of a formal resolution) rarely did (and still rarely do) distinguish between international and internal armed conflicts, and 'the rules of humanitarian law' were and are simply referred to without any specificity, although often with special reference to the need to respect and protect the civilian population.

Apart from adopting resolutions and statements on specific situations, the Security Council has developed a practice of holding general debates on particular issues, based on reports by the Secretary-General. Thus, the Council regularly holds debates on the fate of the civilian population in armed conflicts, and of women and children in particular. Another topic for some time under discussion was the proliferation of small arms and what could be done to stem their rapid spread. Such debates, although not necessarily leading to concrete steps, have proved to be useful policy-setting devices that may spur UN members and others on towards further action in the fields concerned.

In addition to these verbal exercises, the Security Council has also initiated more specific action. Thus, in the 1980–8 war between Iraq and Iran, the Secretary-General, on the instructions of the Council, repeatedly sent missions to the field to verify whether, as alleged, chemical weapons had been used, and the successive reports that confirmed these allegations each time led to sharp rebukes from the Council (which, unfortunately, were not enough to make the accused party change its policy).

The invasion and occupation of Kuwait by Iraq, 1990–1, provided an opportunity for the practical application of the obligation to make reparations for violations of the applicable law, including in respect of individual victims. The Security Council by Resolution 687 (1991) created the UN Compensation Commission and entrusted it with reviewing and awarding claims for compensation for losses suffered as a direct result of Iraq's invasion of Kuwait. Although the Commission deals principally with losses arising from Iraq's unlawful use of force (the *jus ad bellum* aspect), it has also awarded compensation for the consequences of violations of the law of armed conflict, including occupation law, suffered by individuals (such as hostage taking or pillage of private property). Although military costs and the claims of military personnel are excluded from the competence of the Commission, compensation was nevertheless awarded to members of the Allied Coalition Armed Forces held as prisoners of war whose injury resulted from mistreatment in violation of international humanitarian law. (See further Section 5.3.6a.)

While the above actions of the Security Council usually addressed the party or parties concerned, its decisions to establish the Yugoslavia and Rwanda Tribunals, each preceded by reports of commissions of enquiry into the incidence of serious violations of humanitarian law in the respective territories, were based on the notion of individual criminal liability.

A similar case has been the long-term Security Council involvement in the situation of armed conflict in Darfur, a region of Sudan. The Council in 2004 requested an international commission of enquiry to "investigate reports of violations of international humanitarian law and human rights law in Darfur by all parties, to determine also whether or not acts of genocide have occurred, and to identify the perpetrators of such violations with a view to ensure that those responsible are held accountable". In its report of 25 January 2005 the Commission noted that although its findings did not warrant the conclusion that government authorities had pursued a genocidal policy in Darfur, evidence showed that other international crimes, such as crimes against humanity and war crimes, had been committed. Identifying a number of likely suspects, the Commission strongly recommended that the Security Council "immediately refer the situation of Darfur to the International Criminal Court" and that it establish "a Compensation Commission designed to grant reparation to the victims of the crimes, whether or not the perpetrators of such crimes have been identified". The Security Council quickly followed up the first suggestion: on 31 March 2005 it referred "the situation in Darfur since 1 July 2002 to the Prosecutor of the International Criminal Court" (see further Section 5.3.4). In contrast, up to this day it has taken no action to organise compensation for victims.

5.3.1b   The Secretary-General

As mentioned in the previous sub-section, one function of the Secretary-General is to provide the Security Council with reports on a variety of topics, both on the invitation of the Council or independently. Included in the constant stream of reports are those that deal with matters of armed conflict, whether on specific situations of conflict (the Democratic Republic of Congo, Colombia, Sri Lanka, etc.) or on specific issues of combatant behaviour (use of particular weapons, child soldiers, treatment of women and children, etc.). Through this instrument, the Secretary-General is able to exert considerable influence on the decision making at the Council, whether in regard to matters already on its agenda or to issues the Secretary-General wishes to see there.

The need to verify a concrete situation has more than once occasioned the Secretary-General to establish commissions of enquiry. Mentioned just above were the missions sent out to investigate the use of chemical weapons in the 1980–8 war between Iraq and Iran, and the Darfur Commission. Other examples have been the commissions of experts set up to collect information about serious violations of humanitarian law that preceded the establishment of the ad hoc international tribunals for Yugoslavia and Rwanda, dealt with in Section 5.3.3.

Of an entirely different order again was the publication, in 1999, of the 'Secretary-General's Bulletin on Observance by United Nations Forces of International Humanitarian Law'. The Bulletin, the outcome of prolonged debate and negotiations between the UN Secretariat, the ICRC and troop-providing states, entered into force on 12 August 1999, the 50th anniversary of the Geneva Conventions.

Stopping short of rendering the relevant treaties applicable to UN forces, the Bulletin provides guidelines, derived from those treaties, on topics such as protection of the civilian population, means and methods of combat, treatment of detained persons, and protection of the wounded and sick and of medical and relief personnel.

Without addressing the issue of United Nations responsibility for violations by members of its forces, Section 3 of the Bulletin specifies that whether or not there is a status-of-forces agreement between the United Nations and the state in whose territory the force is deployed, the UN "undertakes to ensure that the force shall conduct its operations with full respect for the principles and rules of the general conventions applicable to the conduct of military personnel". On the matter of criminal liability, Section 4 states that "[i]n cases of violations of international humanitarian law, members of the military personnel of a United Nations force are subject to prosecution in their national courts". Since the Bulletin is not a binding instrument, this provision may be little more than a statement of the obvious: the UN does not itself have an in-house judiciary competent to deal with such cases and the troop-sending states are therefore themselves obliged to prosecute and try the perpetrators of such acts. An *a contrario* reading of the provision as excluding the submission of such cases to any other, domestic or international, competent criminal court does not appear warranted.

5.3.2   *The International Court of Justice*

In earlier parts of this book, we encountered the ICJ a number of times, notably in connection with its judgment in the case of *Nicaragua* v. *the United States* (where it held that the United States' mine-laying operations off the coast of Nicaragua had violated the law, see Section 3.3.2). Some other cases that gave the Court the opportunity to express its views on aspects of the law of armed conflict are brought together here for a discussion of those parts that are of relevance in this book.

5.3.2a   Legality of threat or use of nuclear weapons
(Advisory Opinion of 1996)

The most important events relating to the potential use of nuclear weapons that occurred after the adoption of the 1977 Additional Protocols were in the political field, notably, the fall of the Berlin Wall in 1989 and the dissolution of the Soviet Union in 1991. One effect of these events was the diffusion of some of the tension and fear that had persisted throughout the Cold War period as a result of the threat of 'mutual assured destruction'. The two previous antagonists began to dismantle huge numbers of nuclear warheads, without giving up their formidable destructive capacity. At the same time, other states either had already developed, or started developing, a nuclear capacity of their own. Efforts to stem this tendency through the 1971 Non-Proliferation Treaty were not successful.

In these circumstances, the issue of the legality or illegality of a potential use of nuclear weapons retained all its importance. Since it clearly was not going to be solved through an ICRC- or UN-inspired diplomatic conference, the UN General Assembly in late December 1994 decided to submit the issue to the ICJ, requesting its opinion on the following question: "Is the threat or use of nuclear weapons in any circumstance permitted under international law?"

The Court's Advisory Opinion of 8 July 1996 begins by answering several preliminary questions: whether it was competent to give the opinion (answer: yes); whether the request concerned a legal question (again, yes, even though the political connotations of the request were recognised); and, of interest for present purposes, whether the fear of several states was justified that the question as formulated by the General Assembly was vague and abstract and "might lead the Court to make hypothetical or speculative declarations outside the scope of its judicial function". On this, the ICJ opined (para. 15) that to arrive at its advisory opinion, it did not need to write 'scenarios', to study various types of nuclear weapons and to evaluate highly complex and controversial technological, strategic and scientific information. The Court would simply address the issues arising in all their aspects by applying the legal rules relevant to the situation.

This is a remarkable simplification, not of the question as phrased by the General Assembly but of the Court's approach. Whole libraries are filled with literature on the great diversity of weapons that fall under the general heading of 'nuclear weapon': differences in explosive force, primary and secondary radiation, potential conditions of use, short-term and long-term effects of such use, and so on and so forth. It appears a contradiction in terms to state, as the Court did, that it would "address the issues in *all their aspects*" simply by "applying the legal rules relevant to *the situation*". This apparently non-technical approach becomes all the more surprising when the Court observes that "[t]he destructive power of nuclear weapons cannot be contained in either space or time. They have the potential to destroy all civilisation and the entire ecosystem of the planet" (para. 35). Nuclear weapons figure here as an evil force all by themselves.

On the matter of applicable law, the ICJ notes the argument that the use of nuclear weapons "would violate the right to life as guaranteed in Article 6 of the International Covenant on Civil and Political Rights", and the counter-argument that "the Covenant was directed to the protection of human rights in peacetime, [and] that questions relating to unlawful loss of life in hostilities were governed by the law applicable in armed conflict" (para. 24). Rejecting the latter argument, the ICJ states that "the protection of [the Covenant] does not cease in times of war [except for derogable rights; and since the right to life is not derogable], the right not arbitrarily to be deprived of one's life applies also in hostilities". However, when it comes to determining what is an arbitrary deprivation of life, this "falls to be determined by the applicable *lex specialis*, namely, the law applicable in armed conflict which is designed to regulate the conduct of hostilities" (para. 25).

On substance, the ICJ concludes that "the most directly relevant applicable law" to be taken into account is "that relating to the use of force enshrined in the United Nations Charter and the law applicable in armed conflict which regulates the conduct of hostilities, together with any specific treaties on nuclear weapons that the Court might determine to be relevant" (para. 34). While the Charter recognises the right of self-defence against an armed attack, the ICJ holds that the exercise of this right is subject to the customary law conditions of necessity and proportionality, conditions that apply both to the threat and the use of nuclear weapons in self-defence.

Turning next to "the law applicable in situations of armed conflict", the ICJ notes the absence of treaty law expressly dealing with the use of nuclear weapons (para. 37) but at the same time, the existence of a great many rules which are "fundamental to the respect of the human person" and that it regards as binding on all states because they represent "intransgressible principles of international customary law" (para. 79). As for Protocol I, it "recalls that all states are bound by those rules [in it] which, when adopted, were merely the expression of the pre-existing customary law, such as the Martens clause" (para. 84). It rejects the view that nuclear weapons, because of their newness, do not fall under the "established principles and rules of humanitarian law", adding that such a conclusion would be incompatible with the "intrinsically humanitarian character of the legal principles in question which permeates the entire law of armed conflict and applies to all forms of warfare and to all kinds of weapons, those of the past, those of the present and those of the future" (para. 86).

While all this is hardly disputed, the conclusions to be drawn from it (and from the principle of neutrality protecting states not participating in the armed conflict, which the ICJ examines in paras. 88 and 89) are "controversial" (para. 90). It juxtaposes two views: one, that the legality of use of a given nuclear weapon must be assessed on the basis of its characteristics and the specific circumstances of its use (para. 91); and the other, that any recourse to nuclear weapons is prohibited in all circumstances (para. 92).

On the first view, the ICJ observes that its proponents have not "indicated what would be the precise circumstances justifying such use, nor whether such limited use would not tend to escalate into the all-out use of high yield nuclear weapons", and goes on to state that "the Court does not consider that it has a sufficient basis for a determination on the validity of this view" (para. 94.) Here, one wonders how to match this complaint with the Court's earlier statement that it would simply apply the rules to the situation, as if the different modes of use of different types of nuclear weapon were of no relevance.

As for the second view, the ICJ arrives at a similar conclusion: "it does not have sufficient elements to enable it to conclude with certainty that the use of nuclear weapons would necessarily be at variance with the principles and rules of law applicable in armed conflict in any circumstance" (para. 95).

After further references to "the fundamental right of every State to survival, and thus to its right to resort to self-defence", to "the 'policy of deterrence', to which an appreciable section of the international community adhered for many years", as well as to "reservations which certain nuclear-weapons States have appended to the undertakings they have given [under certain treaties] not to resort to such weapons" (paras. 96, 97) the Court, by seven votes to seven by the President's casting vote, arrived at the conclusion (para. 97) that:

> [I]n view of the present state of international law viewed as a whole ... and of the elements of facts at its disposal, the Court is led to observe that it cannot reach a definitive conclusion as to the legality or illegality of the use of nuclear weapons by a State in an extreme circumstance of self-defence, in which its very survival would be at stake.

One notes that the ICJ has been "led to observe" all this because it did not of its own accord set out to discover the facts about possible use of various types of nuclear weapon in different scenarios. Another comment is that the reasoning in the body of the Opinion does not support the tail end of the conclusion with its reference to "an extreme circumstance of self-defence, in which [a state's] very survival would be at stake". Since the ICJ did not feel sufficiently informed to choose between "lawful for some weapons in some circumstances" and "always unlawful", that was the only conclusion it could draw. The rest was a well-meant attempt to give a piece of its own mind – or, at any rate, of the minds of the seven members of the Court who voted in favour of the quoted paragraph in the Opinion.

It is a matter of some regret that this Advisory Opinion has not clarified the issue of legality or illegality of use of nuclear weapons. This may remain an issue that cannot be resolved by law (except in *ex post facto* proceedings, as in the case decided in Japan relating to the use of 'atomic bombs' against Hiroshima and Nagasaki, see Section 3.5.3c). In this situation, one can merely express the wish that nuclear devices will not fall into irresponsible hands, and that the 'responsible hands' now holding them will think, not twice but a hundred times before resorting to the use of these weapons. In this respect, the past, with its long non-use of nuclear weapons even in situations where such use was seriously considered, continues to hold out some hope for the future as well.

5.3.2b   Legal consequences of the construction of
a wall in the Occupied Palestinian Territory
(Advisory Opinion of 2004)

As noted in Section 3.4.6d, in 2002 Israel started building a wall in the Occupied Palestinian Territory (OPT) in an attempt to protect itself better against attacks from the OPT. This led the UN General Assembly to decide on 8 December 2003 to ask the ICJ for its opinion on the legal consequences arising from the construction of the wall. The ICJ delivered its Advisory Opinion on 9 July 2004.

One preliminary objection, raised by Israel and other states, was that "the Court should decline to exercise its jurisdiction because it does not have at its disposal the requisite facts and evidence to enable it to reach its conclusions". On this, the ICJ holds that it has at its disposal "the report of the Secretary-General, as well as a voluminous dossier submitted by him to the Court, comprising not only detailed information on the route of the wall but also on its humanitarian and socio-economic impact on the Palestinian population [as well as] several reports based on onsite visits by special rapporteurs and competent organs of the United Nations" (para. 57). It concludes "that it has before it sufficient information and evidence to enable it to give the advisory opinion requested by the General Assembly", adding that "the circumstance that others may evaluate and interpret these facts in a subjective or political manner can be no argument for a court of law to abdicate its judicial task" (para. 58).

The OPT was occupied in 1967: is it still 'occupied territory'? The ICJ finds the relevant law in customary law as "reflected" in the Regulations annexed to the Hague Convention on Land Warfare of 1907 (to which Israel is not a party): that the Regulations "have become part of customary law ... is in fact recognized by all the participants in the proceedings before the Court" (para. 89). Article 42 considers territory "occupied when it is actually placed under the authority of the hostile army, and the occupation extends only to the territory where such authority has been established and can be exercised" (para. 78). Holding that "subsequent events ... have done nothing to alter this situation", the ICJ concludes that the territories "remain occupied territories and Israel has continued to have the status of occupying Power" (*ibid.*).

Turning to these "subsequent events", the ICJ sets out to determine the law relating to the measures taken by Israel (para. 89). It finds this law, first, in Geneva Convention IV, a treaty which Israel is a party to and which Palestine has undertaken to apply as well (by a unilateral declaration of 7 June 1982 deposited with the Swiss Government: this considered it valid although, as a depositary it was not in a position to decide that it could be counted as an instrument of accession; para. 91). Israel in practice applies major parts of the Convention in respect of the OPT but denies its applicability *de jure* (para. 93). The ICJ notes that, according to Article 2(1), "that Convention is applicable when two conditions are fulfilled: that there exists an armed conflict (whether or not a state of war has been recognized); and that the conflict has arisen between two contracting parties. [It then] applies, in particular, in any territory occupied in the course of the conflict by one of the contracting parties" (para. 95).

Article 2(2) extends the application of Convention IV beyond the case of inter-state armed conflict to "all cases of partial or total occupation of the territory of a [state party], even if the said occupation meets with no armed resistance". Affirming that this text does not restrict the scope of application of the Convention "by excluding therefrom territories not falling under the sovereignty of one of the contracting parties", the ICJ reads the paragraph as merely clarifying "that, even if occupation effected during the conflict met no armed resistance, the Convention is still applicable". This reading, it adds, "reflects the intention of the drafters of [Convention IV] to protect civilians who find themselves, in whatever way, in the hands of the occupying Power". Indeed, while "the drafters of the Hague Regulations [may have been] as much concerned with protecting the rights of a state whose territory is occupied, as with protecting the inhabitants of that territory", "the drafters of [Convention IV] sought to guarantee the protection of civilians in time of war, regardless of the status of the occupied territories" (*ibid.*). The ICJ invokes the ICRC, which on 5 December 2001 declared that it "has always affirmed the *de jure* applicability of [Convention IV] to the territories occupied since 1967 by the State of Israel, including East Jerusalem" (para. 97), and it notes that the UN Security Council and General Assembly have adopted the same position in many of their resolutions (paras. 98–9).

Turning next to the International Covenant on Civil and Political Rights, the ICJ recalls its finding in the Nuclear Weapons Advisory Opinion that the protection of this instrument "does not cease in times of war". Distinguishing three possible situations ("some rights may be exclusively matters of international humanitarian law; others may be exclusively matters of human rights law; yet others may be matters of both these branches of international law"), it concludes that "to answer the question put to it, the Court will have to take into consideration both ... human rights law and, as *lex specialis*, international humanitarian law" (para. 106).

On the basis of the information at its disposal, the ICJ concludes that: "the construction of the wall has led to the destruction or requisition of properties under conditions which contravene the requirements of Articles 46 and 52 of the Hague Regulations of 1907 and of Article 53 of the Fourth Geneva Convention" (para. 132); this "construction, the establishment of a closed area between the Green Line and the wall itself and the creation of enclaves have moreover imposed substantial restrictions on the freedom of movement of the inhabitants of [the OPT] (with the exception of Israeli citizens and those assimilated thereto)", and it has had "serious repercussions for agricultural production" (para. 133). Summing up, the Court repeats that the construction of the wall and its associated regime impede the liberty of movement of the non-Israeli and associated inhabitants of the OPT as guaranteed under Article 12(1) of the International Covenant on Civil and Political Rights; the exercise by the persons concerned of the right to work, to health, to education and to an adequate standard of living as proclaimed in the International Covenant on Economic, Social and Cultural Rights and in the Convention on the Rights of the Child; and lastly, "the construction of the wall and its associated régime, by contributing to the demographic changes [referred to in earlier paragraphs] contravene Article 49, paragraph 6, of the Fourth Geneva Convention and the Security Council resolutions" (para. 134).

The Court next asks whether 'military exigencies' provide an exception from rules of the law of armed conflict applicable in occupied territories even after the general close of the military operations that led to their occupation. In effect, Article 53 of Convention IV, which prohibits the destruction of personal property, provides for an exception "where such destruction is rendered absolutely necessary by military operations". However, on the material before it, "the Court is not convinced that the destructions carried out contrary to the prohibition in [that Article] were rendered absolutely necessary by military operations" so as to fall within the exception (para. 135).

Coming to its conclusions, the ICJ observes that Israel must "put an end to the violation of its international obligations flowing from the construction of the wall in the [OPT]" (para. 150). This implies "the obligation to cease forthwith the works of construction of the wall being built by it in the [OPT], including in and around East Jerusalem" as well as "the dismantling forthwith of those parts of that structure situated within the [OPT], including in and around East Jerusalem" (para. 151).

The ICJ also holds Israel liable to make good for the violation of its international obligations: it is obliged to "make reparation for the damage caused [by the construction of the wall] to all the natural or legal persons concerned" (para. 152), as well as "to return the land, orchards, olive groves and other immovable property seized from any natural or legal person for purposes of construction of the wall" or, if this proves impossible, to "compensate the persons in question for the damage suffered" (para. 153). Quite in general, the Court holds Israel obliged "to compensate, in accordance with the applicable rules of international law, all natural or legal persons having suffered any form of material damage as a result of the wall's construction" (*ibid.*). These findings of the ICJ may support the natural and legal persons affected by the violations in claims for reparation or compensation.

On the state level, the ICJ holds all states obliged "not to recognize the illegal situation resulting from the construction of the wall in the Occupied Palestinian Territory, including in and around East Jerusalem", nor may they "render aid or assistance in maintaining the situation created by such construction". States must also "see to it that any impediment, resulting from the construction of the wall, to the exercise by the Palestinian people of its right to self-determination is brought to an end"; and, "while respecting the United Nations Charter and international law, [they must] ensure compliance by Israel with international humanitarian law as embodied in [Geneva Convention IV]" (para. 159).

The ICJ concludes by inviting "the United Nations, and especially the General Assembly and the Security Council, [to] consider what further action is required to bring to an end the illegal situation resulting from the construction of the wall and the associated régime, taking due account of the present Advisory Opinion" (para. 160).

5.3.2c   Armed activities in the Territory of the Congo
(*The Democratic Republic of the Congo* v. *Uganda*, Judgment of 19 December 2005)

On 23 June 1999, the Democratic Republic of the Congo (DRC) submitted to the ICJ a dispute with Uganda concerning "acts of armed aggression perpetrated by Uganda on the territory of the Democratic Republic of the Congo".

In its first submission, on violations of the UN Charter and other relevant texts, the DRC contends, inter alia, that the Ugandan presence on parts of DRC territory had amounted to belligerent occupation. The ICJ, in its Judgment of 19 December 2005, reiterates its holding that "under customary international law, as reflected in Article 42 of the [Regulations], territory is considered to be occupied when it is actually placed under the authority of the hostile army, and the occupation extends only to the territory where such authority has been established and can be exercised" (para. 172). It concludes from the available data that, while Ugandan troops had indisputably been present on DRC territory, only in one area, the Ituri district, had Uganda "established and exercised authority ... as an occupying Power" and thus had been obliged, as provided in Article 43 of the Regulations, to do what it could "to restore, and ensure, as far as possible, public order and safety in the occupied area ... This obligation comprised the duty to secure respect for the applicable rules of international human rights law and international humanitarian law, to protect the inhabitants of the occupied territory against acts of violence, and not to tolerate such violence by any third party" (paras. 176, 178). As an occupying power in Ituri, Uganda was responsible "for any acts of its military that violated its international obligations and for any lack of vigilance in preventing violations of human rights and international humanitarian law by other actors present in the occupied territory, including rebel groups acting on their own account" (para. 179).

The second submission of the DRC concerns the violation by Uganda of various principles of conventional and customary law, inter alia, "imposing an obligation to respect, and ensure respect for, fundamental human rights, including in times of armed conflict, in accordance with international humanitarian law", and "at all times, to make a distinction in an armed conflict between civilian and military objectives" (para. 181). From the "evidence contained in certain United Nations documents to the extent that they are of probative value and are corroborated, if necessary, by other credible sources" (para. 205, specified in detail in paras. 206–10), the ICJ concludes that "the UPDF troops committed acts of killing, torture and other forms of inhumane treatment of the civilian population, destroyed villages and civilian buildings, failed to distinguish between civilian and military targets and to protect the civilian population in fighting with other combatants, was involved in the training of child soldiers, and did not take measures to ensure respect for human rights and international humanitarian law in the occupied territories" (para. 211). Since "by virtue of the military status and function of Ugandan soldiers in the DRC, their conduct is attributable to Uganda, [t]he contention that the persons concerned did not act in the capacity of persons exercising governmental authority in the particular circumstances, is ... without merit" (para. 213). In addition, given the responsibility of a party to an armed conflict for all acts by persons forming part of its armed forces (Art. 3 of the 1907 Hague Convention on Land Warfare and Art. 91 of Protocol I), it is irrelevant "whether the UPDF personnel acted contrary to the instructions given or exceeded their authority" (para. 214).

Having thus established that the above conduct is attributable to Uganda, the ICJ next examines whether it "constitutes a breach of Uganda's international obligations". It finds the relevant law both in international human rights law and international humanitarian law. As regards "the relationship between international humanitarian law and international human rights law and ... the applicability of international human rights law instruments outside national territory", the ICJ recalls its recent conclusion in the Wall Opinion that "both branches of international law ... would have to be taken into consideration". On that occasion it had also concluded that "international human rights instruments are applicable 'in respect of acts done by a State in the exercise of its jurisdiction outside its own territory', particularly in occupied territories" (para. 216). (Note that, unlike the situation underlying the Wall Opinion, the occupation of Ituri had been of short duration. As is implicit in the quoted phrase, the ICJ holds the application of occupation law solely dependent on whether the requirements of Article 42 of the Regulations are met.)

The DRC's third submission concerns the illegal exploitation, plundering and looting of natural resources, an issue on which the facts again were well documented (para. 237). While finding that the ICJ "does not have at its disposal credible evidence to prove that there was a governmental policy of Uganda directed at the exploitation of natural resources of the DRC or that Uganda's military intervention was carried out in order to obtain access to Congolese resources" (para. 242), it does find enough evidence to support the DRC's claim that Uganda had failed to take "adequate measures to ensure that its military forces did not engage in the looting, plundering and exploitation of the DRC's natural resources" (para. 246). These acts, the Court asserts, violated "the *jus in bello*", and it "notes in this regard that both Article 47 of the Hague Regulations ... and Article 33 of [Convention IV] prohibit pillage" (para. 245). As regards occupied Ituri, Uganda's responsibility covers similar acts by persons who were not members of its military forces as well (para. 248).

As usual, the ICJ Judgment in the case of the *DRC* v. *Uganda* contains a great deal more than could be related here. For these other parts, the reader is referred to the Judgment itself.

5.3.2d Application of the Convention on the Prevention and Punishment of the Crime of Genocide (*Bosnia and Herzegovina* v. *Serbia and Montenegro*, Judgment of 26 February 2007)

On 20 March 1993, Bosnia and Herzegovina requested the ICJ to "adjudge and declare" that the Federal Republic of Yugoslavia (or FRY; since 2006, the Republic of Serbia) "has violated and is violating the Convention on the Prevention and Punishment of the Crime of Genocide, by destroying in part, and attempting to destroy in whole, national, ethnical or religious groups within the, but not limited to the, territory of the Republic of Bosnia and Herzegovina, including in particular the Muslim population" (para. 65). In its Judgment of 26 February 2007 (and after an unusually complicated procedure, marked among other things by both parties changing identities if not characters) the ICJ accepts as "established by overwhelming evidence that massive killings ... throughout the territory of Bosnia and Herzegovina were perpetrated during the conflict [and] that the victims were in large majority members of the protected group [the Muslims], which suggests that they may have been systematically targeted by the killings" (para. 276). Yet, since the ICJ is "not convinced, on the basis of the evidence before it, that it has been conclusively established that the massive killings of members of the protected group were committed with the specific intent (*dolus specialis*) on the part of the perpetrators to destroy, in whole or in part, the group as such", it "finds that it has not been established by the Applicant that the killings amounted to acts of genocide prohibited by the Convention" (para. 277).

The conclusion of the ICJ is different as regards the events at Srebrenica (where in July 1995 more than 8,000 Bosnian Muslim men were abducted and massacred by the Bosnian-Serb army of the Republika Srpska (VRS) under the command of General Ratko Mladić): it finds that the acts of "killing members of the group" and "causing serious bodily or mental harm to members of the group", as defined in Article II(a) and (b) of the Genocide Convention, "were committed with the specific intent to destroy in part the group of the Muslims of Bosnia and Herzegovina as such; and accordingly that these were acts of genocide, committed by members of the VRS in and around Srebrenica" (para. 297). However, the acts "cannot be attributed to [Serbia] under the rules of international law of State responsibility" (para. 415), and neither can Serbia be held responsible for "acts of complicity in genocide" as mentioned in Article III (e) of the Convention. The ICJ concludes that "the international responsibility of [Serbia] is not engaged under Article III as a whole" (para. 424).

This leaves the question whether Serbia had "complied with its two-fold obligation deriving from Article I of the Convention to prevent and punish genocide" (para. 379). As regards the obligation to prevent, the ICJ emphasises that it does not "purport to establish a general jurisprudence applicable to all cases where a treaty instrument, or other binding legal norm, includes an obligation for States to prevent certain acts" (para. 429). It also notes that "the obligation in question is one of conduct and not one of result"; responsibility under this heading can arise "only if genocide was actually committed"; "mere failure to adopt and implement suitable measures to prevent genocide from being committed" may be enough, and it suffices "that the State was aware, or should normally have been aware, of the serious danger that acts of genocide would be committed" (paras. 430–2).

At the time, the "political, military and financial links" of the FRY with the Republika Srpska and the VRS, "though somewhat weaker than in the preceding period, nonetheless remained very close": the FRY had more influence over the Bosnian Serbs than any other state party to the Genocide Convention. Again, "on the relevant date, the FRY was bound by very specific obligations by virtue of the two Orders indicating provisional measures delivered by the Court in 1993". Again, given the information available to them, the Belgrade authorities "could hardly have been unaware of the serious risk [that genocide was imminent] once the VRS forces had decided to occupy the Srebrenica enclave". In view of these facts, "the Yugoslav federal authorities should, in the view of the Court, have made the best efforts within their power to try and prevent the tragic events then taking shape, whose scale, though it could not have been foreseen with certainty, might at least have been surmised". All of this leads the ICJ to conclude that the FRY has "violated its obligation to prevent the Srebrenica genocide in such a manner as to engage its international responsibility" (paras. 434–8).

As regards the question of whether Serbia has complied with its obligation to punish the violation of the Genocide Convention, the ICJ notes that since the Srebrenica genocide was not committed on its territory, Serbia "cannot be charged with not having tried before its own courts those accused of having participated in the Srebrenica genocide" (para. 442). This leaves the alternative, provided in Article VI of the Convention, of trial by an international penal tribunal that has "jurisdiction with respect to those Contracting Parties which shall have accepted its jurisdiction". Article VI implies an obligation upon states to "arrest persons accused of genocide who are in their territory – even if the crime of which they are accused was committed outside it – and, failing prosecution of them in the parties' own courts, [to] hand them over for trial by the competent international tribunal" (para. 443). Such a tribunal is now available: it is the Yugoslavia Tribunal (or ICTY; see Section 5.3.3).

The ICJ raises, and answers affirmatively, two preliminary questions: whether the ICTY constitutes an 'international penal tribunal' within the meaning of Article VI, and whether Serbia must be "regarded as having 'accepted the jurisdiction' of the tribunal within the meaning of that provision" (paras. 444–7). The remaining question is one of fact: whether Serbia "has fully co-operated with the ICTY, in particular by arresting and handing over to the Tribunal any persons accused of genocide as a result of the Srebrenica genocide and finding themselves on its territory". During the oral proceedings Serbia had asserted that "the duty to co-operate had been complied with following the régime change in Belgrade in the year 2000" – and, thus, not before that date. Apart from that, "plentiful, and mutually corroborative, information suggest[s] that General Mladić, indicted by the ICTY for genocide, as one of those principally responsible for the Srebrenica massacres, was on [Serb territory] at least on several occasions and for substantial periods during the last few years and is still there now, without the Serb authorities doing what they could and can reasonably do to ascertain exactly where he is living and arrest him" (para. 448). Finding it "sufficiently established that the Respondent failed in its duty to co-operate fully with the ICTY", the Court concludes that it "failed to comply both with its obligation to prevent and its obligation to punish genocide deriving from the Convention, and that its international responsibility is thereby engaged" (paras. 449–50).

The Court next turns to the question of reparation, first, for the violation of the obligation to prevent genocide. Although at the time of the events, the FRY "did have significant means of influencing the Bosnian Serb military and political authorities", "it has not been shown that, in the specific context of these events, those means would have sufficed to achieve the result which [it] should have sought". Since "a causal nexus between [the FRY's] violation of its obligation of prevention and the damage resulting from the genocide at Srebrenica" cannot therefore be regarded as proven, the ICJ concludes that in this case, "financial compensation is not the appropriate form of reparation" (para. 462). Yet, Bosnia "is entitled to reparation in the form of satisfaction", in the shape of "a declaration in the present Judgment that [the FRY] has failed to comply with the obligation imposed by the Convention to prevent the crime of genocide" (para. 463). The requisite declaration is included in the Operative Clause (para. 471(5)).

As concerns the obligation to punish acts of genocide, Bosnia "asserts the existence of a continuing breach", including the failure to transfer accused individuals to the ICTY, as the reason it maintains its request for a declaration in that sense. Bosnia also asks the ICJ to "decide more specifically that 'Serbia and Montenegro shall immediately take effective steps to ensure full compliance with its obligation to punish acts of genocide ... and to transfer individuals accused of genocide ... to the [ICTY] and to fully co-operate with this Tribunal'" (para. 464). Since the Court is indeed satisfied that Serbia "has outstanding obligations as regards the transfer to the ICTY of persons accused of genocide, in order to comply with its obligations under Articles I and VI of the Genocide Convention, in particular in respect of General Ratko Mladić", it "will therefore make a declaration in these terms in the operative clause of the present Judgment, which will in its view constitute appropriate satisfaction" (para. 465). The Operative Clause (para. 471) duly reflects these two points: the finding of a continuing breach in sub-para. 6, and the order "that Serbia shall immediately take effective steps to ensure full compliance with its obligation under the [Genocide Convention] to punish acts of genocide as defined by Article II of the Convention, or any of the other acts proscribed by Article III of the Convention, and to transfer individuals accused of genocide or any of those other acts for trial by the [ICTY], and to co-operate fully with that Tribunal" in sub-para. 8.

The case before the ICJ of *Bosnia* v. *Serbia* illustrates the point that an inter-state procedure may run simultaneously with procedures before an international criminal body (in this case, the ICTY) against individuals held criminally responsible for the identical facts underlying the inter-state case.

5.3.2e   Jurisdictional immunities of the state (*Germany* v. *Italy*, Application of 23 December 2008)

Mention is made, finally, of the above Application, by which Germany asks the ICJ to declare that Italy:

> [B]y allowing civil claims based on violations of international humanitarian law by the German Reich during World War II from September 1943 to May 1945, to be brought against the Federal Republic of Germany, committed violations of obligations under international law in that it has failed to respect the jurisdictional immunity which the Federal Republic of Germany enjoys under international law.

The Application concerns cases of civil claims brought before Italian courts against Germany, inter alia, by descendants of Italians murdered by German occupation forces after Italy had joined the Allied powers. At the time of writing, the case is still at an early stage. On 20 July 2010, the Court declared inadmissible a counter-claim by which Italy had asked it to "adjudge and declare" that Germany by denying Italian victims of war crimes effective reparation had violated its obligation under international law.

5.3.3 The Yugoslavia and Rwanda Tribunals

The disintegration of Yugoslavia in 1991 has brought about a series of armed conflicts that led to increasingly alarming reports about horrifying crimes, often centring around the practice of 'ethnic cleansing'. As noted in Section 5.3.1b, in October 1992 the UN Secretary-General set up a commission of experts to collect and analyse the available information about these serious violations of humanitarian law. The commission submitted its final report in May 1994. One year earlier, on 25 May 1993, the Security Council by Resolution 827 had established the International Tribunal for the Prosecution of Persons Responsible for Serious Violations of International Humanitarian Law Committed in the Territory of the Former Yugoslavia Since 1991 (the ICTY).

In 1994, less than a year after the creation of the Yugoslavia Tribunal, a major ethnic conflict broke out in Rwanda, in the course of which hundreds of thousands of Tutsis were murdered by members of the Hutu group. The Security Council, in reaction to criticism for having failed to take prompt action to prevent the massacre (and once again after preparation by a commission of experts), on 8 November 1994 adopted Resolution 955, creating yet another international ad hoc tribunal, this time with jurisdiction over genocide and other violations of international humanitarian law committed in Rwanda in 1994 (the ICTR).

5.3.3a Jurisdiction

The Yugoslavia and Rwanda ad hoc Tribunals derive their jurisdiction from resolutions of the Security Council, adopted under Chapter VII of the UN Charter (Action with respect to threats to the peace, breaches of the peace, and acts of aggression). The territorial jurisdiction of the ICTY is limited to the territory of the former Yugoslavia. That of the ICTR covers, apart from the genocidal events in Rwanda, also violations of humanitarian law committed by Rwandan citizens in the territory of neighbouring states but is, on the other hand, temporally limited to acts committed in 1994, with the effect that the subsequent killings of thousands of people who fled the scene of the Rwandan conflict fall outside its jurisdiction.

In contrast, the temporal jurisdiction of the ICTY is open-ended. Article 1 of its Statute refers to "serious violations … committed … since 1991", and the Security Council Resolution by which it was created speaks of such violations committed "between 1 January 1991 and a date to be determined by the Security Council upon the restoration of peace". Its jurisdiction thus has come to include serious violations of humanitarian law committed in 1998 and 1999 in Kosovo, originally a province of Yugoslavia.

The personal jurisdiction of the Tribunals for the former Yugoslavia and Rwanda is limited to natural persons, no matter what their nationality (Art. 6 of the ICTY Statute, Art. 5 of the ICTR Statute). Parties to the conflict and other collective entities, be they states or non-state armed groups, fall outside the jurisdiction of the Tribunals (as had been the case with the Nuremberg Tribunal). Article 7(1) of the ICTY Statute and Article 6(1) of the ICTR Statute extend individual criminal responsibility to any person who "planned, instigated, ordered, committed or otherwise aided and abetted in the planning, preparation or execution of a crime" as defined in the Statutes, and paragraph 2 specifies that an official position, "whether as Head of State or Government or as a responsible Government official, shall not relieve such person of criminal responsibility nor mitigate punishment".

The criminal jurisdiction of the two Tribunals covers "serious violations of international humanitarian law" (Article 1 of both Statutes). The phrase 'international humanitarian law' as used in this article covers war crimes as well as crimes against humanity and genocide, but does not include the crime of aggression. Article 9 of the Statute of the ICTY and Article 8 of the Statute of the ICTR, finally, give the Tribunals primacy over national courts. (On the situation of victims of the "serious violations of international humanitarian law" within the jurisdiction of the Tribunals, see below, Section 5.3.6.)

Article 2 of its Statute gives the ICTY jurisdiction over grave breaches of the Geneva Conventions, while Article 3 empowers it to prosecute violations of "the laws or customs of war". Article 3 non-exhaustively lists "employment of poisonous weapons or other weapons calculated to cause unnecessary suffering; wanton destruction of cities, towns or villages, or devastation not justified by military necessity; attack or bombardment, by whatever means, of undefended towns, villages, dwellings, or buildings;

seizure of, destruction or wilful damage done to instruction dedicated to religion, charity and education, the arts and sciences, historic monuments and works of art and science; plunder of public or private property" – all of this, language copied from the 1907 Hague Regulations.

In its case law, the ICTY has consistently taken the position that it could only apply rules of customary law. It argued that, either, treaty provisions only provide for the prohibition of a certain conduct, not for its criminalisation, or the treaty provision itself insufficiently defines the elements of the prohibition it criminalises and customary international law has to be relied on for the definition of those elements. Even where a treaty applicable between the parties prohibits conduct and provides for individual criminal responsibility and, thus, could provide the basis for its jurisdiction, in practice the ICTY has preferred to ascertain that the treaty provision in question is also declaratory of custom. In this reliance on custom, the Tribunal even interpreted the notion in Article 3 of 'laws or customs of war' as applying in internal armed conflicts as well. (For a critical comment on this extended reliance on customary law, see Section 1.2.)

As the Rwandan situation was seen from the outset as a purely internal conflict, Article 4 of the Statute of the ICTR explicitly lists serious violations of common Article 3 of the 1949 Geneva Conventions and of Protocol II as punishable crimes. The recognition that violations of humanitarian law applicable in internal conflicts entail individual criminal liability is a historic event. Until that time, the notion of 'war crime' was generally held to have no place in internal armed conflict. Accordingly, neither common Article 3 nor Protocol II addresses individual responsibility. Thus, the establishment and work of the ad hoc tribunals has significantly contributed to diminishing on this score the relevance of the distinction between the two types of conflict.

5.3.3b   Superior responsibility

An important issue concerns superior responsibility, a matter dealt with earlier in Articles 86 and 87 of Protocol I of 1977 (see Section 4.3.4b). Article 7(3) of the ICTY Statute and Article 6(3) of the ICTR Statute provide that:

> The fact that any of the acts referred to in articles 2 to 5 of the present Statute was committed by a subordinate does not relieve his superior of criminal responsibility if he knew or had reason to know that the subordinate was about to commit such acts or had done so and the superior failed to take the necessary and reasonable measures to prevent such acts or to punish the perpetrators thereof.

Articles 7(4) of the ICTY Statute and 6(4) of the ICTR Statute reject the notion that a subordinate who has committed a crime may be relieved of responsibility by proving that they acted pursuant to orders of a superior. At the same time, superior orders "may be considered in mitigation of punishment if the International Tribunal determines that justice so requires".

Both Tribunals have dealt with numerous cases involving issues of superior responsibility. Clarifying one particular aspect of the superior–subordinate relationship, the ICTY has held that this hinges on the existence of a relation of authority, and it found that apart from formal authority, this may also be a de facto position of authority. On the standard of 'reason to know', the ICTY held that this was met when a commander "had information placing him or her on notice of a likelihood that such offences were being committed, or were about to be committed, and indicating the need for additional investigation" (Delalic *et al.*, trial judgment, paras. 384–6). In the same judgment, the Trial Chamber held that the duty of a commander to take the "necessary and reasonable measures" goes no further than to the measures that were "within his powers" (para. 395).

5.3.3c   Role and rights of the victims

At the post-Second World War Nuremberg and Tokyo Tribunals against the top officials of the Axis powers, victims figured hardly at all: they could not submit claims for reparation, and few were called to testify. On the matter of reparation, as noted before, reliance at the time was rather placed on the practice of lump-sum agreements, leaving the task of dealing with individual losses to the victims' nation states.

The proceedings, half a century later, before the ICTY and ICTR present a very different picture, with large numbers of victims being called to testify in virtually every case. The Statutes of both Tribunals provide measures for the protection of witnesses, including *in camera* proceedings and the protection of witness identity (Art. 22 of the ICTY Statute, Art. 19 of the ICTR Statute).

As regards compensation, while the Statutes of the Tribunals do not provide for claims by, or on behalf of, victims, they do enable the Tribunals to "order the return of any property and proceeds acquired by criminal conduct, including by means of duress, to their rightful owners" (Art. 24(3) of the ICTY Statute, Art. 23(3) of the ICTR Statute). Apart from that, the matter of compensation to victims is again left to the national states. To facilitate their task, Rule 106 of both Tribunals' Rules of Procedure and

Evidence provides that "[t]he Registrar shall transmit to the competent authorities of the States concerned the judgement finding the accused guilty of a crime which has caused injury to a victim"; and for the purposes of such a claim, "the judgement of the Tribunal shall be final and binding as to the criminal responsibility of the convicted person for such injury".

5.3.3d   Exit strategy

The Security Council had already in 2003 imposed an 'exit strategy' on both Tribunals, requiring them to work towards their closure "by the end of 2010" – a goal that soon proved to be beyond reach. Even so, it did lead to the referral of an increasing stream of cases to national courts of the countries concerned, accompanied by an extensive programme of support where necessary in developing these courts' capacity to handle wartime cases.

On 22 December 2010, the Security Council adopted Resolution 1966 by which it took a number of measures to speed up the closure of the Tribunals. To this end, it decided to establish a new body, the International Residual Mechanism for Criminal Tribunals, with two branches: one, for the ICTR, scheduled to start functioning on 1 July 2012, and the other, for the ICTY, on 1 July 2013. It adopted the Statute of the Mechanism, as set forth in Annex 1 to the Resolution. It ordered the ICTY and the ICTR to "expeditiously complete all their remaining work as provided by this resolution no later than 31 December 2014". And it agreed on a set of transitional arrangements (Annex 2).

Without going into too much detail, the following points may be noted. The Tribunals remain competent to "complete all trial or referral proceedings which are pending with them as of the commencement date of the respective branch of the Mechanism" (Transitional Arrangements, Art. 1(1); this includes the long-lasting trial of Karadžić). If a fugitive indicted by either Tribunal (e.g. Mladić) is arrested before the respective branch of the Mechanism has started to function, the length of time before that date determines whether the case will be tried by the Tribunal or the Mechanism. If the date of arrest falls on or after the commencement date of the Mechanism, this is solely competent to deal with the case (Transitional Arrangements, Art. 1(2–4)).

The Mechanism "shall continue the material, territorial, temporary and personal jurisdiction of the ICTY and the ICTR" as set out in the Statutes of those bodies (Statute, Art. 1). Except for cases of contempt of court, its power is restricted to existing indictments; it will take up cases against indicted persons who fall into the power of a Tribunal only if they belong to the most senior leaders suspected of being most responsible for crimes, or if all reasonable efforts to refer their case to a national court have remained without success (Statute, Arts. 2, 3).

Meanwhile, Resolution 1966 once again "urges the Tribunals and the Mechanism to actively undertake every effort to refer those cases which do not involve the most senior leaders suspected of being most responsible for crimes to competent national jurisdictions" (para. 11).

With this set of measures, and as expressed in the fifth preambular paragraph of Resolution 1996, the Security Council intends to reaffirm "its determination to combat impunity for those responsible for serious violations of international humanitarian law and the necessity that all persons indicted by the ICTY and ICTR are brought to justice", while at the same time considerably reducing the staggering expenditure involved in this undertaking.

5.3.4   The International Criminal Court

Shortly after the establishment of the ICTY and profiting from the favourable political momentum, the International Law Commission finally completed the work on a statute for an international criminal court it had begun in the early years of the United Nations. In 1994 it submitted the draft statute to the UN General Assembly. After a committee set up for this purpose had prepared a text that might be broadly acceptable, the General Assembly at its fifty-second session decided to convene a diplomatic conference in Rome from 15 June to 17 July 1998, "to finalise and adopt a convention on the establishment of an International Criminal Court". On 17 July 1998 this Conference adopted the Statute of the ICC, which was subsequently signed by 139 states. On 1 July 2002, after ratification by sixty states, the Rome Statute (as it is usually called) entered into force. On 11 March 2003, the first court was inaugurated at The Hague, where it has its seat. At the time of writing, 111 states are party to the Statute. The United States of America, long a staunch opponent of the ICC, has recently changed its position into one of positive cooperation.

While the ad hoc tribunals for the former Yugoslavia and Rwanda, given their territorially and temporally limited jurisdiction, might be accused of selective justice, the ICC, as a permanent court with in principle worldwide jurisdiction, may hope to develop into an institution not open to such criticism. Yet its reputation will come to depend on its record in acquiring and dealing with actual cases.

5.3.4a Jurisdiction

The opening words of Article 5 on 'Crimes within the jurisdiction of the Court' state that "[t]he jurisdiction of the Court shall be limited to the most serious crimes of concern to the international community as a whole". Its jurisdiction encompasses war crimes, crimes against humanity and genocide. It also includes the crime of aggression; however, since there was no agreement at the time on the conditions for the exercise of jurisdiction over this crime, Article 5 adds that the Court shall exercise its jurisdiction over the crime of aggression only after agreement has been reached on the definition of the crime and on the conditions for the exercise of this part of the Court's jurisdiction. This thorny issue, which includes the difficult problem of the relations between the jurisdiction of the Court and the powers of the Security Council, was finally resolved by the Review Conference held in May–June 2010 in Kampala, Uganda. As the actual exercise of jurisdiction under this heading is still a long time off, this matter is discussed separately in Section 5.3.4f.

Article 8 defines the jurisdiction of the Court in respect of war crimes. Paragraph 1 indicates that it shall have jurisdiction over such offences "in particular when committed as part of a plan or policy or as part of a large-scale commission of such crimes". This phrase poses a certain threshold to the exercise of jurisdiction of the Court, although not an absolute one, as the words "in particular" indicate: the Court retains the power to deal with isolated war crimes.

Article 8(2) defines four different categories of war crime, with the first two applying to international conflicts and the last two to internal conflicts. In so doing, the Statute maintains the distinction between the two types of situations (as is done in the Statutes and practice of the two ad hoc tribunals).

Paragraph 2(a) lists grave breaches of the Geneva Conventions, and paragraph 2(b) "other serious violations of the laws and customs applicable in international armed conflict". The quite extensive list in the latter sub-paragraph contains rules of warfare already recognised in the nineteenth century, but equally takes into account recent developments in international humanitarian law, some of which are laid down in Protocol I: for instance, the provisions criminalising various acts against UN peace-keepers and humanitarian organisations, their installations, material, units and vehicles; the transfer by an occupying power of civilians into or out of certain territories; rape, sexual slavery, enforced prostitution, forced pregnancy, enforced sterilisation or any other form of sexual violence; intentional starvation of civilians as a method of warfare; and conscripting or enlisting children younger than fifteen into the national armed forces or having them actively participating in the hostilities.

As regards the employment of prohibited weapons, the list is confined to two items: poison or poisonous weapons, asphyxiating, poisonous or other gases, and all analogous liquids, materials or devices, and bullets which expand or flatten easily in the human body. According to paragraph 2(b)(xx), the employment of "weapons, projectiles and material and methods of warfare which are of a nature to cause superfluous injury or unnecessary suffering or which are inherently indiscriminate in violation of the international law of armed conflict" will not in general fall under the jurisdiction of the ICC, but only once such weapons and methods of warfare "are the subject of a comprehensive prohibition and are included in an annex to this Statute" by a proper amendment in accordance with the relevant rules. This means that the ICC has no power to determine that employment of a particular weapon violates these principles and is therefore punishable as a war crime. This includes nuclear weapons: any reference to these weapons was ultimately kept out of the Statute.

The list of war crimes in internal armed conflicts in Article 8(2), though considerable, is far shorter than that for international armed conflicts. Paragraph 2(c) mentions serious violations of common Article 3, the provisions of which are thus for the first time made the subject of a penal treaty provision. Paragraph 2(e) renders punishable as "other serious violations of the laws and customs applicable in armed conflicts not of an international character", a series of acts that are drawn from Protocol II as well as from provisions of customary law in the Hague Regulations, the Geneva Conventions and Protocol I. Like the provisions on international armed conflict, those on internal conflict include the protection of UN and other humanitarian personnel and assets, and gender-based crimes. The inclusion of "conscripting or enlisting children under the age of fifteen into armed forces or groups or using them to participate actively in hostilities" also runs parallel with the provision on such use in international conflicts. The use in an internal conflict of weapons classified as prohibited in the context of international armed conflict is not, however, listed among the war crimes that fall within the jurisdiction of the ICC.

As for the conditions for applicability of the provision criminalising serious violations of common Article 3, paragraph 2(d) prescribes that it shall not apply to "situations of internal disturbances and tensions, such as riots, isolated and sporadic acts of violence or other acts of a similar nature". Paragraph 2(f) repeats the same form of words in relation to paragraph 2(e), adding that this only "applies to armed conflicts that take place in the territory of a State when there is protracted armed conflict between governmental authorities and organised armed groups or between such groups". This language, based in principle on Article 1(1) of Protocol II, deviates from that article in several respects. It includes conflicts between non-state armed groups (which are also included in common Article 3 but were left out of Article 1 of the Protocol), and it leaves out the element of control over a part of the state's territory enabling a group "to carry out sustained and concerted military operations and to implement [the] Protocol". While these are significant improvements, paragraph 2(f) unfortunately adds the qualification 'protracted', which finds no basis in Protocol II (and which has been copied from a judgment delivered by the Yugoslavia Tribunal in an early phase of its first case, the *Tadić* case (jurisdiction)).

Paragraph 3 of Article 8 is derived from Article 3 of Protocol II, stating that nothing in the paragraphs dealing with internal conflicts "shall affect the responsibility of a Government to maintain or re-establish law and order in the State or to defend the unity and territorial integrity of the State, by all legitimate means".

Concerned that crimes defined in the Statute might not meet the requirements of the principle of legality, Article 9 stipulates that "Elements of Crimes shall assist the Court in the interpretation and application" of the articles containing the crimes. After due groundwork by a Preparatory Commission, the Assembly of States Parties on 9 September 2002 adopted the requisite list of Elements of Crimes (ICC-ASP/1/3, Part II-B).

5.3.4b Exercise of jurisdiction, complementarity

One of the core issues confronting the ICC concerns the effective exercise of its jurisdiction. Article 12 of the Statute lays out the "preconditions". The general requirement is, either, that the state on whose territory the crime was committed or the state of nationality of the accused has accepted the jurisdiction of the Court, or that the Security Council acting under Chapter VII of the UN Charter refers a case to it. A state which becomes a party to the Statute thereby accepts the Court's jurisdiction. It is also possible for a state to accept its jurisdiction ad hoc, with respect to a particular crime. It may be emphasised that in cases referred by the Security Council the Court may have jurisdiction over a crime committed in a state that is not a party to the Statute and by a national of such a state.

Provided the preconditions for exercise of jurisdiction are met, the next question is who or what triggers the actual exercise of jurisdiction. Article 13 mentions three possibilities: a state party or the Security Council may refer a case to the Court, or the prosecutor may take the initiative for an investigation. This latter possibility is provided in Article 15, stating that "[t]he Prosecutor may initiate investigations *proprio motu* on the basis of information on crimes within the jurisdiction of the Court". The Court may also be expected to come into play when national institutions have broken down, as was the case in Rwanda in 1994.

The ICC is not meant to replace or supersede national courts. The preamble of the Statute recalls "that it is the duty of every State to exercise its criminal jurisdiction over those responsible for international crimes", and Article 1 lays down the principle that the Court "shall be complementary to national criminal jurisdictions". As specified in Article 17(1), the ICC is supposed to take over only when a state which has jurisdiction over a case "is unwilling or unable genuinely to carry out the investigation or prosecution", or when a state's decision not to prosecute the accused "resulted from [its] unwillingness or inability ... genuinely to prosecute". Such situations are particularly likely to arise when international crimes involve the direct or indirect participation of individuals linked to the state, as the authorities often lack the power or the political will to prosecute high-level officials; this a fortiori when the crimes are committed in execution of a set government policy.

As far as exercise of jurisdiction is concerned, the ICC is still in its infancy. But even when it has more fully developed, it probably will not be able to take up all the cases that might fall within its jurisdiction. If the state concerned takes no action either, the risk persists that very serious crimes go unpunished. In this regard, the 2010 Review Conference reaffirms its "determination to combat impunity for the most serious crimes of international concern as referred to in the Rome Statute", and it "stresses the obligations of States Parties flowing from [the Statute]": that is, states' obligations to deal effectively with such crimes. It also encourages all "stakeholders, including international organizations and civil society to further explore ways in which to enhance the capacity of national jurisdictions to investigate and prosecute serious crimes of international concern", all of this with a view to reducing the evil of impunity (RC/Res.1, 8 June 2010).

5.3.4c General principles, including superior responsibility

Part 3 of the Statute sets out the general principles of criminal law. These include the principles of *nullum crimen sine lege* and *nulla poena sine lege* (no crime nor punishment without previous legislation); the principle of non-retroactivity of criminal law (no criminal responsibility for conduct prior to the entry into force of the Statute, i.e. 1 July 2002); the various forms of individual responsibility; the responsibility of superiors; the mental element; and the grounds for excluding individual criminal responsibility.

The ICC has jurisdiction over natural persons (as distinguished from juridical persons (Art. 25(1)). Paragraph 2 emphasises that "[a] person who commits a crime within the jurisdiction of the Court shall be individually responsible". Far from being restricted to the actual perpetration of the act, the notion of 'committing a crime' is elaborated in paragraph 3. This lists a wide range of forms of committing (whether as an individual or jointly), contributing, facilitating and assisting in the commission of a crime, including: ordering, soliciting, inducing, aiding, abetting or providing the means for the commission of a crime. Contributing in any other way to the commission or the attempted commission of a crime by a group of persons acting with a common purpose is also punishable when the contribution is intentional and is made with the "aim of furthering the criminal activity or criminal purpose of the group" or "in the knowledge of the intention of the group to commit the crime". Especially in respect of genocide, the direct and public incitement of others to commit genocide (as was done in Rwanda) is brought under the notion of 'committing a crime'.

Article 25(4) provides that nothing in the Statute "relating to individual criminal responsibility shall affect the responsibility of States under international law". Evidently, the reverse is equally true: a person belonging to the state apparatus who has committed a crime within the jurisdiction of the Court is not exempted from criminal responsibility under the Statute by the fact that the state is internationally responsible for the act. Article 27 specifically provides in this respect that no official capacity, including that as a head of state or government, exempts a person from such criminal responsibility under the Statute.

Article 28, on superior command responsibility, distinguishes between "military commanders or persons effectively acting as a military commander" and other "superior and subordinate relationships". As regards the military commander or person effectively acting as such, the article provides under (a) that such person:

> shall be criminally responsible for crimes ... committed by forces under his or her effective command and control, or effective authority and

control as the case may be, as a result of his or her failure to exercise control properly over such forces, where:

(i)   That military commander or person either knew or, *owing to the circumstances at the time, should have known* that the forces were committing or about to commit such crimes; and

(ii) That military commander or person failed to take all necessary and reasonable measures within his or her power to prevent or repress their commission or to submit the matter to the competent authorities for investigation and prosecution.

With respect to the other "superior and subordinate relationships" Article 28(b) contains a similar provision. The difference lies in that, instead of the broad rule on information in (a)(i), the rule in (b)(i) is that "[t]he superior either knew, or *consciously disregarded information which clearly indicated*, that the subordinates were committing or about to commit such crimes". An additional requirement, laid down in (b)(ii), is that "[t]he crimes concerned activities that were within the effective responsibility and control of the superior"; a requirement that in respect of the military commander need not be made.

An important point is that the doctrine of superior responsibility as defined in the Statute applies equally to international and internal armed conflicts. One implication is that in internal armed conflicts, the political and military leaders of non-state armed groups may come to fall under the terms of this article.

Article 29 provides that "[t]he crimes within the jurisdiction of the Court shall not be subject to any statute of limitations". Conceivably, such a crime may be subject to a statute of limitations under the domestic legislation of the state concerned, so that this state, in the terms of Article 17(1), is "genuinely unable to carry out the investigation or prosecution" of that crime. That would make the case admissible to the ICC – and impunity will result if the case is not taken up at the ICC.

Articles 31 and 32 address grounds for excluding criminal responsibility, including self-defence and mistake of law.

Article 33 deals with superior orders, or, more precisely, with crimes committed "pursuant to an order of a Government or of a superior". It provides that such orders do not relieve a person of responsibility, unless that person was (a) legally obliged to obey the order, (b) did not know that the order was unlawful, *and* (c) the order was not manifestly unlawful. Note that the three conditions are cumulative. In respect of condition (c) in particular, paragraph 2 adds that "[f]or the purposes of this article, orders to commit genocide or crimes against humanity are manifestly unlawful". Apart from that, if all three conditions are fulfilled, a valid defence will have been established freeing the accused from criminal responsibility.

5.3.4d The victims

The Statute goes on to provide for the composition, administration and work of the Court (Parts 4 to 8), international cooperation and assistance (Part 9), the enforcement of sentences (Part 10), the Assembly of States Parties (Part 11), financing (Part 12) and final clauses (Part 13). Out of this abundant material, attention goes here only to the situation of the victim as it emerges from the Statute and the Rules of Procedure and Evidence adopted by the Assembly of States Parties in its first (2002) session (ICC-ASP/1/3, Part II-A; hereinafter the Rules). Rule 85 defines victims as "natural persons who have suffered harm as a result of the commission of any crime within the jurisdiction of the Court" – a definition that logically presupposes the existence of an alleged perpetrator "within the jurisdiction of the Court". The victim may figure in an ICC procedure as a witness: a provider of evidence, who may seek to spur the procedure on as well; or as a claimant, seeking reparation for the harm they suffered.

Giving evidence, whether during or after an armed conflict, is a risky activity that may entail all kinds of harassment. The Court must therefore take "all appropriate measures to protect the safety, physical and psychological well-being, dignity and privacy of victims" as of other witnesses; measures that may include "procedures *in camera* or … the presentation of evidence by electronic or other special means" (Art. 68(1, 2)).

Where the "personal interests" of victims in particular are affected, the Court must "permit their views and concerns to be presented and considered at stages of the proceedings determined to be appropriate by the Court and in a manner which is not prejudicial to or inconsistent with the rights of the accused and a fair and impartial trial" (Art. 68(3)). In addition, the Statute provides for the establishment, within the Registry, of a Victims and Witnesses Unit, which is required, in consultation with the Office of the Prosecutor, to provide "protective measures and security arrangements, counselling and other appropriate assistance", and its staff must include expertise, inter alia, in "trauma related to crimes of sexual violence" (Art. 43(6)).

To be admitted to the procedure, a victim must "present [his or her] views and concerns" in writing to the Registrar – in practice, the Victims Participation and Reparation Section of that office. The Registrar submits the application to the relevant Chamber (i.e. the Chamber assigned to handle the case against the alleged perpetrator). It is for this Chamber to decide on his or her admission (Rule 89). Once admitted, the victim may participate in all stages of a case, from the prosecutor's early investigations to the proceedings before the Pre-Trial, Trial and Appeal Chambers. To this end, the victim is "free to choose a legal representative" (Rule 90(1)); given the expected complexity of ICC procedures, this will often be a dire necessity. If there are a number of victims, they may, "for the purposes of ensuring the effectiveness of the proceedings", be requested "to choose a common legal representative or representatives" (Rule 90(2)).

The victim as a claimant is the subject of Article 75. The "principles relating to reparations to, or in respect of, victims, including restitution, compensation and rehabilitation" referred to in the article are specified in Rules 94–8: the victim's request must be in writing and filed with the Registrar; it must contain information on the victim, on the harm suffered, on the incident, including, if possible, the identity of the perpetrator, etc. (Rule 94). A decision on the request can only be expected once the Court arrives at the stage of convicting the perpetrator. Given the large number of victims to be expected with every single crime before the Court; given as well that, for some time to come, convictions will be few and the convicted perpetrators not necessarily wealthy, the conclusion lies ready at hand that not much should be expected of this modality of achieving reparations.

A Chamber may also award reparations on its own motion, but once again only in the process of convicting the perpetrator whose conduct is held to have caused the harm (Rule 95). The same comment applies: for the time being, nothing much should be expected of this capacity of the Court.

The Statute provides a third road towards reparations, in the shape of the Trust Fund for Victims "for the benefit of victims of crimes within the jurisdiction of the Court, and of the families of such victims" (Art. 79). Established on paper in 2002 (ICC-ASP/1/Res.6), the Fund was actually set up and started its work in 2005. Money can arrive at the Fund in two ways. First, awards decided by a Chamber may be made through the Fund (Rule 98(1–4)). However, Rule 98 in a brief closing sentence adds that "[o]ther resources of the Trust Fund may be used for the benefit of victims subject to the provisions of article 79" (para.5). This open-ended reference to "other resources" has been interpreted as a mandate for the Fund to accept money independent of Court awards – a possibility that has been eagerly exploited.

Under its mandate, which does not require the availability of a convicted person, the Trust Fund for Victims is providing support to several thousand victims in the shape of reconciliation workshops, or reconstructive surgery, for example.

The 2010 Review Conference dealt with the multiple aspects of the situation of victims as well. The relevant resolution, entitled "The impact of the Rome Statute system on victims and affected communities", reaffirms the importance of the Statute in the fight against impunity for the perpetrators of the crimes under the ICC mandate. Then, while states are encouraged to implement the Statute provisions "relevant to victims/witnesses", the Court is urged to "continue to optimize ... its field presence in order to improve the way in which it addresses the concerns of victims and affected communities".

The Resolution underlines the need "to ensure that victims and affected communities have access to accurate information about the Court ... as well as about victims' rights under the Rome Statute, including their right to participate in judicial proceedings and claim for reparations". "Governments, communities and civil organizations" are encouraged to "play an active role in sensitizing communities on the rights of victims", in particular those of "victims of sexual violence"; all of this, once again, so as to "combat a culture of impunity". Then, on the matter of retribution, the Resolution stresses the importance of "regular exchanges [of the Trust Fund for Victims] with the international community, including donors and civil society, so as to promote the activities of the Trust Fund and contribute to its visibility", and "States, international organizations, individuals, corporations and other entities" are called upon to contribute to the Fund (RC/Res.2, 8 June 2010).

5.3.4e   Cases before the Court

To date, three states parties to the Rome Statute: Uganda, the Democratic Republic of the Congo and the Central African Republic, have referred situations within their territories to the ICC. In addition, the situation in Darfur, which the Security Council referred to the ICC in 2005, concerns a state, Sudan, which is not a party to the Statute (see Section 5.3.1a). Again, the prosecutor, acting *proprio motu* under Article 15 of the Statute, on 26 November 2009 sought authorisation from the Pre-Trial Chamber to start an investigation into the post-election violence in Kenya in 2007/8 – a period of internal unrest that does not appear to have amounted to an internal armed conflict and therefore is not dealt with here.

The Uganda case is currently being heard before a Pre-Trial Chamber, with the four suspects still at large. The Central African Republic case is in the pre-trial stage. In the situation in the Democratic Republic of the Congo, three cases are being heard, with three suspects in custody and one at large; in one of these cases, the *Prosecutor* v. *Thomas Lubanga Dyilo*, the accused is charged with "enlisting and conscripting children under the age of 15 years into [a non-state armed group] and using them to participate actively in hostilities" in ongoing armed conflicts – the first time this type of conduct has been brought before an international court.

The Darfur referral concerns a situation of internal armed conflict. It was a very difficult case from the outset, and even more so when in July 2008 the Prosecutor decided to seek the indictment of Omar Hassan Ahmad Al Bashir, who was – and, after re-election, still is – the President of Sudan. On 4 March 2009, the Pre-Trial Chamber granted the request of the Prosecutor and duly issued an arrest warrant against Al Bashir, for crimes against humanity and war crimes (though not for genocide). As of this writing, the warrant has not led to the apprehension and detention of President Al Bashir. Indeed, on 25 May 2010, the Pre-Trial Chamber formally informed the Security Council about the total lack of cooperation by the Republic of Sudan "in the case of the Prosecutor v. Ahmad Harun and Ali Kushayh" (as the case is styled).

5.3.4f   The exercise of jurisdiction over the crime of aggression

Article 123 of the ICC Statute provides that seven years after its entry into force, the UN Secretary-General "shall convene a Review Conference to consider any amendments" to the Statute. The Review Conference was duly held in Kampala (Uganda) from 31 May to 11 June 2010. Among the issues before the Conference, the one to be dealt with here concerns the Court's exercise of jurisdiction with respect to the crime of aggression. Other items, notably complementarity v. impunity and the position of victims in criminal procedures before the ICC as well as before domestic courts, are mentioned in Sections 5.3.5 and 5.3.6 below.

As mentioned above, for the Court to exercise jurisdiction over the crime of aggression requires adoption of a provision "defining the crime and setting out the conditions" for this task (Article 5). In effect, the UN General Assembly adopted a definition as long ago as 14 December 1974. Recalling that it is for the Security Council to "determine the existence of any threat to the peace, breach of the peace or act of aggression", Resolution 3314 (XXIX) defines aggression as "the use of armed force by a State against the sovereignty, territorial integrity or political independence of another State, or in any other manner inconsistent with the Charter of the United Nations". It goes on to explain that a state's first use of such force "shall constitute prima facie evidence of an act of aggression although the Security Council may, in conformity with the Charter, conclude that a determination that an act of aggression has been committed would not be justified in the light of other relevant circumstances, including the fact that the acts concerned or their consequences are not of sufficient gravity".

While the General Assembly in 1974 left it to the Security Council to decide that an attack is not 'aggression', practice shows that such an express Security Council decision is not always required. A case in point was the war Eritrea started in 1998 against Ethiopia. The claims commission that investigated this two-year armed conflict concluded that Eritrea had not committed an act of aggression: it did not have the requisite intent, and the Security Council had treated the situation as an ordinary armed conflict between equal partners. (See also Section 5.3.7b.)

For the Review Conference to arrive at its definition of the crime, including the element of sufficient gravity, to anchor the crime of aggression into the Statute, and to define the conditions for its effective application in terms that guaranteed impunity for leaders of states that did not, or not yet, want to accept this new development, has required a series of steps, provisions and clauses that will not all be rendered here (the complete information can be found in the Conference document RC/Res.6). Suffice it to state, first, that Art. 8 *bis* defines the crime as follows:

1. For the purpose of this Statute, "crime of aggression" means the planning, preparation, initiation or execution, by a person in a position effectively to exercise control over or to direct the political or military action of a State, of an act of aggression which, by its character, gravity and scale, constitutes a manifest violation of the Charter of the United Nations.
2. For the purpose of paragraph 1, "act of aggression" means the use of armed force by a State against the sovereignty, territorial integrity or political independence of another State, or in any other manner inconsistent with the Charter of the United Nations. [etc.]

Two further articles regulate the Court's exercise of jurisdiction over the crime of aggression: Article 15 *bis* with respect to state referral or *proprio motu*, and Article 15 *ter* with respect to Security Council referral.

Years must pass before the ICC actually will be able to exercise jurisdiction over the crime of aggression. First, thirty states parties must have accepted the amendments. A further decision confirming the recent decision must be taken after 1 January 2017 by a two-thirds majority of the

states parties to the Statute. Even then, a state party will be able to block
the ICC's exercise of jurisdiction over the crime of aggression by lodging
with the Registrar a declaration to the effect that it does not accept this
jurisdiction. Even so, the 2010 Review Conference has achieved a major
step forward in filling the gap left by the impunity for aggression.

5.3.5   Mixed tribunals

Since the ICTY and the ICTR, the Security Council has established no
further international ad hoc tribunals of the same order of magnitude.
On the other hand, a variety of mixed bodies have been set up, combining
international and domestic elements.

5.3.5a   Extraordinary Chambers in the Courts of
Cambodia (ECCC)

The ECCC, a 'hybrid' or 'internationalised' tribunal functioning partly as
an international and partly as a domestic court, is the product of an agreement between the United Nations and the Government of Cambodia
signed in 2003. In 2004, Cambodia ratified the agreement, passing a 'Law
on the Establishment of the Extraordinary Chambers in the Courts of
Cambodia for the Prosecution of Crimes Committed during the Period of
Democratic Kampuchea'. The ECCC is to try "senior leaders" and "those
most responsible" for the atrocities committed during that time. To date,
it has indicted five persons: Kaing Guek Eav (alias Duch), Nuon Chea,
Ieng Sary, Ieng Thirith and Khieu Samphan.

The jurisdiction of the ECCC extends over the period of Democratic
Kampuchea, from 17 April 1975 to 6 January 1979. It may try suspects
for the international crimes of genocide, crimes against humanity, grave
breaches of the 1949 Geneva Conventions, destruction of cultural property during armed conflict, and crimes against internationally protected
persons, as well as for the domestic crimes of homicide, torture and religious persecution. The inclusion of 'grave breaches of the 1949 Geneva
Conventions' implies a power of the ECCC to deal with such crimes committed in the context of the international armed conflict with Vietnam
that began in May 1975. The conflict lasted until December 1989, but large-
scale fighting occurred in particular during the Democratic Kampuchea
period when Vietnamese forces had invaded Cambodian territory: events
that led the General Assembly to note with concern "that the armed con
flict in Kampuchea [had] escalated and [was] seriously threatening the
peace and stability of South-East Asia".

The ECCC is competent to deal with individual claims, in particular, of victims of a crime within the jurisdiction of the Court who have personally sustained a real physical, material or psychological injury as a direct consequence of the offence. Rule 23 of the Internal Rules of the ECCC (which are in turn based on the Cambodian Criminal Code) defines the purpose of the civil party actions as: to (a) participate in the proceedings by supporting the prosecution, and (b) seek collective and moral reparations. These reparations may take the form of an order to publish the judgment in any appropriate news or other media at the convicted person's expense; an order to fund any non-profit activity or service that is intended for the benefit of victims; or other appropriate and comparable forms of reparation. However, civil parties are not entitled to individual compensation.

On 26 July 2010, Kaing Guek Eav was sentenced to thirty (but effectively nineteen) years in jail. Appeal against the sentence is pending.

5.3.5b   Special Court for Sierra Leone (SCSL)

The SCSL is another 'hybrid' or 'internationalised' tribunal. It stems from Security Council Resolution 1315 of 14 August 2000, requesting the Secretary-General to negotiate an agreement with the Government of Sierra Leone. The agreement was drafted that same year (S-G Report of 4 October 2000, including the text of the agreement and the Statute of the Special Court) and was signed on 16 January 2002.

The SCSL was established to deal with crimes committed in the territory of Sierra Leone after 30 November 1996, the date of a peace agreement between the Government of Sierra Leone and the Revolutionary United Front (RUF) that brought a temporary cessation of hostilities in an ongoing internal armed conflict. Its jurisdiction includes both international crimes (crimes against humanity, violations of common Article 3 of the 1949 Geneva Conventions and of Protocol II of 1977, and other serious violations of international law) as well as domestic crimes (abuse of girls under the 1926 Prevention of Cruelty to Children Act, and wanton destruction of property under the 1861 Malicious Damage Act). Its personal jurisdiction covers "those who bear the greatest responsibility for serious violations of international humanitarian law and Sierra Leonean law", including "those leaders who, in committing such crimes, have threatened the establishment of and implementation of the peace process in Sierra Leone".

Three cases before the SCSL were against leaders of the Civil Defence Forces (CDF), the RUF and the Armed Forces Revolutionary Council

(AFRC). A fourth (and the most conspicuous) indictment was issued against Charles Taylor, the one-time president of neighbouring Liberia. For security reasons, the trial of Taylor has been moved to The Hague; the other trials were/are conducted in Freetown, the capital of Sierra Leone.

The trials of the AFRC, CDF and RUF leaders have been completed, including the appeals phase, with sentences of up to fifty years imprisonment in the first case, up to twenty years in the second and up to fifty-two years in the third. The remaining case, of Charles Taylor, is in the trial phase. The Prosecution rested its case in February 2009 and the Defence opened its case on 13 July 2009. The expectations are that a judgment will be delivered sometime in 2011.

Rule 105 of the SCSL Rules of Procedure and Evidence refers to domestic courts instances where victims may submit claims for reparation based on successful prosecutions. Article XXIX of the Lomé Peace Agreement concluded in 1996 between the Government of Sierra Leone and the Revolutionary United Front of Sierra Leone provides for a special fund for the rehabilitation of war victims – many of them amputees. The effects of this provision are unknown.

5.3.5c   The Special Panels for Serious Crimes (SPSC) in East Timor

In 1999, the Indonesian occupation of East Timor came to an end, and in 2002 East Timor (renamed Timor-Leste) gained independence. Between those dates, the United Nations took over authority and to that end established the UN Transitional Authority in East Timor (UNTAET). UNTAET set up an Investigative Commission of Inquiry, which, focusing in particular on the violence by Indonesian military and pro-Indonesian militias that had followed the September 1999 referendum in favour of independence, reported that hundreds of civilians had been killed, property had been destroyed on a large scale, and thousands of people had been driven from their homes. The Commission's proposal to establish an international tribunal, along the lines of ICTY and ICTR, was rejected in favour of Special Panels for Serious Crimes established within the national legal system (the District Court in Dili, the capital of the country) and each consisting of three judges, two international and one East-Timorese. The Panels were invested with authority over serious international and national crimes committed between January and October of 1999. The international crimes listed included genocide, war crimes and crimes against humanity. UNTAET also set up a Serious Crimes Unit charged with the investigation and prosecution of the crimes in question.

Following independence in May 2002, the Special Panels continued under the authority of the Timor-Leste Government. Then, in May 2005, with the withdrawal of much of the UN infrastructure, the Special Panels suspended operations indefinitely. They had issued indictments for almost 400 people, and held 55 trials involving 88 accused persons, out of which 4 were acquitted and 84 convicted, with 24 pleading guilty. With the suspension of operations, several hundred cases remained untried.

A Commission of Experts established by order of the Security Council reported in 2005 on the functioning of the Special Panels as well as on a Commission for Reception, Truth and Reconciliation that had performed its task coincidentally with the Special Panels. It concluded that a great deal of work had remained undone, not least because of the refusal by Indonesia to cooperate in bringing some high-ranking officers to trial. It saw as one possibility that the Security Council, acting under Chapter VII of the Charter, create an ad hoc tribunal for the prosecution of the outstanding cases. The suggestion was seconded by the International Federation for East Timor, a federation of non-governmental organisations (NGOs) actively engaged in the decolonisation process of Timor-Leste, in a letter of 18 February 2009 addressed to the Security Council.

5.3.5d   The mixed courts of Kosovo

On 10 June 1999, at a time of violent armed conflict in Kosovo between Albanian Kosovars and the Serbian armed forces, the Security Council by Resolution 1244 established the UN Interim Administration Mission in Kosovo (UNMIK). To try alleged perpetrators of atrocities committed during the armed conflict, UNMIK issued regulations permitting international judges to serve alongside domestic judges in existing Kosovar courts, and international lawyers to act together with domestic lawyers in the prosecution or defence of individual war crimes cases. After an initial phase of limited numbers of international judges sitting on panels with a majority of Kosovar judges, UNMIK Regulation 2000/64 provided for panels composed of at least two international judges and one Kosovar judge (hybrid mechanism) to adjudicate cases where it is "necessary to ensure the independence and impartiality of the judiciary or the proper administration of justice". The 'Regulation 64 Panels', which generally adjudicate cases involving serious crimes committed during the conflict, have meanwhile conducted more than two dozen war crimes trials, including those of Miloš Jokić and Dragan Nikolić, both indicted for genocide – and both found not guilty.

5.3.6 Claims commissions

5.3.6a The UN Compensation Commission

In the wake of the Iraqi 1990–1 invasion and occupation of Kuwait, the Security Council by Res. 687 of 3 April 1991 decided that Iraq was "liable under international law for any direct loss, damage, including environmental damage and the depletion of natural resources, or injury to foreign Governments, nationals and corporations, as a result of Iraq's unlawful invasion and occupation of Kuwait" (para. 16). As mentioned in Section 5.3.1a, it also decided "to create a fund to pay compensation for claims that fall within [that paragraph] and to establish a Commission that [would] administer the fund" (para. 18). On 20 May 1991, following a report of the Secretary-General, the Council by Res. 692 established the UN Compensation Commission (the UNCC) as one of its subsidiary organs, as well as the UN Compensation Fund.

Located in Geneva and comprising a governing council, panels of commissioners and a secretariat, the UNCC has verified and valued claims arising as much from the *jus ad bellum* argument of unlawful invasion and occupation of Kuwait as from acts violating the applicable *jus in bello*. It also administers the payment of compensation. Claims were not submitted by the thousands of individual and corporate claimants themselves but bundled by their national governments. Moreover, as noted by the Secretary-General in his report to the Security Council of 2 May 1991, the UNCC could not be "a court or an arbitral tribunal before which the parties appear". Rather, it examined claims on the basis of documentation as presented and, where necessary, supplemented with what could be discovered with expert help. Obviously, the higher the claimed amount, the more deep probing the verification. Altogether, the almost 2.7 million claimants who saw their claims honoured were allotted more than 52 billion US dollars in compensation.

A vast number of the claims for common matters such as forced departure or personal injury could be decided in bulk, on the legal ground of unlawfulness of the invasion and occupation, and with the aid of statistics. Rules of the law of armed conflict came into play, for instance, when a person claimed to have been detained as a prisoner of war and the question was whether they had qualified for that status.

5.3.6b The Eritrea–Ethiopia Claims Commission

From May 1998 to June 2000, Eritrea and Ethiopia waged a war at vast expense and with a huge number of casualties. The hostilities ceased with an agreement concluded at Algiers on 18 June 2000, and on 12 December 2000, a peace agreement was signed at the same place. Article 5(1) of the 'December Agreement' provides for the establishment of a "neutral Claims Commission". This was given the mandate to decide all claims for loss, damage or injury, whether by governments or by natural and juridical persons who were nationals of one of the parties. Claims must be related to the conflict and must "result from violations of international humanitarian law, including the 1949 Geneva Conventions, or other violations of international law". Excluded were "claims arising from the cost of military operations, preparing for military operations, or the use of force, except to the extent that such claims involve violations of international humanitarian law".

The Eritrea–Ethiopia Claims Commission (the EECC) was established in 2001 as a treaty body under the aegis of the Hague-based Permanent Court of Arbitration, which also served as its registry. It was composed of five lawyers, two of them appointed by each party and the fifth selected by these four. Claims could be submitted by the parties on their own behalf and on behalf of natural and juridical persons who were their nationals or of Ethiopian or Eritrean origin. The claims were filed under six headings: (1) unlawful expulsion or (2) unlawful displacement of natural persons, (3) mistreatment of persons held as prisoners of war, (4) unlawful detention or mistreatment during detention of civilians, and any other claims of (5) persons or (6) governments for loss, damage or injury. Under the sixth heading, Ethiopia brought claims for Eritrea's violation of *jus ad bellum* in opening the hostilities. The EECC, while honouring the claims, did not regard Eritrea's attack as aggression, given the absence of the requisite intent. Note that the claims before the EECC were state, not individual, claims.

The EECC divided its work over two phases: issues of liability, and damages. In the first phase, starting out with the mistreatment of prisoners of war, the EECC placed on record that both parties evidently "had a commitment to the most fundamental principles bearing on prisoners of war". Their troops were trained and instructed on the requisite procedures, and "in contrast to many other contemporary armed conflicts", they "regularly and consistently took POWs", and enemy personnel *hors de combat* were "moved away from the battlefield to conditions of greater safety". Indeed, "although these cases involve two of the poorest countries in the world, both made significant efforts to provide for the sustenance and care of the POWs in their custody" (Partial Award, Prisoners of War, Ethiopia's Claim 4, 1 July 2003, para. 12). Even so, the EECC found Eritrea, and to a lesser degree Ethiopia, liable for significant violations of this part of the law.

One question was where to find the law. While Ethiopia was a long-standing party to the Geneva Conventions of 1949, Eritrea acceded only on 14 August 2000. The applicable law was therefore the customary law of war. While all parties agreed that most of the Third Convention had that character, Eritrea listed a few ostensibly minor exceptions, not-ably, one regarding the ICRC's claimed right of access to prisoners of war. This, it argued, is a treaty-based right, and the relevant language in Convention III belonged to the "detailed or procedural provisions" that had not acquired the status of customary law. The Commission notes that the ICRC did not agree, as demonstrated by a press statement of 7 May 1999 in which "it recounted its visits to POWs and interned civilians held by Ethiopia and said: 'In Eritrea, meanwhile, the ICRC is pursuing its efforts to gain access, as required by the Third Geneva Convention, to Ethiopian POWs captured since the conflict erupted last year'". The EECC, for its part, argues that far from being procedural, the visits to POW camps belong to the ICRC's essential humanitarian func-tions, and it held Eritrea liable for the suffering caused by its refusal to permit the ICRC to "send its delegates to visit all places where Ethiopian POWs were detained, to register those POWs, to interview them with-out witnesses, and to provide them with the customary relief and ser-vices" (Partial Award, Prisoners of War, Ethiopia's Claim 4, 1 July 2003, paras. 55–62).

The issue of applicable law arose again with respect to claims arising from military operations and occupation. Here, the EECC accepted, and neither party contested, that the 1907 Hague Regulations and most of Protocol I of 1977, including the 'safety net' provisions of Article 75 on fundamental guarantees of humane treatment, reflect customary law. As for the use of anti-personnel landmines and booby traps, the EECC felt that the 1980 Conventional Weapons Convention with its annexed Protocols were too recent, and state practice too varied, for these instru-ments to have expressed customary law applicable in the armed conflict at issue. Exception was made for some rules in the 1980 Mines Protocol on minefield recording and the prohibition of indiscriminate use: rules that "reflect fundamental humanitarian law obligations of discrimination and protection of civilians" (Partial Award, Central Front, Eritrea's Claims 2,

4, 6, 7 and 22, 28 April 2004, para. 24). With all due respect, this form of words is more suggestive of principle than custom.

Both parties had actually used landmines, usually as a defensive measure around military positions. Such use, the EECC notes, "has been common and permissible under customary international law". This requires "reasonable precautions, such as fences or warning signs ... to protect civilians remaining in the area wherever they were at risk of entering those defensive mine fields". It was not known whether such precautions had been taken, but claims had arisen from the effects of anti-personnel landmines left behind when forces were forced to withdraw from their positions. On this, the EECC notes that "[w]hen troops are compelled to quit their defensive positions by force of arms ... it is understandable that they may be unable to remove or otherwise neutralize their mine fields. On the contrary, they may depend on those mine fields to slow their attackers or to channel their attacks sufficiently to allow defense and escape". Indeed, the risk thus posed to civilians from perfectly lawful minelaying operations went to underscore "the importance of the rapid development in recent years of new international conventions aimed at restricting and even prohibiting all future use of antipersonnel landmines" (Partial Award, Central Front, Ethiopia's Claim 2, 28 April 2004, paras. 50, 51). It may be a while before the "new international conventions" that are now on the book have acquired the status of customary law.

Out of the wealth of cases dealt with by the EECC, mention is made here of one case that concerns aerial bombardment. On 5 June 1998, Ethiopian aircraft attacked the Asmara airport, and Eritrean aircraft, the Mek'ele airport. If only because both airports also housed military aircraft, they were legitimate military objectives. Ethiopia claimed, however, that Eritrean aircraft had also dropped cluster bombs "in the vicinity of the Ayder School ... in Mekele town", killing or wounding a number of civilians, including schoolchildren; and it alleged that this had been done intentionally. Eritrea in the end conceded that cluster bombs had been dropped in the vicinity of the school, but this, it contended, "was an accident incidental to legitimate military operations, not a deliberate attack".

Focusing on the available "rather limited key facts and pieces of evidence", the EECC in the end holds that the third and fourth of four sorties flown by Eritrean aircraft dropped cluster bombs in the vicinity of the Ayder School. However, it is "not convinced that Eritrea had deliberately targeted a civilian neighbourhood"; it had "obvious and compelling reasons to concentrate its limited air assets on Ethiopia's air fighting capability – its combat aircraft and the Mekele airport"; it is "not credible that

Eritrea would see advantage in setting the precedent of targeting civilians, given Ethiopia's apparent air superiority"; its programmers and pilots had "little experience" with the "computerized aiming systems" on board its single-pilot aircraft; it is unlikely that "two consecutive sorties mak[e] precisely the same targeting error", and many "types of human error ... could have resulted in the bombs being released at the wrong place".

So, no malicious intent, but the dropping of cluster bombs in the vicinity of the Ayder School doubtless amounted to an attack as defined in Article 49(1) of Protocol I: were the acts also justifiable? The EECC finds the yardstick in Article 57 of Protocol I, on 'precautions in attack': this "requires all 'feasible' precautions, not precautions that are practically impossible". Carefully weighing the limited available evidence, the EECC ultimately concludes that "failure of two ... bomb runs to come close to their intended targets clearly indicates a lack of essential care in conducting them". Thus, since Eritrea has not taken "all feasible precautions ... in its conduct of the air strikes on Mekele", the EECC "finds that it is liable for the deaths, wounds and physical damage to civilians and civilian objects caused in Mekele by the third and fourth sorties on June 5, 1998" (Partial Award, Central Front, Ethiopia's Claim 2, 28 April 2004, paras. 101–13).

At the end of the second phase of its work, the EECC allotted damages to both parties for each of the violations of applicable law it had established. For the Mek'ele affair alone, with 60 persons killed and 168 injured, it awarded 2.5 million US dollars (Final Award, Ethiopia's Damages Claims, paras. 154–61). It concludes this Final Award, as the other ones, with a reiteration of "its confidence that the Parties will ensure that the compensation awarded will be paid promptly, and that funds received in respect of their claims will be used to provide relief to their civilian populations injured in the war".

5.3.7   Human rights bodies

International human rights bodies are often carrying out their activities in, or in respect of, theatres of armed conflict. In such theatres, rules of humanitarian law are applicable, usually alongside other branches of law. One such other branch is human rights law, a body of law remarkably similar in substance to certain rules and principles of the law of war (for example, principles of the right to life, or of the inviolability of the human person). The two branches are very different, however, in respect of orientation (with in particular the civil and political human rights law providing the individual person with rights against the state) and of scope of application (with human rights treaties tending to limit this to the territory of the state).

Intergovernmental human rights bodies derive their mandate from a treaty or comparable document, and NGOs, from an equally constitutive text emanating from the organisation or movement they belong to. Of interest for present purposes are two questions: what law are the human rights bodies mandated to apply: human rights law, or humanitarian law, or both? And how is their jurisdiction defined? The number of international human rights bodies is legion – we confine ourselves here to a few of the most important ones.

5.3.7a Applicable law

From among the intergovernmental organisations with worldwide activity, two UN agencies are mentioned here: the Office of the High Commissioner for Human Rights and the Human Rights Council (formerly the Commission on Human Rights, composed of states periodically elected by the General Assembly). Although operating under the banner of human rights, they both come across humanitarian law, for instance, when rapporteurs (on torture, on summary executions, on the position of women and children, etc.) sent out to countries involved in armed conflict couch their reports in terms of the law of war as well.

This is particularly the case with the branch office of the High Commissioner for Human Rights in Colombia, a country that is the scene of protracted internal armed conflict. The office is expressly mandated to collect information and receive claims about violations of human rights and humanitarian law, whether committed by the army or other state agency or by one of the non-state armed groups active in the country. The office entertains direct contacts with the central authorities and it reports, in general terms and through the High Commissioner's Office in Geneva, to the UN.

The Human Rights Council, composed of forty-seven states elected by the General Assembly, is a more political body. While this may taint its discussion of the issues on the agenda, its discussions and resolutions may nonetheless act as an incentive towards improved behaviour, including in terms of respect for the law of armed conflict.

On 3 April 2009, in reaction to recent events in the Middle East, the Human Rights Council established a commission headed by Judge Richard Goldstone and mandated "to investigate all violations of international human rights law and international humanitarian law that might have been committed at any time in the context of the military operations that were conducted in Gaza during the period from 27 December 2008 and 18 January 2009, whether before, during or after". The commission's report of 30 September 2009, entitled 'Human Rights in Palestine and other Occupied Arab Territories', formulates a series of recommendations on 'collective' and 'individual' accountability for serious violations of humanitarian law and human rights law. The recommendations of this 'Goldstone Report' are addressed to various UN organs, to Israel, the 'responsible Palestine authorities' and 'Palestinian armed groups', as well as to the Prosecutor of the International Criminal Court. In furtherance of these recommendations, UN General Assembly Resolutions of 2 November 2009 and 23 February 2010 give Israel and the Palestine authorities three months to undertake "independent, credible investigations" into the alleged violations. The resolutions also ask the Secretary-General to report back within three months on their implementation, with a view to considering further action by relevant UN bodies. As of this writing, it is not yet clear what effect the report may have on the parties to the conflict.

In contrast to the above two UN bodies, the Human Rights Committee can only express itself in terms of human rights. It is established under the regime of the International Covenant on Civil and Political Rights (or ICCPR). Since this treaty is only concerned with human rights, so too has the Committee an equally restricted mandate: states parties would not allow it to directly apply other rules such as international humanitarian law.

The Committee's mandate is to examine and comment on reports submitted by states parties on the implementation of the rights contained in the treaty. In addition to the reporting procedure, Article 41 of the treaty provides for the Committee to consider inter-state complaints with regard to alleged violations. Apart from that, an Optional Protocol to the Covenant, adopted in 1966 and in force since 1976, enables the Committee to consider individual complaints (called 'communications') as well. The ICCPR tends to keep an eye in particular on situations of serious political trouble or armed conflict, including military occupation, and on situations where troops are taking part in peacekeeping operations.

Down to the regional level, the relevant human rights bodies in the Americas are the Inter-American Commission on Human Rights (IACHR) and the Inter-American Court of Human Rights (IACtHR). The Commission was created in 1960 by a meeting of American Ministers of Foreign Affairs, incorporated as a principal organ in the Charter of the Organization of American States in 1967, and given a place in the American Convention on Human Rights of 1969. This Convention also created the Court. The applicable law is found in the Convention as well as in the American Declaration of the Rights and Duties of Man of 1948: regarded at the outset as a non-binding text, both the Court and the Commission have since recognised the Declaration as a source of international obligations for member states of the Organization of American States.

Both the IACHR and the IACtHR have a wide practice of dealing with situations of armed conflict. Where human rights law is insufficiently equipped to cope with the particularities of armed conflict, these bodies revert to relevant rules of the law of armed conflict as a 'source of authoritative guidance'. The IACHR also applies this law directly in assessing the conduct of non-state armed groups (which it regards as non-accountable under human rights law). However, when it attempted to apply the law of armed conflict to the state as well and hold Colombia responsible for violations of Article 3 common to the Geneva Conventions, it was stopped by the Court (*Las Palmeras*, judgment on preliminary objections, 4 February 2000).

In the European region, the main intergovernmental human rights body is the European Court of Human Rights (ECHR), created under the European Convention for the Protection of Human Rights and Fundamental Freedoms (Rome, 1950). Apart from state complaints, the ECHR may receive individual applications from any person, NGO or group of persons claiming to be the victim of a violation by a state party of the right set forth in the Convention. While the Court has had to deal with complaints arising from situations of armed conflict it has adjudged such cases solely in terms of human rights. Examples include the Turkish military occupation of northern Cyprus and the internal armed conflict in Chechnya. On 24 February 2005, the Court issued two judgments on claims arising out of the conduct of hostilities in the armed conflict in Chechnya (*Isayeva, Yusupova & Bazayeva* v. *Russia*, App. Nos. 57947–49/00, and *Isayeva* v. *Russia*, App. No. 57950/00). While the conduct of hostilities is often seen as the exclusive realm of the law of armed conflict, the Court directly applied human rights law without so much as referring to that other body of law.

Among non-governmental human rights bodies, Human Rights Watch has been the first to openly investigate and report on situations of armed conflict in terms of both human rights and humanitarian law. As an NGO, its competence to act is not based on (nor limited by) any treaty.

It is therefore free to, and actually does, 'accuse' any parties or individuals of violations of these bodies of law. In doing so, it strives to be, and to be seen as, a credible source of information. Amnesty International, for its part, is equally capable of speaking out against violations of the law of war committed by any party.

5.3.7b   Extraterritorial jurisdiction

The treaty bodies in the above paragraphs (ICCPR, IACHR and IACtHR, and ECHR) depend for their territorial jurisdiction on the terms of the respective treaties. Thus, Article 2(1) of the ICCPR provides that "[e]ach State Party to the present Covenant undertakes to respect and to ensure to all individuals within its territory and subject to its jurisdiction the rights recognized in the present Covenant". Reading this provision, with its dual requirement of "within its territory" and "subject to [a state's] jurisdiction", is of particular interest to states taking part in armed conflicts outside their own territory. The ICCPR has decided that the text requires states parties "to respect and to ensure the Covenant rights to all persons who may be within their territory and to all persons subject to their jurisdiction. This means that a State party must respect and ensure the rights laid down in the Covenant to anyone within the power or effective control of that State Party, even if not situated within the territory of the State Party" (para. 10 of General Comment No. 31 [80] adopted on 29 March 2004).

The 1948 American Declaration of the Rights and Duties of Man contains no provision delimiting its scope of application; indeed, the preamble severs the application of human rights even from a person's link of nationality to a given state, considering instead that the rights "are based upon attributes of his human personality". In contrast, Article 1(1) of the American Convention on Human Rights provides that "[t]he States Parties to this Convention undertake to respect the rights and freedoms recognized herein and to ensure to all persons subject to their jurisdiction the free and full exercise of those rights and freedoms". In effect, issues of scope of application in situations of armed conflict needed not be expected in the southern part of the American hemisphere, where most armed conflicts were internal ones.

The situation is different as regards the northern half, with the United States and Canada frequently involved in armed conflicts beyond their borders, whether as a state party or in a peacekeeping role. Since neither state is a party to the Convention, issues of interpretation of Article 1(1) could not arise either before the IACtHR. However, the possible extraterritorial effect of the American Declaration has arisen more than once in reports of the IACHR.

One case arose from the invasion, in October 1983, by US and Caribbean armed forces into Grenada, where they deposed a revolutionary government that had taken power after the murder of the prime minister and a number of his associates. Seventeen individuals arrested and detained by the US forces in the first days of the operation and turned over again to the Grenadian authorities in November 1983, lodged complaints about maltreatment with the IACHR, invoking the Declaration as the basis of their claims. The IACHR notes in its report on admissibility that:

> under certain circumstances, the exercise of its jurisdiction over acts with an extraterritorial locus will not only be consistent with but required by the norms which pertain ... Given that individual rights inhere simply by virtue of a person's humanity, each American State is obliged to uphold the protected rights of any person subject to its jurisdiction. While this most commonly refers to persons within a state's territory, it may, under given circumstances, refer to conduct with an extraterritorial locus where the person concerned is present in the territory of one state, but subject to the control of another state – usually through the acts of the latter's agents abroad. In principle, the inquiry turns not on the presumed victim's nationality or presence within a particular geographic area, but on whether, under the specific circumstances, the State observed the rights of a person subject to its authority and control. (*Coard et al.* v. *the USA*, para. 37)

Another situation arguably involving the issue of 'authority and control' arose in the wake of '9/11', with the USA detaining on Guantánamo Bay a large number of individuals captured in Afghanistan and elsewhere. In 2002, the IACHR received a request for 'precautionary measures' on behalf of these people. One argument in its decision to impose such measures was that "where persons find themselves within the authority and control of a state and where a circumstance of armed conflict may be involved, their fundamental rights may be determined in part by reference to international humanitarian law as well as international human rights law". Since it was well known that the USA, in contrast, held that humanitarian law, as the *lex specialis*, was the only law applicable on Guantánamo Bay, but that the individuals detained there did not qualify for protection under the Geneva Conventions, the IACHR argued that in such a situation where "the protections of international humanitarian law do not apply ... such persons remain the beneficiaries at least of the non-derogable protections under international human rights law. In short, no person, under the authority and control of a state ... is devoid of legal protection for his or her fundamental and non-derogable human rights" (Decision on Request for Precautionary Measures (Detainees at Guantanamo Bay, Cuba), 12 March 2002). While the argument about "authority and control" was well placed, the attempt to impose precautionary measures was bound to fail, given that neither the American Convention on Human Rights (not applicable anyway) nor the Organization of American States Charter grants the IACHR a power to order precautionary measures.

The European Convention on Human Rights provides that "[t]he High Contracting Parties shall secure to everyone within their jurisdiction the rights and freedoms defined in Section I of this Convention" (Art. 1). The Court has held that while "jurisdiction" under this provision is primarily territorial, it may exceptionally be extraterritorial. This is most markedly the case when "as a consequence of military action – whether lawful or unlawful – [a state] exercises effective control of an area outside its national territory", as in the case of the Turkish military occupation of northern Cyprus (*Loizidou* v. *Turkey*, judgment on preliminary objections, 23 March 1995, para. 62). In contrast, in a case arising from the aerial bombardment by NATO forces of the Serbian Radio-Television station in Belgrade, the Court went out of its way to explain that such an act – a typical example of conduct of hostilities as opposed to a situation of occupation – did not mean that the attacking states had jurisdiction within the meaning of Article 1 of the ECHR. The Court stated that "had the drafters of the Convention wished to ensure jurisdiction as extensive as that advocated by the applicants, they could have adopted a text the same as or similar to the contemporaneous Articles 1 of the four Geneva Conventions of 1949" (*Bankovic* v. *Belgium et al.*, Grand Chamber Decision on admissibility, 12 December 2001).

In sum, although the practice of human rights bodies described above is still limited, it provides a welcome addition to the admittedly limited array of international means to enforce compliance with international humanitarian law by parties to armed conflicts. The strength of these bodies lies in their capacity to speak out openly, to reprimand, to exhort and to find violations. Their weaknesses are that they are not all equally well versed in humanitarian law, and that at all events they have no power to authoritatively hold parties responsible for violations of that law. Therefore, while their interest in international humanitarian law should be supported and encouraged, their activities in this area do not remove the need to develop supervisory mechanisms specifically mandated to enforce compliance with humanitarian norms.

5.3.8   National jurisdictions

In 1907, the Second Hague Peace Conference introduced into Article 3 of the Convention on Land Warfare the principle that a belligerent party is liable to pay compensation for violations of the law of war. While under one interpretation, this rule equips the victim with a tool to claim damages from the responsible adverse party, the usual reading of Article 3 is that it applies only on the international plane, where the individual victim has no standing. Practice appears to confirm the latter interpretation.

In the aftermath of the Second World War, Japanese courts were seised in the 1990s of a series of cases specifically concerning the above question brought by individuals who at the time of the Second World War had been ill-treated by the Japanese armed forces, whether as prisoners of war, civilian detainees or 'comfort women' (forcibly prostituted women and girls in occupied territory). Some had earlier received some token payment from their national authorities out of money paid by Japan on the basis of lump-sum agreements concluded after the war; in other cases no such agreement existed, or, as in the case of a group of Philippine 'comfort women', the victims had not earlier been able to speak at all about their sufferings. The cases were all rejected, mainly on the argument that foreigners cannot bring such claims based on the law of war against the state of Japan. One positive point is that the effort was made at all, not just by the claimants but by their Japanese voluntary counsel as well – and, indeed, by the courts, which gave the cases serious consideration.

Elsewhere, and in reaction to the events in various recent armed conflicts, states are showing a greater readiness to take up matters relating to violations of international humanitarian law than has long been the case. Thus, the first case to come to the ICTY, against a Bosnian Serb named Duško Tadić, began with his arrest in 1994 in Germany and by the German authorities on suspicion of having committed offences in Bosnia-Herzegovina, including torture and aiding and abetting the commission of genocide, which, both in terms of substance and of jurisdiction, could be tried in Germany. A formal Request for Deferral brought the case to the ICTY.

Since then, numerous cases arising out of the events in the former Yugoslavia and Rwanda have been dealt with in various national jurisdictions, in situations where the Tribunals saw no grounds for asking for a deferral. In Rwanda in particular, the vast majority of the cases arising out of the massacres of 1994 were left for the national courts of that country to deal with. Even though the events of 1994 had left the judicial system largely destroyed in terms of personnel and infrastructure, by 2006 some 10,000 genocide suspects had been tried. In an effort to deal with the enormous backlog (with over 120,000 suspects awaiting trial by 2000 in Rwanda's prisons and communal jails) a third approach was launched in 2002: 'Gacaca', or 'judgment on the grass'. Inspired by indigenous models of local justice, Gacaca represents a model of restorative justice through which genocide suspects are tried and judged by neighbours in their community. By the end of 2009, when the system had to be brought to a close, Gacaca courts had dealt with over a million cases, securing over 70,000 convictions. While the system has been criticised on procedural grounds, with the accused having no right to see their files or be legally represented, it is assessed to have contributed to reconciliation in Rwanda, bringing genocide perpetrators face to face with the survivors.

Also as a consequence of recent events in the former Yugoslavia, Rwanda and elsewhere, it has been realised anew that a state's criminal laws and rules on jurisdiction must enable the prosecution and trial of serious violations of humanitarian law committed outside that state by nationals of another state who subsequently are found in its territory (as Tadić was in Germany). In several states, existing legislation has been adapted; in other states, this work is in progress, where required, with the assistance of the ICRC Advisory Services (see below, Section 5.3.9b). States that have been actively seeking to exercise universal jurisdiction in the fight against impunity for cases of torture, war crimes, crimes against humanity and genocide include Belgium, Denmark, France, Germany, the Netherlands, Norway, Spain and the United States.

In Belgium, an Act for the punishment of grave breaches of international humanitarian law was amended in 1999 to include universal jurisdiction over war crimes, crimes against humanity and genocide. Attempts to bring this jurisdiction to bear on high-ranking officials such as former Prime Minister of Israel Ariel Sharon, former Chinese President Jiang Zemin and former US President George H. W. Bush having led to vehement negative reactions, the Act was amended in April 2003, providing for immunity "in accordance with international law". Following further pressure, the Act was repealed altogether in August 2003 and its provisions concerning international crimes were incorporated into the Belgian Criminal Code.

In a similar pattern, a law of 1985 conferred on Spanish courts universal jurisdiction over genocide and any offence that Spain was obliged to prosecute under international treaties, including the Convention against Torture and the 1949 Geneva Conventions and Protocol I of 1977, and crimes against humanity were brought under the Spanish Criminal Code in 2004. When a number of high-profile cases (e.g. against former Chinese President Jiang Zemin, former Peruvian President Alberto Fujimori, former Israeli officials, and former officials of the US administration) had met with increasing international pressure, the Spanish Congress on 25 July 2009 passed a law that limits the competence of the High Court (Audiencia Nacional) to cases in which Spanish nationals are victimised, the alleged perpetrators are on Spanish territory, or there is another relevant link to Spain.

In the Netherlands, the International Crimes Act of 19 June 2003, in force since 1 October of that year, empowers the courts to exercise universal jurisdiction over genocide, war crimes, crimes against humanity and torture, provided the perpetrator is present in the country and the crimes were committed after the entry into force of the act. International crimes committed before that date have to be dealt with under previous law, the Wartime Offences Act of 10 July 1952, the Genocide Convention Implementation Act of 1964 or the Act implementing the Convention against Torture of 1988.

Finally, reference should be made to two cases brought in the USA under the Alien Tort Claims Act by a group of Bosnian Muslims who sought compensation from Radovan Karadžić for acts of genocide, rape, forced prostitution, torture and other cruel, inhuman and degrading treatment committed under his command during the conflict in the former Yugoslavia. At the jurisdiction stage the court held that the Act gave it jurisdiction over claims based on genocide and war crimes, which it considered to include violations of common Article 3 of the Geneva Conventions. Judgments entered against Karadžić in 2000 awarded the victims $4.5 billion. With Karadžić on trial at the ICTY, it remains to be seen how the judgments might ever be executed.

In a parallel development, the United Nations General Assembly on 21 March 2006 adopted Resolution 60/167 on "Basic Principles and Guidelines on the Right to a Remedy and Reparation for Victims of Gross Violations of International Human Rights Law and Serious Violations of International Humanitarian Law". Opening with a discussion of states' "obligation to respect, ensure respect for and implement" the twin bodies of law listed in the title, the Resolution exhorts states to incorporate the relevant rules of international law into their domestic legal systems, and to adopt procedures that provide effective access to justice and adequate remedies. It sets forth the duty of states to investigate and prosecute "gross violations" of these bodies of law – a duty which in respect of international humanitarian law is limited to such violations that "constitut[e] crimes under international law". Turning next to the victims of gross violations of human rights law or the law of war, the Resolution defines them as those persons who individually or collectively have suffered any type of harm, including, where appropriate, the immediate family and other dependants. And it makes the point that victims should be treated with "humanity and respect for their dignity and human rights".

In subsequent sections, Resolution 60/167 develops victims' rights to three types of remedy: access to justice, reparation for harm suffered, and access to information. Access to justice means "equal access to an effective judicial remedy as provided for under international law". It also implies access to administrative and similar bodies, as well as "measures to minimize the inconvenience to victims and their representatives", etc. In addition, states "should endeavour" to develop group claims procedures. A final clause to this section specifies that to be adequate, effective and prompt the judicial remedies "should include all available and appropriate international processes in which a person may have legal standing". Significantly, the text passes over in silence the issue discussed above, of the victim seeking access to an (ex-)enemy legal system.

Reparation for harm suffered is subdivided into restitution (whenever possible to the original situation), compensation (for any economically assessable damage), rehabilitation (including medical and psychological care as well as legal and social services), satisfaction (through such disparate steps as verification of the facts, search for the whereabouts of the disappeared or killed, a public apology, etc.) and guarantees of non-repetition (through a list of measures that will at the same time contribute to the prevention of further violations).

Apart from the mass of detail in elaborating the various sections of Resolution 60/167, its main import lies in its incessant emphasis on the duties of states, that is, governments and all other parts of the public state system, to do whatever is required to turn the notion of victims' rights to a remedy into a living reality.

5.3.9 The International Red Cross and Red Crescent Movement

5.3.9a The structure of the Movement

Among the institutions referred to in the foregoing, the ICRC is certainly the one cited most often, whether alone or in one breath with other parts of the 'Red Cross family'. The original component parts of this family are the ICRC and the national societies, whether Red Cross or Red Crescent (and now including the Israeli Magen David Adom, or Red Shield of David, as well). The societies are organised under the umbrella of the International Federation of Red Cross and Red Crescent Societies (which, like the ICRC, has its seat at Geneva). All components are bound by the Fundamental Principles of the Movement proclaimed in 1965 by the 20th International Conference: humanity, impartiality, neutrality, independence, voluntary service, unity and universality.

The national societies, originally devised as auxiliaries to the military medical services, today find their tasks, domestically, mostly in the fields of healthcare and assistance to those most in need, and in disaster preparedness. On the international level, they may provide assistance to the victims of man-made or natural disasters, through the national societies concerned or, depending on whether the disaster is 'man-made' (armed conflict) or natural, the ICRC or the Federation. Many societies are also increasingly active in the dissemination of international humanitarian law.

The Statutes of the Movement, adopted in 1986, identify the ICRC, the national societies and the Federation as its components. Yet their first section deals with the states parties to the 1949 Geneva Conventions (as mentioned earlier, today all existing states plus the Vatican), thus recognising the close links between the community of states and the Movement. These links find their expression in particular in the International Conference of the Red Cross and Red Crescent, "the supreme deliberative body for the Movement" (Art. 8). At the Conference, which in principle meets every four years (Art. 11), state delegations have the same voting rights as the delegations of the components. This makes the Conference an interesting forum for states, where they can vote on issues, say, of humanitarian law without becoming formally bound.

The Statutes mention two further organs of the Movement: the Council of Delegates (where the representatives of its components "meet to discuss matters which concern the Movement as a whole" (Art. 12), which meets on the occasion of an International Conference) and the Standing Commission of the Red Cross and Red Crescent, defined as "the trustee of the International Conference between two Conferences" (Art. 16). The Standing Commission is composed of five representatives of national societies and two of the ICRC and the Federation each (Art. 17). Its main functions are: preparation of the next Council and International Conference, and settling problems and conflicts that might arise between components – most often between the ICRC and the Federation (Art. 18).

With Geneva being the city where the international components of the Movement are located, this is also one of the main venues for states' diplomatic contacts with the ICRC and the Federation, or among themselves, about matters of humanitarian concern. (The other venue is New York, at the United Nations Headquarters.)

5.3.9b   The ICRC

Both the ICRC and the Federation have their own organisational structure, which need not be exposed in detail here. Yet, given the purpose of this book, some further information about the ICRC is in order. Founded in Geneva in 1863 (as recalled in Article 5 of the Statutes) it is formally recognised in the Geneva Conventions and by the International Conference as an independent humanitarian organisation, with a status of its own (often indicated as *sui generis*, setting the ICRC apart from non-governmental organisations).

The ICRC is governed by its own Statutes. Article 4(1) lists a series of functions that "in particular" fall within its role, first and foremost: "to maintain and disseminate the Fundamental Principles of the Movement". Roles we encountered frequently in the course of this book are "to work for the faithful application of international humanitarian law" and "to work for the understanding and dissemination of knowledge of [this law] and to prepare any development thereof" – in short, to act as guardian and promoter of humanitarian law.

Another essential function is "to endeavour at all times … to ensure the protection of and assistance to military and civilian victims of [armed conflicts or internal strife] and of their direct results". One practical feature is the role of the ICRC's field delegates, who monitor the application of humanitarian law by the parties to conflicts. In case of violations they attempt to persuade the relevant authority – be it of the state or of a non-state armed group – to correct its behaviour. Whenever necessary, such efforts may be reinforced from the ICRC headquarters. Through this work, the ICRC endeavours to build a constructive relationship with all involved in the violence, and it conducts what could be called 'discreet diplomacy'.

Given the element of confidentiality required in this work, the ICRC maintains that neither its delegates nor the institution itself can be obliged to provide evidence before national or international courts. This claim has been honoured by the ICTY and the ICC, and a clause to this effect is included in headquarters agreements establishing its privileges and immunities in the states where it has a presence.

That said, if all confidential interventions fail to produce the desired results, the ICRC reserves its right to publicly denounce the violations.

The aim of speaking out is not to single out individual responsible persons but, rather, to appeal to the parties to the conflict to respect humanitarian law. The ICRC also frequently appeals to other states to intervene with the parties concerned.

Article 4(2) reaffirms that the ICRC may take any humanitarian initiative that comes within its role as a specifically neutral and independent institution and intermediary, and may consider any question requiring examination by such an institution. To this end (and as also recognised in the Geneva Conventions) it may offer its services to parties to armed conflicts. Two instruments may be mentioned in this respect. One we encountered in earlier parts of this book (Sections 3.4.3, 3.4.5, 3.4.6f) is the Central Tracing Agency that, dating back to 1870, acts as an intermediary between parties to an armed conflict, transmitting information on prisoners of war and interned civilians and detainees to the other party in the conflict, who in turn inform the relevant families. The system is also used to inform families of combatants who have died.

The other instrument is the relatively novel Advisory Service on International Humanitarian Law that, as part of the ICRC's legal division, serves to advise and assist states in their efforts to adopt national measures of implementation. Apart from this, ICRC legal experts at its headquarters in Geneva and in the field provide states with technical assistance, for example, on legislation to prosecute war criminals or protect the red cross and red crescent emblems.

Although states have primary responsibility for the teaching of humanitarian law, over the years the ICRC has developed a considerable expertise in that field and its delegates often give courses, especially to armed and security forces, state employees and diplomats as well as civilians in general. In these activities, the ICRC whenever possible cooperates with the local Red Cross and Red Crescent societies, as, indeed, with the International Federation.

6

Conclusion

The international humanitarian law of armed conflict, rather than being an end in itself, is a means to an end: the preservation of humanity in the face of the reality of war. That reality confronts us every day; the means remains therefore necessary.

The preceding chapters provide a sketch of the development of the international humanitarian law of warfare and of some of its problems. These problems are more varied and complicated than usually emerges in public debate, with its tendency to take notice of humanitarian law only in the context of given 'topics of the day': the potential use of nuclear weapons; the position of guerrilla fighters in wars of national liberation; the fate of the civilian population in contemporary armed conflict; or the wanton attacks on Red Cross or Red Crescent personnel. Important though each of these issues may be, we should not lose sight of the overall picture.

This overall picture is dominated by the perennial problem of balancing humanity against military necessity. The tension between these two notions is tangible throughout the impressive structure of customary and treaty law brought about in just over a century. This is not to suggest that now everything has been regulated to everyone's satisfaction: this indeed appears impossible, and new demands on the international legislator cannot fail to arise in the wake of future events.

It should immediately be added that neither the adoption of treaty texts nor even their gradual incorporation into the body of international customary law of armed conflict is a guarantee of their application in practice. Observance of the obligations restricting belligerent parties in their conduct of hostilities is rarely an automatic thing: more often than not, it must be fought for step by step, so as to prevent armed conflict from degenerating into the blind, meaningless death and destruction of total war. This battle for humanity is not always won. Yet each even partial success means that a prisoner will not have been tortured or put to death, a hand grenade not blindly lobbed into a crowd, a village not bombed into oblivion: that, in a word, man has not suffered unnecessarily from the scourge of war.

The above-mentioned goal of the humanitarian law of armed conflict, to preserve humanity in the face of the reality of war, is a secondary one: our primary goal must be to prevent armed conflict. The complete realisation of this primary goal, no matter how earnestly sought by many, appears to lie, as yet, beyond our reach. It is for this very reason that the present authors felt justified in drawing the reader's attention to the often awkward relationship between war and humanity.

INDEX